Mrs. Velvet AND THE BLUE STRING Theory

BOOK ONE | **QUEEN OF HER FATE**

To Alllee
with Love,
Linda

LOVE x1.618

THE BOOK THAT WILL CHANGE THE WORLD
LINDA HEART

ISBN 978-0-615-67193-2

This book is also available in ebook format.
Please go to www.lindaheart.com to purchase the ebook version.

Cover design by Glyphics Design • www.glyphicsdesign.com
Interior design by Krause Creative • www.krausecreative.com
Interior illustrations by Igor Brezhnev • www.igorbrezhnev.com
Editing by Mary Holden • www.marylholdeneditor.com

All correspondence to the publisher should be addressed to:
Heart Productions, LLC
10115 E. Bell Rd., Suite 107-#186
Scottsdale, Arizona 85260
www.LindaHeart.com

CONTENTS

ACKNOWLEDGEMENTS

"It's gratitude!"
the poet cooed.
"And turning ear
to love –not fear."
For you, to you
And you and YOU!
From me to us
She says it thus:
Thank you to friends
who've helped me be
Purveyor of Curiosité!

John White — Thank you for holding the door open for me to find my greater self. What a journey it continues to be! This piece of art would have never happened without you. Thank you from the bottom of my heart for all our deep discussions on life and your consistent belief in me breaking boundary layers to go further into my creative self.

Mary L. Holden — Thank you for editing my books and keeping my voice. Thank you for all the 4 x 4 poems you were inspired to write which then reinspired me. Thank you for your unwavering belief in this book, your friendship, and our discovery of true magic!

Tom Bird — Thank you for teaching me how to get in touch with my voice. I am forever grateful!

Christine Alexandria — Thank you for your unwavering belief in me and for your uplifting and insightful conversations that keep me moving forward in my discovery.

Sharon Loeff — Thank you for your amazing artwork that takes my words to vision.

CC — Thank you for your support and consistent statement, *"the book will be done when the book will be done."*

Mom and Dad — Thank you for giving me the space to be me as I transformed through the years of discovery.

Angela and John — Thank you for your love and support through the years as I searched and searched for something more in life.

Thank you to all my many friends who have assisted me: **Mandy, Alana, Laurel, April, Rob, Brian, Ron, Barry, Lisa Renee, David, Igor**. Thanks also to my siblings **Jonathan, Christina, Jason** and my extended family. *I love you all dearly.*

I dedicate this book to all the people in the world who still believe in the magic of love.

The Golden Ticket: Your Passport To This Novel

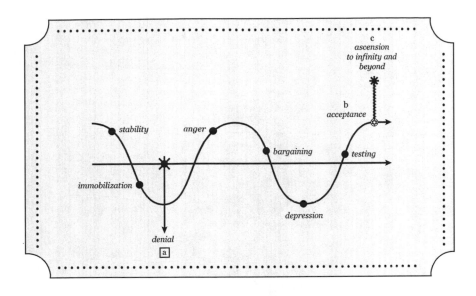

This book is set up to get you from point a to point b to point c. It is written in a unique and non-linear style that weaves over 99 stories *backwards* and *forwards* so that your logical mind cannot follow it 100 percent. For the ease of flow of information through your mind along new and old neurological tracks, there are no quotations used for dialogue. The intention of this book is *set up* to have your mind unlocked and opened to greater possibilities as it works you through the stages of grief about the human condition. The journey takes you from the third dimension, in which we live, into the fifth dimension of no time and relative space, allowing you to step into your greater potential and align with your infinite *Creative Genius*.

You have been given a Golden Ticket to enter a story where your mind tells you YOUR story as you read the story.

Be aware of the sections that make you PAUSE, the sections that make you upset, the sections that make you smile and most importantly the sections that make you get stuck…making you unable to TURN THE PAGE. It is here in these sections that you can learn the most about yourself…because this journey you are on is all about accessing the greater YOU!

TAKE NOTE: Take a notebook and write the new life events you experience while you read the story. This allows you to MATCH BACK your life experiences with the story.

STORY #144: **Our Final Inning**

A key, antique and brass, in the shape of a cross within a cross and a star at the end fit perfectly into the keyhole that was shaped like a circle with a triangle underneath. I wanted to peer in without entering because I knew there was something beyond the door that I was not prepared for. I checked my watch. It read 10 **o**'clock p.m. I turned the key and held my breath. I slowly released the air in my lungs as I entered the apartment. When I stepped over the threshold and through the door I walked into an entirely different reality. I saw that Mitchell, my husband of seven years was living a parallel reality *without* me. I was devastated, yet on some level I knew.

I felt so betrayed.

My immediate thought was how much I had given of myself to this relationship that was now a lie. I had put all my dreams on hold to help him achieve his dream of becoming a professional baseball player. He made it to the big show. Now I was seeing the curtains pulled up to unveil the *real* big show.

The seams of his career and our marriage started to come apart in his very last professional game. That one pitch—that one moment when he threw out his shoulder—also threw out the SEQUENCE in our relationship.

He left me behind, 576 miles away, and went to Las Vegas, the city of sin, to rehabilitate his injury. I now saw how having one's identity wrapped up in a game could take the whole house of cards down. He had his identity wrapped up in baseball and I had my identity wrapped up in him. The ball of string was unraveling. I was now seeing a gigantic ball of string rolling down a hill, unable to be caught.

I thought, this wasn't the life I envisioned for myself. I dreamed my whole life about love, finding that perfect someone to share my life with. When I was younger I used every spare moment to dream about my future husband and the love we would share. I didn't know what he looked like but I knew he was going to love, love, love me.

We were going to fall asleep holding hands and touching our big toes together. When we woke up we were going to be so excited the other was there. We would say, I adore you even more today. We would kiss and kiss and kiss. We would write each other love notes and poems. Poetry is the ultimate expression of love because it is not bound by meaning. He would write me love letters in the morning and *I would kiss the mirror and write backward a message of love to him.* We would speak foreign languages to one another, dance to "Quando, Quando, Quando" by Engelbert Humperdinck, www.youtube.com/watch?v=2QNIflxg5Cs, in the kitchen, while dinner was cooking, all while drinking the finest wine. We would write a special message within each other's napkin so we would have a surprise when we opened them. We would play Frank Sinatra and Edith Piaf and transcend to another era, when life was simple and love was grand. We would hold hands and take long walks on the beach. He would caress my face and tell me a thousand times how beautiful I was to him.

When did my romance take a 90-degree turn into another reality?

I knew we weren't doing great in our relationship. But don't all relationships have their ups and downs? I grew up believing you stay married forever. You don't divorce. Only losers divorce. We were going a little our own way, but isn't that what marriage allows you to do? You twist and turn and grow in unusual ways. It's okay because the other person has your back. They're going to be there for you. I did a quick mental flashback and saw all the signs. They were all there. One came the night before when I dreamed of him having sex with someone else. That is why I was there at the apartment in Las Vegas but nothing could have prepared my soul for the scene before my eyes.

I walked in. He wasn't home. The entire apartment looked like it had not been cleaned in a month. There was a video camera set up facing the couch. The bed was soiled with funky stains and my favorite painting hung above it, "The Great War on Facades," by René Magritte. She hung sideways by three nails. She had witnessed it all…or maybe not. She was a woman in a white dress holding a white parasol with a bouquet of purple flowers covering her face.

I went to the kitchen and searched for a knife. I saw the block of knives Mitchell had purchased for me for my Christmas present. The red bow was still on them. Who buys their wife knives? I remembered hating that gift and thinking how insensitive he was. Maybe I knew then. I pulled the sharpest one out of the block and just held it in front of me. I stared at my reflection in the stainless steel blade. The air in the room was so still you could cut it with a knife. I went over to the painting, came out of my daze, and cut her with precision from the frame. She was going with me. She was mine! How dare he allow her to witness all of this! I threw the frame on the ground.

I went into the bathroom. It had the 4 foot by 4 foot gold-leafed mirror from the bedroom lying on the counter by the sink. A mound of cocaine was in the middle of it. I turned the water on and watched it travel backward down the drain with my dreams. I began to shake uncontrollably as I slid down the back of the bathroom door. I felt the fresh tattoo of a red sun over my tailbone painfully absorb the pressure of every inch I traveled down to the floor. The tattoo symbolized my life force.

I wept for the pain I just self-induced. I wept for me, for my life, for all my broken dreams. That's what life is, just a lot of dreams linked together. Some of them work out and some of them don't. It's all about the dream. That's what my girlfriend Mandy always said to me. It's all about the dream.

I saw a flash in my mind of the king and queen from the top of my wedding cake get sliced in half by a huge knife. The king fell on his back losing his crown and the blue diamond came out of the center. He turned into a frog and hopped away. The queen wobbled *back* and *forth*, losing her balance, desperately trying to hold on to her 12 jewelled, 7-pronged, red heart tipped crown. One prong broke off leaving only 6. The red heart fell from the prong to the ground in slow motion. Once there it turned to a drop of blood. She desperately tried to hang on. She caught the crown by her index finger and spun it around her wrist, creating the sound of *ut, re, mi, fa, so, la.*

I crawled over to the toilet and threw up. I began to cry. I cried for me now. I cried for that little girl inside of me who just had her dream squished, stomped out and deflated. I cried…and cried…and cried. I didn't stop for hours.

Mitchell finally arrived. What he saw was a shell of my former self. I just sat there glassy eyed and dumbfounded. I really couldn't even speak. I just couldn't believe he betrayed me, and our life together. I knew it would never be the same…never, ever, ever.

He wasn't apologetic. He wasn't in the mood to have a heart-to-heart. I guess he made up his mind a while ago, but just forgot to tell me. He shapeshifted right before my eyes from my best friend to someone I didn't even know. He said words that were so detached. I wondered if he was on some type of drug. How could anyone be so blasé? Our lives were totally changed. Did he not care at all?

He stood up and messed with his hair in the mirror and said, I have to go. I have to meet some people. He kissed my forehead and walked out.

What? Hello. Is there anyone in there? I am your wife and you are just walking out? Do you not care about me? Just like that he was gone. I just received the kiss of death. This had to be the ultimate betrayal.

I stayed a bit longer before going to the hotel across the street. I could not stay at the scene of the crime. I could not stand the dead silence. Everything was in slow motion. I went over to the CD player and flipped the switch. Everything seemed to come into e-motion. I took the remote control and pressed play. The CD was from the band Faithless. I played track number 1, "Everything Will Be Alright Tomorrow," www.youtube.com/watch?v=gzTKGDiG3qw. Not in the mood to hear that right now, I thought as I hit the fast forward button and track 5 played, "I Want More," www.youtube.com/watch?v=SQZ2KrpZpMk&feature=related.

I hit track 2 and it played, "No Roots," www.youtube.com/watch?v=-Ww-WdADx518.

I hit track 3 and it played, "Giving Myself Away," www.youtube.com/watch?v=Wry9X5JCfxo.

I hit track 6 and it played, "Reverence," www.youtube.com/watch?v=jiDAIoEvekA. That word stuck in my head. I thought, I have to look up the meaning of that later.

I continued and hit track 4 and it played, "Take The Long Way Home," www.youtube.com/watch?v=nkK1zEGL7uk.

I played track 7 and it played, "In the End," www.youtube.com/watch?v=ex7N1bhP68U. I pressed PAUSE and then I played track 8 and it played, "Weapons of Mass Destruction," www.youtube.com/watch?v=v1TsCud9QhU.

I opened up the CD player, ripped the disk out and hurled it across the room. It didn't break so I went and picked it up and broke it into 8 pieces. I threw it on the floor and then picked each piece up and put them in my pocket. I contemplated for a moment. I thought, this moment of betrayal will be memorialized by this broken record.

I decided it was time to go. I picked up my bag and painting and headed for the door. As I passed the gigantic globe in the hallway I thought, where am I going? I spun it and pointed my finger to a spot. It landed on water. So, I did it again. It landed on water again. I did it a third time and it landed on Egypt. I thought, I am going to do something outrageous. I am going to Egypt tomorrow.

I looked down at the coffee table and saw his ring with the zodiac symbols around it in an ashtray. I thought how apropos. We had said we would be together through the ages. I laughed as I saw the unity candle from our wedding alongside the ashtray. I remembered that moment at the ceremony when we both lit our individual candles and then together lit the center one. What a joke that ritual is. As I scoffed I saw all 6 wedge shaped pie pieces from the Trivial Pursuit game creating a circle next to a game card. I picked up the card and read the question: What is the golden rule? I flipped it over and read: Treat others as you would like to be treated.

I checked into the hotel across the street and decided to leave on the first flight out in the morning. When I got into the hotel room I lay on the bed and cried. I started to speak to God for the first time in a long time. I said, God I have a 9-1-1. You have to help me. I can't go on. I need you to help me. I know the last time I asked for a miracle I had paralysis in my legs and feared I would never walk again. Yes, I remember I made a lot of promises back then. I know I didn't keep them all. I promise I will, but I think this may be bigger than that. I don't think I can go on. I think I want to die right now. I have nothing to live for.

I got up off the bed and went and searched my bag for something sharp. I only had a plastic razor. I beat it against the sink in the bathroom. I was weak from crying and so desperate for that blade. I couldn't get it loose for anything. I was hysterical by now. Exhaustion had washed over me. I stopped and looked in the mirror and caught sight of myself and stopped.

I took a deep breath and then had a heart-to-heart with myself. A little voice inside my head said, Gabriella do you really want to end your life over a man? Really?

And my answer was a very quiet no. I want to do the things I have always wanted to do. I want to travel. I want to solve ancient mysteries…I want to live in Paris where romance is at every corner.

The voice said, ok then go do it. You are being given a chance. There is nothing stopping you now. I felt my life force return to me. It ROSE UP from DEEP WITHIN me.

I surrendered to what was and went and climbed into bed. I was thinking about all the signs that had been there. The last time I had visited Mitchell in Las Vegas we were not connecting. I was reading *The Keys of Enoch* by Dr. J.J. Hurtak and the *Emerald Tablets* by Hermes and he said that I was too out there. I had taken an interest in sacred geometry, ancient history, current events, spirituality and politics and how they all meshed together. I started feeling guilty for who I had become. I felt guilty that I wasn't there for him. I felt guilty because I wanted to explore myself. I felt all this guilt stick to me like a wet blanket.

My last thought before I fell asleep was, isn't it interesting I always call on God in the midst of trauma.

I finally dozed off at 4:40 a.m. only to hear the alarm go off at 5. I decided I was going to go to the airport and take the first flight out to Egypt.

STORY #89: Flight 440 to CairO

I woke up and put my best red dress on. I attached a red rose to it. I wore my favorite pair of red Manolo Blahnik's and carried my black leather Gucci handbag with silver studs. I was still going to look fabulous no matter how much pain I was in. Isn't that what everyone in this world does? We all dress up and go out to face the world with a mask on, hiding all our pain. I was just like everyone else today.

I walked through the lobby hearing nothing but the

CLICK

CLICK

CLICK

CLICK

CLICK

CLICK

CLICK

CLICK

of my red heels hitting the marble floor until I heard Mayer Hawthorne's voice singing "I Wish It Would Rain," www.youtube.com/watch?v=JYHYAwvdHzY. I felt like he was singing just to me. I barely made it through the lobby, walked outside and stood in the rain. I opened my red umbrella to meet the taxi. My umbrella got caught up IN the wind and turned inside OUT. I was staring at the silver spokes underneath. They looked like a beach cruiser bicycle wheel that was turning backwards. They shapeshifted into the ceiling of a cathedral and then to the canopy of a tree with a view from the ground. The raindrops fell on my face. It felt like the tears of the world were falling on me. I felt hopelessness. The water shapeshifted into blood.

I got in the back seat of the cab and reached in my purse for my lipstick and said, under my breath, why did I take the backseat to my own life? What made me forget my dreams? How did I ever allow a man to take away my sunshine? What on earth have I done with my life? One tear slid down my cheek, followed by two more. I brushed them aside.

The Palestinian taxi cab driver was watching from his rear view mirror. He said, are you going to shrine him? He looked in the mirror and adjusted his black turban.

What?

He said, you know…memorialize him. He pointed to the magnets on his dashboard. Mother Mary was placed next to Jesus who was next to Muhammad who was next to Tweety Pie.

I thought, war is being fought over religion and here the prophets sit side by side in a yellow taxi. I blankly stared at Mother Mary in her white and baby blue robe with gold rays coming off her.

He said, you know…only remember the good times. That's what a lot of women do. He put his foot on the gas. My head whipped backwards and I felt like I had whiplash. He said, don't forget you can put lipstick on a pig, but it's still a pig.

I glanced down and saw a headline from a newspaper someone had left behind: *The President Swears Transparency.*

I finished applying my #528 red Dior lipstick called Red Rose thinking, I can put this lipstick on but it could never mask the pain inside me. I felt as if my insides were bleeding—worse yet—hemorrhaging.

The taxi driver turned up the volume when "Let It Be," www.youtube. com/watch?v=0714IbwC3HA by the Beatles played on the radio. He said, that is what this country does. It shrines events in history. It forgets all about all the terrible things it does. He said, you know if Jesus did return, your country would blow him up and somehow the event would be sold to you as protection from terrorists. Thank God the Divine is coming back as an energy signature you won't be able to see. You will just be able to feel. Religion has been used as a distraction for far too long.

I went to put my lipstick away and saw my *Webster's Unabridged Dictionary* wrapped in a homemade cover made out of a brown paper grocery bag with a black eightball drawing on it. Below the drawing, it said *don't get behind the eightball.* My Grandpa had given it to me for my first communion in the Catholic church. He wrote a note inside saying: *There are two kinds of facts. The kind you look up and the kind you make up.*

I pulled it out and looked up the definition for *reverence:*

1. Honor or respect felt or shown.

2. Gesture of respect (as a bow).

3. The state of being revered.

When we arrived at the curbside check-in he said, the ticker says $32.00. Your ticker, he was now pointing to my heart, should not let him weigh you down. We both got out of the cab. He handed me my overweight baggage.

A blackbird flew over and pooped on my head. He smirked and said, that means good luck in my family. It's all how you look at things. Or maybe it means you need to take a bird's eye view of life. Everything has more than one meaning. He handed me my receipt. I stepped off the curb and looked down at the receipt, which read: *One's real life is often the life that one does not lead.* —Oscar Wilde. I turned my head 90 degrees but that cab and driver was a distant memory. All I saw was a yellow blur of the taxi and the black and white checkered flag. I walked to the ticket counter with a CLICK

CLICK

CLICK

CLICK

CLICK

CLICK

CLICK

CLICK

CLICK

CLICK

CLICK

I reached the ticket counter and was greeted by a distinguished brunette lady standing behind the counter dressed in a red dress accessorized with a silver pin on her lapel of wings with the initials S. **O**. S.

I said, hello. You have a ticket in your top drawer for me.

She said, are you sure?

I said, without a shadow of doubt, yes ma'am I am sure.

She said HERE?

I said, yes ma'am.

She said, we are in a code red as she rummaged through her top drawer keeping her head bent down. She said, do you still want the ticket?

I said, what does code red mean?

She said, high terror.

I laughed and said yes…I still want the ticket. I am having a personal code red in my marriage, but that isn't going to stop me from taking flight.

She said, oh…code 639…fight or flight?

I paused and said, yes. I thought, all women understand the hijacked family values code which should be renamed the betrayal code of the world, 6 3 9.

She found the ticket and was surprised it was THERE in the top drawer. She pulled it out and examined it. The ticket read, First Class. She handed it to me along with an envelope attached to it. I took both and immediately opened the envelope.

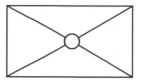

Inside I found a Golden Ticket 8 ½ x 6 inches long with a Grief Graph imprinted on it. I looked back at her with respect. My eyes zeroed in on her lapel pin of silver wings that now read: _Self Empowerment_

S. **O**. S.

She said, once the string of lies starts to unravel you will see how betrayal runs through your life. I believe it started during the John F. Kennedy era, the JFK era. That was such a pivotal point, that's when _We the People_ were sold down the river.

I nodded, not quite understanding anything anymore.

She said, YOU are a pillar of strength! Get on your way! Head up the escalator to your right. Follow the arrows.

As I picked up my bags and took two steps forward I looked back and saw her pass the word around to the other women working check-in. They all looked my way and gave me the thumbs up.

I nodded at them and felt a powerful energy wash over me. I stood straighter and walked with my head held high. I thought, I am taking flight!

I walked to security, removed all my personal possessions—belt, shoes, watch, laptop computer, lipstick and my 2 oz. bottle of Chanel No. 5—and placed them on the conveyor belt. After passing through security I gathered my possessions while watching the TSA security guards unnecessarily grope other travelers. I thought, this is psychological warfare. It is conditioning people to believe they are not safe. Security is a concept just like marriage. Marriage gives you that fake sense of security until you have the rug pulled out from underneath you, then you realize it is all made up! As I was putting everything back together, I looked up and saw a sign that read _Recombobulation Area_. I thought, how interesting! My life with my husband discombobulated me and now I am recombobulating myself.

I looked at my watch. I had 3 hours until flight 440 boarded so I did what all women do in a crisis…I shopped.

I was drawn to a shop with a window display of hundreds of goldfish in individual bowls in the configuration of a pyramid. I went in the store and just stared. The fish at the top of the pyramid was a different type of fish. It was a blowfish in dirty water. I thought to myself, a life span in captivity. Then one of the fish jumped out of its fishbowl. I thought, he didn't realize he was in that fishbowl until he jumped.

I grabbed a red fish-shaped water bottle as a symbol. For what, I wasn't sure yet. I remembered the time I was in Cornwall, England, the home of King Arthur. I was following his footsteps, trying to find something, I wasn't sure what. I stayed in a castle that didn't heat well so they gave me a hot water bottle. I couldn't believe how it soothed me. It was almost like a warm body was lying next to me.

As I left the store I looked back and saw a huge magnifying glass looking at all the goldfish with a huge eye on the other side. I did a double take and saw a satellite instead. I shook my head and walked off. As I walked past the window at a 90-degree angle I saw a bluebird in a cage with its left wing clipped.

I called Mom and told her what had happened in my marriage and then I told her I was going to Egypt.

She said, oh Gabriella are you ok?

I said, I am going to be fine. I just need to figure some things out.

She said, Gabriella, why are you doing this to me? Are you trying to put me in my grave early? Why don't you just come home? You know we all love you…right?

I thought, if I went home I would need to be put 6 feet under.

Bye Mom. They are calling my flight. I will not be in touch unless something goes terribly wrong. I have to work some things out in my head. I don't want anyone's opinions or judgments messing with me.

I learned a long time ago to keep my cards close to my chest. Otherwise, I would hear everyone else's fear overlayed on me. I knew when that happened their fears would stick in my mind and take me away from living *my* life the way I desired.

Before hanging up Mom said, whatever you do don't take an unsecured taxi! Who knows where you'll end up? Remember when you were a little girl I told you that whoever would kidnap you would turn you loose by morning?

I said yes.

She said, I lied. I just said that to toughen you up.

I thought, I wonder how many other lies she told me and how many other lies my husband had told me. How long had I been living a lie?

Thanks for the tip, Mom. Gotta go.

Bye. Love you Gabriella.

Love you Mom…and I mean it.

As soon as I got in my first-class seat I took a deep breath and allowed myself to relax. I sank deep within the leather seat. I felt exhausted holding all my pain inside. I realized I had absolutely no plan. I didn't really even know what the hell I was doing. I was in the flight of the fight-or-flight stage.

The flight attendant, a 40 year old woman dressed in a '60s style red dress and matching red scarf and pill box hat, came into the aisle and said, buckle up this is going to be the ride of your life. No doubt when we land this bird you will not be the same. If you should need oxygen pull down your mask and breathe deeply. Breathe IN what you desire and OUT what you don't. In case of an emergency go to the exit row. You have the CHOICE between going LEFT or RIGHT.

She then held up the flight manual. The back read: Fight or Flight. Which do you choose? It's a personal choice.

I opened my envelope and pulled out my Golden Ticket and followed the Grief Graph. My eyes followed an oscillating line that charted out the stages of grief. Depending on your emotional response you could be *over* or *under* the line. It started with stability *over* the line to immobilization *under* the line; then there was denial on the line to anger *over* the line to bargaining, which was slightly *over* the line to depression, which was well *under* the line to testing which was slightly *over* the line to acceptance over the line.

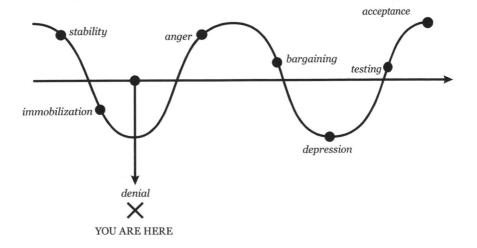

I decided I was right on the line. I was in denial. I felt as if a yellow Post-it note flew through the air that said, YOU ARE HERE! right on the line. You are in denial of that which is. I slowly turned the paper over in contemplation and saw a drawing of an old tree with a large root system made up of several s r a e f / f e a r s and many capital A's. My eyes traveled up the canopy of the tree and noticed it was filled with many capital B's and the words *TRUST* and *FAITH*. My eyes traveled back down to the bottom of the tree where the caption read *Trees Heal*. $a^2 + b^2 = c^2$.

I closed my eyes and thought, two negatives always create a positive. It will all work out. It always does. Have faith and trust. I always wanted to go to Egypt and now I am on my way. As one door closes another opens. Thank God I had my passport. I opened my eyes and clicked on the light bulb symbol above my head. I grabbed my purse to double check that I had my passport. Getting to a foreign country without my passport would be hell. I panicked. I rummaged through my purse and then found it inside the inner pocket. I thought, how many times have I panicked only to realize I was fine. I had everything I needed. I looked down at it and an eagle stared back at me.

How had I never seen this before? I pulled out my small round magnifying glass that I always carry and saw stars over the head of the eagle. They were in the shape of a pyramid, one facing up and one facing down with a star in the middle. I saw the sequence of 14341. The eagle held 13 arrows in its left talon that glowed with red tips. In the right talon it held an olive branch. I thought, what a duality that signifies, war and peace. Then my eyes rested upon the words *E Pluribus Unum*.

I pulled out my *Webster's Unabridged Dictionary*. I looked up the phrase *E Pluribus Unum*. It said: *Out of many, one*. I then looked up the word *passport* and it said, from the Latin word *portus; permission or authorization to go somewhere*.

I thought, we are nothing more than goldfish trapped in a pyramid. I didn't realize it until I jumped out of the fishbowl. My fish water bottle represented an escape from captivity. How beautiful.

I put my black eye mask on that read *blinders* and drew a fish symbol *over* and *over* and *over* and *over* and *over* and *over* and *over* and *over* and *over* and *over* and *over* and *over* and *over* with my index finger on the hem of my dress. It was a soothing habit taken from what my grandmother always used to do on my nightgown while she told me bedtime stories. I drifted into a thick mist of sleep.

As I awoke I thought, when did life get so complicated? Where's the riddle in this? How did I not know? I got the message in a dream when I saw my husband with a naked woman. Holy shit! Life is a riddle and I got the message in my dream. I realized that everything is speaking to me at all times, it's just if I have my receptor on or not. Everything is speaking to everybody all the time. I was just missing a lot of riddles.

The intercom came on saying, Flight 440 is due to land in Cairo, Egypt in twenty minutes. I reached into the pocket of the seat and grabbed a newspaper to do the crossword puzzle to put my mind into another frame. 12 down, 4 letters, starts with an F and ends with an E. The description was *an inevitable course of events.*

Then 15 across, the third letter in was E. The description was *in chess the most powerful piece.* I solved a few more riddles from the puzzle and then tossed the newspaper into the empty seat next to me.

As I was exiting the plane, something caught my eye. The headline of that newspaper said: *Get Ready for the Dawn of a New Red Day.* I thought, I know the meaning of this, but from where?

The crossword puzzle shapeshifted into the periodic chart of elements highlighting the H1 and **O**8 and then it shapeshifted into a 64-squared chessboard and then became some kind of 3 dimensional grid. I grabbed it and threw it in my blue and white striped retro carry on bag. I shook my head thinking, am I losing it?

As I walked off the plane I saw a woman in the airport who was wearing a sky blue skirt with gold stars on it. I counted 9 rows of 8 stars, 72 stars. The skirt reminded me of my cousin, Carmen, who read my tarot cards when I was a little girl. She used to dress in skirts and was the hippie of our family. I loved her. She taught me about astrology, reincarnation and the unseen world coexisting with us. I thought, what if your life is *set up* for you and you are just walking through the steps for the experience, the journey. Now, that would be the grand *set up!*

STORY #55: Tarot Cards and 639

I kissed my index finger and placed it on the gold magnet of Mother Mary before dad started the ignition. Dad followed. He had a ritual of kissing his right index finger and then placing it on a gold magnet of Mother Mary before starting his green and white Chevrolet Suburban. He said that it kept us all safe from a car accident. He never missed a kiss. I thought it was a miracle we hadn't been in an accident since he was always on the far right, right on the edge…of a ditch…more than once. My big brother, 13-year-old Jonny and I teased him about this on more than one occasion. He said he preferred everything a little to the RIGHT including his politics.

As we drove to Uncle Dave's, Jonny and I made hats out of the newspaper that Dad was toting around. It was like his security blanket. It made him feel like he was grounded in this reality. He knew what was true through the newspaper. He had a subscription to every *SUN NEWS* paper under the sun. We never understood why he believed the paper enlightened him. We couldn't understand because there was no one proofing the paper for the truth. It was just someone's opinion and what if they were paid off to write something? How did Dad not get that? Jonny and I decided our parents didn't know as much as they thought they did. We kept that to ourselves. We called it the *hornshwaggle*. We even had a symbol for it…our first two fingers crossed. If we made that sign it meant someone was trying to pull a fast one on us.

As we drove we sang, *over the river and through the Bretton Woods to someone else's agenda we go.*

Jonny said, Dad, tell us a story of cock and bull.

I said, do you need the paper to create your story?

Jonny said, how about the *Wall Street Journal?* He lifted up the paper with a pull quote in bold: **The main enemy of the open society, I believe, is no longer the communist but the capitalist threat.** –George Soros.

Our father had no idea what we were really saying. We laughed in the back seat and whispered, grown-ups live cock and bull. In unison we both lifted our crossed fingers and said hornshwaggle. Jonny made his hat out of a cartoon section. I made mine out of the crossword section. When I inspected Jonny's hat I noticed a cartoon on the side that said, "Hell Hath No Fury Like A Woman Scorned." I laughed.

He said, what is so funny?

I whispered, check out the cartoon. It has a lady in red, madder than hell.

He checked it out and we both laughed.

He said, she must have caught him in bed with another woman.

Every cell inside me seemed to boil. At the age of 12 I never knew what betrayal was like but I could imagine it. I could *feel* that sensation of betrayal. I thought to myself, this must be stored in my cells from a past life. Why else would I feel this terrible?

When we got to Uncle Dave's Jonny took off for the river with Dad. He shouted to me, come on let's see if we can make your hat float like a boat. He pointed to his and said, I have to wear mine because I am President of the *Sun News*, better known as the *Hornshwaggle News*. He laughed as dad took a dollar bill and quickly folded it into the shape of a boat. George Washington's face looked like he was steering the boat.

Jonny took it laughing and said, let's send this President, G.W., down the river.

I said, I am only interested in the Love Boat. I can't go. I have to speak with Carmen. It's about girl stuff.

Jonny pointed to his hat and laughed as he ran sideways to the lake. He sang:

> Row, row, row your boat,
> Gently down the stream,
> Merrily, merrily, merrily, merrily
> Life is but a dream.

When I went inside I immediately looked for Carmen. She was aunt Nel's daughter from a previous marriage. She sometimes came to stay with my aunt and uncle. She was 32 but treated me like I was the same age as her. I didn't have an older sister so I really enjoyed talking with her. She read tarot cards, something I found fascinating. I wanted to hear what she had to say about this feeling I was having. I entered her room hoping she would read my tarot.

Carmen was standing in her bedroom. They never changed the décor when she moved out and grew up. Mom said it was weird, but I thought it was cool. She always got to remain her younger self even when the crows feet came in. She was 5'10" and yoga thin with purple streaked hair, a beautiful face with brown almond shaped eyes and slightly large lips. She wore black, extra large square-framed glasses with a piece of black electrical tape on the right side. She said that the electrical tape and extra large glasses made her smarter than the average bear. She was what Dad called a hippie chick. Her room was filled with vintage framed posters of musical groups I had never heard of.

I walked in and marveled at all the groups. I wondered if at night they came out of the posters and played concerts just for her. I listened intently to see if I could hear one group playing now. All I could hear was "Quando, Quando, Quando" playing way out in the distance. I thought, maybe I should get a picture of Engelbert Humperdinck and see if he would play for me at night.

Carmen was dressed in a long violet skirt with tiny bells hanging on a red string around her ankles. She was adjusting a black lava lamp in the shape of a brain. Instead of the unusual globs of colors this one was made up of a myriad of colored strings that looked like wires. They were bouncing all over the place. When she saw me she said, come touch it on the forehead and watch it balance all the wires.

I touched it and all the light strings went into one oscillating yellow line at the point where my finger touched it. I took my index finger and touched my own forehead. I tapped my forehead with a

$$T^2app$$
$$T^2app$$
$$T^2app$$
$$T^2app$$
$$T^2app$$
$$T^2app$$
$$T^2app$$

Carmen said, that is how you focus your mind leading you down the Yellow Brick Road to your Providence. Pretty cool huh?

I nodded and thought, maybe that's the secret to hearing the bands at night or maybe that's the secret to everything…you just have to focus on it.

She bent down and whispered, I heard you were coming so I set aside all my time for you. What would you like to do?

I smiled and said, of course read the tarot.

She acted like she knew I was going to ask her this. She pulled out her sky blue tablecloth with 72 stars on it from under her bed and put it over her nightstand. She pulled out a deck of tarot cards in a blue velvet pouch from inside the nightstand and placed them on the table. The cards  were purple with an image of a geometric shape on one side. She removed a blue celestite crystal from inside a white leather pouch hanging from around her neck. She ran it over the top of the cards as she spread them out. She said, tarot means *royal* path.

I thought, hippie chicks are so freaking cool! Everything they do just seems different from the ordinary. I thought, who would want ordinary?

Carmen broke my train of thought when she said, we shall use the tarot from Rider-Waite. This one is not filled with black magic. She whispered, the Thoth deck is distorted. It is filled with the symbology of the dark forces.

I said, who is Thoth? I bet he wouldn't have wanted his work to be distorted.

Carmen said, Thoth was an Egyptian god who was about divine magic and alchemy. He worked as a scribe to the gods and introduced writing to the world. Later he was known as the Greek god, Hermes.

I said, I love writing, especially poems.

Carmen smiled and continued, Thoth drew the original 44 tarot cards depicting the 22 major arcana cards, representing UPPER Egypt and 22 minor arcana cards, representing lower Egypt. Added together, the UPPER and lower cards equal 44, which is the number of chromosomes at the lowest level of consciousness. You may not understand this, Gabriella, but your soul does, so bear with me.

Carmen continued as I twisted a ring on my finger that looked Egyptian that I had taken from Mom's jewelry box without permission. She said, the pictures on this tarot card deck illustrate the great wisdom of the ancient temple mystery cult of Egypt. She held up her index finger and said, but the 8 most important tarot cards that depict the keys to ascension are missing.

I looked up and said, so we are working with a half deck?

Carmen laughed and said yes. These 8 cards depict 8 programs that you run that keep you from realizing YOU, your true potential.

I asked, what is being your true potential?

Carmen said, being your true potential is ascension and ascension is when you are connected back up to the God force energy realizing YOU ARE DIVINE and you have abilities *beyond* the ordinary. It is when you know your real YOU and you are not hiding. It is when you become free.

I said, are you free?

Carmen said, of course! That is why everyone thinks I am a hippie chick!

I fist pumped and said, we can all be hippie chicks!

Carmen laughed.

I said, so…connecting back up to the Divine is like calling God up on the phone? I put my thumb and index finger up to my right ear and said, God I need you. I have a 9-1-1. I need you to answer me. I'm tired of the dead line.

Carmen smiled and said, these 8 cards have to do with the original 3 atoms of humans that were distorted. The father, son and holy ghost, which were really the male, female and God energy that combined together making us Divine, illuminating our inner sun. This is what connected us to the God force energy through a tri-wave.

I said, so that's what holy ghost means. I knew that holy ghost stuff didn't make sense. As a light bulb went off in my head, I whispered, they hid our true potential because of our power. I looked at Carmen and said, I think we speak the same language, Carmen. I also think my science teacher is smarter than I thought. He said atoms can turn into waves and waves can turn into atoms. They are interchangeable. The problem is when they accumulate as standing waves. He said, the CERN collider is a waste of Billions with a capital B. It's just a way to keep the greatest science minds distracted. He said, the God particle is within all of us. We just need to REMEMBER how to reconnect. I am going to have to start paying more attention in science class. I started daydreaming about beakers in a laboratory filled with yellow and white flowers.

Carmen coughed to get my attention and then continued, these pictures were hung under the right paw of the Sphinx or in a labyrinth called the Double House of Life or the Circle of Gold. She whispered, a person who was an initiate into the mysteries was led between 2 pillars and would have the meanings of the pictures explained to her by the initiator. Her voice changed as she said, the information and symbols got passed down through generations, but most of it was lost or skewed. It is our mission, the Goddesses of the past, to REMEMBER this. It is what will bring us out of separation and back into being whole.

I stared at Mom's ring and noticed an ankh on the side of it. I said, will it give me my magic powers back?

She said yes.

I sat up taller and said, I am up for the job then. I can handle anything that can do that. I am a Goddess of the past and the future.

Carmen said, let's see if the cards can help guide you in remembering what you once knew because everything is recorded in vibrational form. All knowledge is available. We just need to REMEMBER. Now, take a deep breath, concentrate on any questions that may assist you in remembering and shuffle the deck. When you get the feeling to stop, cut the cards into 3 piles going LEFT to RIGHT. Pick up the piles from RIGHT to LEFT.

I shuffled and cut the cards. I placed them in 3 piles going LEFT to RIGHT.

Carmen picked the cards up from RIGHT to LEFT and then laid out the cards in a SEQUENCE. She said, hmm…very interesting. The 6, 3 and 9 are the cards we will focus on. These are the universal numbers that will be returned to their original power in our lifetime. They will show up in your life repeatedly. Pay attention to these numbers throughout your life.

She held up the 3 card. It was the Empress. It was a picture of a beautiful woman sitting in a chair. Carmen said, this my dear, is a power card. She is the Empress, the Madonna, Great Mother, Queen of Heaven and Earth. Her picture shows her holding a golden eagle. You will encounter the many different meanings of the eagle in your life. She pointed to the card and said, she is holding the golden rod and staff joined together. This shows she has the ability to connect heaven and earth.

I said, I would like to be a queen and wear a crown like her. I counted 1, 2, 3, 4, 5, 6, 7 stars on her head.

Carmen took a crown hanging from a post on the headboard of the bed and placed it on my head. She said, there you go.

I said, that was easy. I pointed to the top of the rod and asked, what is that? It looks like a pinecone.

Carmen said, the pinecone represents the pineal gland. It is an endocrine gland located in the middle of your brain. It used to be the size of a ping-pong ball but is now the size of a dried up seed, because we forgot how to use it.

I said, use it or lose it.

She smiled and said, in its natural state it looked like a multi-faceted crystal eyeball. It was round and had an opening on one portion. In that opening was a lens for focusing light. It was hollow and had color receptors inside. It looked upward toward heaven. It could look as much as 90 degrees away from upwards. Inside were all the sacred geometries and understandings of how our reality was created.

Carmen took a deep breath, then she continued. We stopped breathing through our crowns, the tops of our heads, so the pineal gland dried up like a seed. Instead of taking in prana, energy, life force, through the pineal and circulating it UP and DOWN our central pillar, the hara line, we started breathing through our nose and mouth. This caused us to sidetrack the pineal gland, which resulted in our seeing things in a totally different way, a different interpretation. This perception is called polarity. It is demonstrated through right and wrong, good and evil, black and white, male and female, left and right. This made us have the perception we are inside a body looking out, separated from everyone and everything. Something happened to us that shouldn't have. We went through a mutation, a chromosome breakage within our DNA. We have been sidetracked from our true selves. We have been in code red for a long time…for 13,000 years.

What is code red?

It's a code that has beings from all over the Universe standing in line, in queue to help us REMEMBER who we truly are.

I sat with my mouth open and said, who are we? I paused and said, who am I?

She said, galactic spiritual beings with talents beyond what we can even imagine.

Wow! I want to REMEMBER.

Carmen smiled and said, so do I. We all do at our soul level. It's what drives our life.

Dad told me that money drives our life.

Carmen said, that is what most men think. They are wrong. They need to learn to search deeper within themselves to find what is *really* driving them.

I pointed to the 3 and said, what does that represent?

She said, that represents the sacred trinity. The mother, father and child. The past, present and future. The mind, intellect and ego. The father, mother and SUN. Osiris, Isis and Horus. Solar, lunar and Earth. Solid, liquid and gas. Space, time and matter.

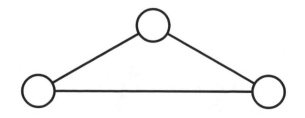

I said, in school we are learning about the proton, electron, and neutron. My science teacher said they are the great trinity.

Carmen said, yes, in all of these the third member acts as an equilibrating factor. The 3 creates a triangle, a positive, negative and neutral. Beginning, middle and end. In the future when you REMEMBER how to use the energy from the resurrected tri-field you will be able to tap into a field of consciousness where everything is located. She looked over her glasses and said, you know things without studying.

I said, like running my hands along the spine of books and understanding them? If I had a super power I would want that.

Yes, but this is even easier. You don't have to run your finger along the spine of a book. You just have to sit quiet and GO INSIDE yourself.

I sat quietly and went inside to tap my super power.

Carmen smiled and said, the Empress represents creativity. She can take a blank piece of paper and all of sudden cover it with words and codes. She may take her life and connect it to the past and future to create something in the present moment that is perfect.

The Empress turns INWARD for there she finds the mysterious inner world that is incorruptible as gold. The Empress connects with the INNER KNOWING that is far more important than the masculine left-brain logic. Women and men are wired differently. She pointed at the lava lamp brain. I watched a myriad of colored lines shoot all over the brain like lightning bolts in a static electric storm.

Carmen said, men spend a lot of time in their logical left-brain mind. The left-brain is about SEQUENCE, patterns, analysis, rationality, objectivity. Women spend a lot of their time in their right brain, which is the imagination, intuition, synthesizing, subjective thought, looking at the whole rather than the parts. Original ideas come to women from out of thin air, images and daydreams. The Empress is a bridge for these ideas.

Mom says I am a big dreamer, I said with a smile.

Carmen smiled and said, the Empress is touched by Venus. She loves beauty in all forms and is often eclectic in her tastes, combining the old and the new to create the future in the past and the past in the future.

That's me! I am the Empress!

She held up the next card. It was a picture of a man and woman with a beautiful woman, in the form of a red sun who stood in between them with a wreath of red roses around her head. She said, number 6. Six is unique because 0, 1, 2 and 3 add up to equal 6. God created the world in 6 days with 6 tones of *ut, re, mi, fa, so, la.* Symbolically the 6 is pictured as a 6-pointed star. The star is composed of 2 triangles, 1 facing UP and 1 facing DOWN.

 I said, one facing to heaven and one facing to earth.

Carmen said, it's where the macrocosm and microcosm intertwine.

I lifted my left hand DOWN to my LEFT side and my right hand UP to my RIGHT side and said, *as above so below.*

Carmen continued, 6 is also the Lovers card.

I thought, now this is what I want to hear about. I whispered, go on.

Carmen said, this card has 2 women involved with 1 man with the god Eros hovering over them with his love arrows. I regret to tell you, you shall have an experience where your husband chooses to go with another woman outside of your marriage. You will be devastated and as a result of this you will d i v o r c e.

I felt lightheaded. I started to see stars swirl around my head. She continued while I counted the stars and heard Charlie Brown's teacher's voice say d i v o r c e *over* and *over* and *over.* After a while all the letters merged together into a tone of ddddoooo.

Carmen said, this card presents the ego with a challenge that marks an important step in your cycle of life. Your challenge will be to CONNECT WITHIN to your true self at this time. If you choose to do the work and accomplish this, a new energy of LOVE WITHIN will radiate out into all your relationships with others. It all depends if you CHOOSE TO GO IN. She lifted the card and said, in the picture you see Eros with his love arrows. He is the god of LOVE connected to FATE.

I mumbled to myself, the god of love connected to fate.

Carmen said, he upsets the apple cart in your life. He upsets old patterns so you can allow new energy in. He is necessary in the great work of self-discovery. An involvement of the heart usually marks a significant turning point in our journey. Such a love appears or disappears as an act of fate to break a cycle. We all experience the arrows of love and they are all leading us back to our true self, which is located at our CENTER. She bowed her head and touched her RIGHT hand between her breasts.

I said, Carmen. This is a lot for me to handle. I haven't even kissed a boy yet. I whispered, even though I have practiced with my pillow. All this makes me not feel so good. I can't imagine my husband doing that.

Carmen laughed. She said, my love you will find out your betrayal runs deeper than a stack of cards. It runs all the way back to the beginning of the human race. Now, let's continue. The number 9 represents spiritual advancement. This card shows a man carrying a lantern to illuminate his path. This represents the universal human potential. The golden flame inside the lantern represents the spirit inherent in all of life. Once humans learn to GO WITHIN they will realize they can affect change within themselves and within the world. Sir Isaac Newton spent his life trying to achieve the alchemy of himself, the philosopher's gold, that nugget buried deep within us all connecting us back to the Divine. She pointed to the card and said, the hermit card is to shed light on ancient mysteries. You will witness the breakdown of society and it will be essential to come back to the inner knowledge represented through this card.

Carmen knocked on the table. Is there anybody in there?

I had gone into another reality. Carmen just told me something I didn't think I could handle. How could I, the girl of love, be betrayed? I left my body and was daydreaming in a field of purple wildflowers. I was dressed in a white dress and a white-feathered hat having a picnic of cheese and green apples with Sir Isaac Newton. He was tossing a green apple UP and DOWN. It would hide his face for a split second and all I could see were his eyes.

He poured his affections over me. It felt like gold sparkles filled with love were being decanted from a Kool-Aid pitcher, sprinkling like rain. It made my toes tingle and my heart go p-p-pitter pat. He held a white parasol over me as I used a pink butterfly net to catch bright orange and yellow butterflies. Sir Isaac said, to catch a miracle is to believe in one. He pinched their wings with his index finger and thumb and laid them upon my hand.

He handed me a tiny magnifying glass on a steel stem with a loop at the top and at the bottom. He said, this is for you. It is very important. It is a magnifying glass I invented. He dropped his eyes down to the ground. He was quite modest. He said, play with it!

I put it up to my RIGHT eye and closed my LEFT then I put the magnifying glass up to my LEFT eye and CLOSED the right. Then I did it back and forth fast. My eyes got confused. They couldn't keep up with what I was thinking. I turned the loops 90 degrees and put my finger through the loop. I poked myself in the RIGHT eye. I squealed with delight.

He smiled and said, I love how you play. Don't ever lose that. Life is a mystery to be played with so you can OPEN UP your world as you OPEN UP your eyes.

I could feel his love for me grow.

He said, let's look at the beautiful geometric patterns of the butterflies. He twirled his set of magnifying glasses in his fingers. He made them flip over so perfectly. I watched in awe of how his fingers moved. I thought, I bet he could tie an eyelash 3 times with those nimble fingers.

He said, you are the only one who really understands beauty…even in the smallest things.

He whispered, the butterflies are made up of the mathematical equation PHI. He pointed to every little bend in their legs, the length and width of their wings. Every little part was made up of 1.618. He touched my belly button and said, it is the same for you, too. You are made up of PHI proportions. Your top half is a mirror image of your bottom half from the belly button.

I said, I am the same as a butterfly!

He said exactly. We are all made in the same likeness. I looked back down and my belly button shapeshifted into the city of Jerusalem.

A brilliant blue dragonfly landed on my right shoulder. Sir Isaac took a piece of parchment paper from his pocket and said, look at 10 o'clock. Do you see a resemblance? The parchment was a round circle with 7 stars around it and 1 in the middle on top of a beam. At 10 o'clock there was an outline of a dragonfly's body.

I looked through my magnifying glass and said yes.

He said, it is the star constellation Orion, guiding you to Sirius. Look for

it tonight in the sky. This parchment is the Seal of Solomon.

It's the key to understanding your betrayal.

He waved the parchment in the air. He said, it ended with Solomon and it shall begin again with Solomon as he relinquishes his power. He took a green apple and held it in his hand. He said, this is Earth. The center of the apple is the equator. A little above and below the equator is 19.47 north and south latitude. He sliced the apple at the equator. He held the two halves in front of his eyes and said, what do you see?

I said, I see a 5-pointed star made out of seeds on both hemispheres of the world.

He said, that is the star Sirius, the home of the goddess. He gave me one half and said, you are the return of the goddess. He put the second half in his shirt pocket and took out a book of poetry by Rumi. He read:

Two Forms, One Soul

Happy is the moment, when we sit together,

With two forms, two faces, yet one soul,

you and I.

The flowers will bloom forever,

The birds will sing their eternal song,

The moment we enter the garden,

you and I.

The stars of heaven will come out to watch us,

And we will show them

The light of a full moon –

you and I.

No more thought of "you" and "I."

Just the bliss of union –

Joyous, alive, free of care, you and I.

All the bright-winged birds of heaven

Will swoop down to drink of our sweet water –

The tears of our laughter, you and I.

What a miracle of fate, us sitting here.

Even at the opposite ends of the Earth

We would still be together, you and I.

We have one form in this world,

Another in the next.

To us belongs an eternal heaven,

The endless delight of you and I.

He pulled a bouquet of purple flowers from thin air and placed them in my face.

Carmen knocked again. Is anybody in there?

I snapped back into reality holding a small magnifying glass within my fingers.

Carmen said, you may do this to awaken your Hermit within.

I said, what do you do?

She got frustrated and said, that is all little one. You weren't even listening.

I said, I was. Please don't stop.

She said, not until you are older will you understand.

I started to cry. I said, I do understand. I am going to have my heart broken and I can't handle it. Hell hath no fury like a woman scorned! I sank into the chair. I bent over and felt as if I were a shrinking violet. I am different. I have no fury to unleash. I am empty. My cup doesn't runneth over.

She said, then you should fill a Kool-Aid pitcher up every night with love and empty it into your heart through a red funnel. You must learn to have a cup that runneth over. A woman without love wilts like a flower without sun. Learn to walk with your heart leading and not your head. It's all in the posture.

She took a gold necklace with a silver charm of Mother Mary from around her neck and gave it to me. You are very special. Wear this. It will help you REMEMBER.

Dad walked in carrying his newspaper and said, Gabriella it's time to go home. Jonny was by his side with the wet dollar bill pasted to his forehead. George Washington was staring right at me.

Jonny said yea, it's time! You should have come. It was great! You should be more like Christopher Columbus. He wasn't afraid to veer out more than 90 degrees into the open sea. He took a chance! You don't have to stay close to the bank, that's a false sense of security. What are you afraid of, Gabriella? Why do you have to play safe? FLIP THE SWITCH!

I looked at Carmen and she said, go on. It will all work out. Let it be love.

As we drove home, I became very ill. I felt all my red blood cells were erupting inside my body. I asked Jonny for his hat and threw up all over the cartoon of the scorned woman.

Jonny said, that cartoon really set you off didn't it? It really sent your head swimming. You know, there are a lot of fish in the sea.

I looked up at him with tears in my eyes and vomit all over my mouth and said, I don't even know why.

He said, I do. You got seasick. Your vomit looks like Kool-Aid.

When I looked down all I saw was blood. Dad pulled over and got a red bucket out of the back and said, here throw up in this. My dad believed everyone should carry a bucket and a can of gas in their cars at all times. He grew up having to thumb it to school every day. Now he carries a bucket and can of gas with him to help people in need on the side of the road because someone was always there to pick him up. He calls it *The Pick Up Theory* because when someone is in need you pick them up.

As I threw up again I thought, maybe he does know what he is talking about. This bucket came in handy. The tag on the bucket read: *99 cents. Make every second count. Ace Hardware.*

STORY #34: Mrs. Velvet and the Piggy Bank

When I got home, I raced to Mrs. Velvet's house. She was from France but she lived next door. Our houses shared an underground connection through a tunnel-like walkway between our basements. I always thought of myself traveling through a black hole to get to her. I named the tunnel *the Schwarzschild*.

Mrs. Velvet was the most amazing woman I had ever met. She was so beautiful. She had the most beautiful skin, always intensified with perfect make-up. Her dark eyelashes were long, and bordered deep green-blue eyes. Her hair was pink, twisted up into a precise beehive that resembled an ice cream cone. She often put things in it for me to notice, saying they all had significant meaning. She had such a lovely demeanor. Her house always held fresh wildflowers arranged everywhere in Mason jars, illuminated by glistening chandeliers that were so beautiful they could have hung in museums. She had a library, devoted to walls of shelves entirely covered in books. I often found her reading by candlelight about far-off places and fascinating people. She always had a chess game set up, but we never did play. I always wondered about that.

Tonight I found her in bed, popping bon-bons from a silver tray. She was dressed in a white nightgown, her pink beehive adorned in purple flowers, orange butterflies and one white dove. She was listening to "Les Miserables." I had barely placed a foot inside when she called, in here, love.

I recounted my tarot reading with Carmen. She listened intently, then said, you have gotten your red blood cells in a thither. Let me fix you some tea so you can relax.

I plopped on the bed while she made tea. Her bed was so comfortable. It was like reclining on a cloud. Her white Egyptian cotton linens and comforter seemed very expensive. She came back and handed me my cup of tea. I noticed the tag hanging to the left read *Egyptian Remembrance Tea*.

She went to her vanity and picked up her gold-plated hairbrush, then gently ran it through my hair. It felt so soothing. She said, now, tell me everything.

Talking made me feel less upset, and more at peace. She listened to me, unlike most adults. I asked, is fortune telling always right?

She responded, fortune telling says something must happen. Divination, such as with tarot cards, never tells what must happen. It states the probability of something happening if you continue on the same track. You have FREE WILL and FREE CHOICE. The outcome is always up to you.

When Carmen read my tarot, she told me that another woman would break up my relationship with my future husband.

My dear, it's never about the other woman. It's always about you and your relationship with yourself. You must learn to love every thread of your being. Even the things you wish you could change, the things you hate. She bent over and kissed my cheek. If this does happen you will learn a lesson in that relationship that will allow you to find your true self 22 divided by 7 times faster. It may sting like a bee, but because of it, you will REMEMBER EVERYTHING YOU EVER DREAMED OF BEING.

If you learn to love all your bits before you grow up you won't have to undergo that lesson. The CHOICE is yours. She bent down so I could see the card nestled in her hair. It read, 8^2 = the squaring of one's possibilities.

Learn to love everything about yourself. She patted her rump as she said that. From your bumps and humps to your flashy eyes. Learn to love the way you do things; the way you think, the way you brush your teeth, the way you write, the way you sleep, the way you sneeze, how you walk, how you dance! How you talk, the way you open your heart, the way you answer the phone. She danced around the room like a butterfly. The way your teeth look. She took a mirror off her vanity, looked at herself, and smiled. She held it in front of me and said, LOOK AT YOU AND LOVE YOU! Anything you see that is not perfect is truly perfection. You are a child of God. You were made perfect just the way you are!

She went over to her vanity and picked up a pink piggy bank. You have to fill up your love bank first. What you put in is what you get out. She shook out 13 quarters. If you want something different you have to put something different in.

I reached in my pocket and pulled out 2 pennies. I said, I have 2 cents.

Mrs. Velvet smiled and said, you will have plenty of time to give your 2 cents, love. Later in life, you will see more women WAKE UP to their true self. They will step up to the plate. They will learn to love themselves. They will learn the code of honor between women. It will be the code 639. Watch this. She extracted a pen and piece of paper from her hair, then combined the 6 and 9, then overlaid the 3, creating an 8, symbolizing eternity. She rotated it 90 degrees, creating infinity. She then squished them together, creating the vesica pisces. She dropped a diamond in the center that created a third loop. She said, that is the new infinity. It's a tri-wave connecting to the celestial.

It will bond women together in a new, unique way and you will be a part of that. So don't fret, my love. REMEMBER you have to love every golden thread of your being first, because that is the true meaning of divine union. You can then enter into a divine union with a man who reflects that back to you. The new paradigm of relationship will be based on faith and trust where loyalty to oneself and each other is based in love, not fear.

It's funny how women treat each other. They all want the same thing; love with the highest respect, yet they treat one another disrespectfully when it comes to men. When women BOND, they can affect change. This will create a symphony of music. She turned up the music and asked, shall we dance?

We danced on the bed in a circle, holding hands, filling the room with love notes as we sang from "Les Miserables," "I Dreamed a Dream," www.youtube.com/watch?v=U_xFNa7YKDw.

We did one final JUMP and SPIN on the bed and landed with our feet in the air. We sent all the feathers flying from the feather bed and pillows. The room was filled with white feathers, gold sparkles and the scent of Chanel No. 5.

After the feathers settled, Mrs. Velvet looked at me, adorned with a feather mask, and I looked at her with one on my face too. She slipped out of bed, leaving feathers floating above me. I pulled back the comforter, revealing a silver lining, and folded it around myself.

She came back with a scroll. We lay in bed as she unrolled it. It showed a beautiful painting of a woman dressed in a white gown and white hat. She was holding a white parasol as well as a huge bouquet of purple flowers covering her face. She said, this is a gift for you. It is from the artist René Magritte. Keep it as a reminder of this moment.

She whispered, may you always see your true self reflected back to you. May you always stop to smell the flowers. May you see the mystery in all things hidden and visible.

I loved the painting. I loved what it represented. I promised to always have it near me. I asked, what's it called?

"The Great War of Façades."

So what do I do if I find myself in the situation that Carmen said?

Do something outrageous! That will help you break the cycle!

I went home and passed Mom who was doing the laundry. She asked, do you have any whites to put in? This cycle is getting ready to SPIN.

I noticed that the dryer door was open. It looked like a giant magnifying glass. I laughed and walked on, thinking, it's all how you look at things.

I went to my room where I had taped to the walls my black and white charcoal drawings of abstract women's faces in my own unique Picasso-ish style. I slipped on my white cotton nightgown, and got into bed as all eyes were on me. Mom came in and gave me a spoonful of medicine for my stomach. I swallowed it and held onto my silver medallion of Mother Mary for dear life. I heard her say, *let it be.* I let go and drifted into a deep sleep.

STORY #21: Blueprints and Red Hearts

I dreamed of 32 ravens typing on old-school *Royal* typewriters. Their beaks created a beat as they hit the keys. One raven said to the others, we need to clean the keys. There are shadows in the keys. The instrument is not clear. Maybe we should change the ribbon from red to black.

The head raven said, the message is clear. That is all that matters.

As each raven finished, they hit the lever with their left foot and sent the 8 ½ x 11 papers flying. The head raven gathered the papers as they wafted through the air. They were imprinted with the code 639 typed *over* and *over* in the shape of a heart. The head raven sent them down an assembly line made up of another 32 ravens, who cut out the codes with their scissor shaped beaks and stored them in silver titanium briefcases. When they finished the last one, they shut all the briefcases in unison with a loud clap and formed a circle.

One woman entered the circle in a white dress, hat and parasol, then she split into 2. The 2 women danced to "Survivor" by Destiny's Child, www.youtube.com/watch?v=Sd2RIDz1tzy. The 2 women split to 4, then 8, then 16, then 32 and then 64. The 64 women shapeshifted into white bowling pins with red stripes around their necks. They created a triangle pattern. The bowling pins stood firm until they were knocked down by an enormous black three-holed bowling ball with the number 8 on it, which changed into a wrecking ball with the words World Bank/IMF imprinted on it. The pins toppled on top of one another, creating a pyramid that reached 99 feet high. The pins shapeshifted to ballerinas dressed in size o white tutus and red corsets that were self-lacing up their backs as they stood in formation. As each corset passed through each eyelet, red herrings that read IN *the interest of the dynasty*, jumped OUT. Each woman wore a red wig and red ballet lace up slippers matching their red Dior #528 lipstick. The ballerina on top of the others reached up and grabbed a braided red ribbon hanging from the sky. As the ribbon was pulled, 12 red ribbons that were intertwined released. The ballerinas disassembled from the pyramid and 12 of them grabbed a red ribbon and swung through the air acrobatically catching 32 7-pronged heart tipped crowns, engraved with the date of invention, 1111, and 32 silver titanium briefcases and passed them out to the others.

The ballerinas shapeshifted into tap dancers with bright red hearts beating loudly to the tune of p-p-pitter pat. They tap danced in a SEQUENCE, dressed in 1960s-style white swimsuits and white flowered swim caps, which then changed shape to purple crash helmets. Half of the women carried silver titanium briefcases, while the other half wore gold crowns as they shifted into a line dance. They were clicking their heels with a

CLICK CLICK

CLICK CLICK

CLICK CLICK

CLICK   CLICK

CLICK CLICK

CLICK   CLICK

and clapping their hands with a

CLAPP   CLAPP

CLAPP   CLAPP

CLAPP   CLAPP

CLAPP   CLAPP

CLAPP   CLAPP

CLAPP   CLAPP

exchanging items back and forth as their clothes changed from white dresses to 1960s swimwear to the tune of "Don't Let Me Be Misunderstood," by Nina Simone. www.youtube.com/watcj?v=9ckv6-yhn1y.

In the shadows, the members of the shadow government, the 100 Knights Templar International Bankers, all dressed in black suits, red and white-checkered ties, and bowler hats traded black titanium briefcases with the communist symbol: a blazing sun rising over the mountains in the east. The words: *The Invisible Empire* were clearly visible under the sun.

The World Bank suits, who were a part of the Knights Templar International Bankers led the others with their fingers crossed behind their backs, they passed their briefcases between one another to a lower octave beat as Nina Simone's "Sinner Man (Felix Da Housecat House Mix)," www.youtube.com/watch?v=PrK35KKorM4 was playing. Their hearts, all showing through their white collared shirts were black and beat to a slow tock tick with no empathy. Their backs showed that their 7 chakra centers were seals plugged into by off world cable sources, directing their every move in accordance with the negative alien agenda. Blueprints hung out from their briefcases, stating:

- GREED

- POWER

- FRAUD

- EXPLOITATION

- ENSLAVEMENT THROUGH DEBT CONTROL

- FEDERAL RESERVE – PRIVATELY OWNED by BANKERS IN THE CITY OF LONDON, WHICH IS NOT BOUND BY LAWS.

- WAR – *SOLD AS PROTECTION (for the elite)*

- HIDDEN ANCIENT KNOWLEDGE USED AGAINST HUMANITY

- 2012 DECEPTION – KEEPING you IN THE DARK

- 2030 REPORT – POSTGLACIAL REBOUND

- SECRET SPACE PROGRAM – NAZI RUN

- SECRET FUNDED BLACK OPERATIONS including low flying self repairing/self replicating nano satellite orbiting systems

- WORLD BANK / IMF RULE THE WORLD THROUGH DEBT ENSLAVEMENT

- PSYCHOLOGICAL WARFARE SUPPRESSING CONSCIOUSNESS

- USE OF THE PLANETARY GRID FOR NUCLEAR WARFARE

- EARTHQUAKE WARS / ENERGY WARS

- THE SAGA OF THE counterfeit BEARER BONDS

- CLONE WARS

- THE GREAT TIME WARS

As they passed the briefcases between one another, the communist symbol changed into millions of logos, flashing each time they changed hands. The logos involved corporations, cities, states, countries, flags, religions, movies, entertainment and music. The logos all showed the blazing sun rising over the mountains of the east, faintly emblazoned in the background. It was a worldwide movement. Under the logos, it read:

A Dawn of a New Day.

The typing black ravens shapeshifted into crows and swirled in a circle above the shadow government group. Their briefcases fell to the ground, opening up and exposing hundreds of counterfeit $1,000,000,000 Kennedy bearer bonds. One side of the bond showed Kennedy's face, the other side showed the space shuttle going to the moon. The shadow government group fell to the ground and gathered up their bonds. A digitized debt clock, in the shape of a giant piggy bank, ran up in the background. Above the piggy bank was a sign that read:

National Debt = Enslavement.

The shadow government group went DOWN an escalator marked 14,832. The women in white passed through a turnstile and went UP a parallel escalator marked 12,960. Their escalator was made out of the 13-month calendar based on the original moon cycles. The women in white handed them their white hankies as they passed one another. The women going UP followed a 90-degree arrow that pointed to a sign that read: *To Greener Pastures.*

Beyond the sign, I saw a spiraling yellow brick road that said *Make Your Own Providence.* It led to green grass, clean water, fresh air and a place where there was a fine mist of Chanel No. 5 glistening in the air.

The shadow government members followed an exit sign that read: *Road to Destruction.* They waved their white hankies while all the women in white outstretched their arms and pointed their fingers at them, as if they were hands on a clock pointing to 4 o'clock. The crows descended upon the shadow government and led them to a feast of humble pie. The shadow government fought over the pie. Each one wanted a bigger piece. The pie shapeshifted into PI, then shapeshifted into suns.

Once there, the black crows shapeshifted into a circle of PHI and then the constellation Corbus, the crow, as the film of JFK's murder by Zapruder played in slow motion. The film showed the alteration in the SEQUENCE in the film frames at 1.618 intervals throughout, using Gestalt psychology techniques that changed the perception of the event through optical illusion.

The scene of the black 1961 Lincoln coming around the corner with the right wheel hitting the curb, sending it into a wobble and braking, *was spliced.* The loud sound that made the driver hit the brakes a second time *was spliced.* The scene of the President standing up and saying, "Oh my God I've been shot," *was spliced.* The black Lincoln shapeshifted into a black box with the code SS 100x written on the side…and then into a black coffin.

After it ended, two black and white Polaroid photos, one of JFK and one of Officer J.D. Tippit, who was killed 45 minutes after JFK, *were spliced* together, showing their resemblance. They looked like brothers. The lips were joined together with a bright red color. The picture flipped over, revealing the Warren Commission Report. The report stated that the original autopsy for J.D. Tippit was the same as JFK's. At the bottom it read: Date of Death: November 22, 1963. *THE ANSWER LIES IN TIMELINES.*

The subtitle read: *The Big Event = Ancient history reenacted as Act I of the*

Dark Tragedy, the Egyptian myth of Osiris versus Set. Osiris's assasination by his brother Set and 72 accomplices. Osiris, who represented order of the world was snuffed out by Set, who represented chaos/destruction of the world. This Dark Tragedy resulted in the 4 parts of Act I: Death, Disorder, Darkness, Destruction being played out since the time of the pharoahs. The planet earth has been operating out of this closed system of life. It is where chaos and destruction have fed

back and *forth*

into

one another

over and *over*

because the 3rd loop, which opens UP the closed system of the feedback loop, was cut off from the Divine feminine energy. This happens in Act II of the Big Event when the female, represented by Isis, realizes the power she holds and reveals the codes she holds.

The shadow government group shapeshifted to the face of their fathers and grandfathers, criminals in 3 piece suits, framing the beginning of deception. They froze in time, then shapeshifted to framed pictures of René Magritte's, "The Son of Man," which is a picture of a man in a bowler hat with his face hidden by a sour green apple.

Then they shapeshifted to "The Man with the Bowler Hat," which is a picture of a man in a bowler hat with a white dove covering his face. The white dove shapeshifted into a vulture as the sun rose in the east emitting a coronal mass ejection in the form of Trivial Pursuit pie pieces at 19.47 north and south latitude, burning the vulture and turning him into a buzzard. He made the sound, peeee-uu, as the Trivial Pursuit pieces reorganized into a pie

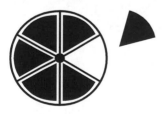 chart of the true government spending, including black operation projects. The largest piece, over 80 percent was for Project Bluebeam, the fake alien invasion planned to create world domination of a few over the many by skewing the truth of extra terrestrial life *in their favor.*

The woman in red from the grassy knoll in Dallas who saw the entire crime of JFK's murder revealed herself in the black and white Polaroid of JFK and J.D. Tippit. She was morphed into the painting as the ruby red lips. She stood up, gathered her red dress and walked out of the Polaroid. She turned into Marilyn Monroe in a red dress and then walked into a black and white film of 64 pictures of the comic strip "Hell Hath No Fury Like A Woman Scorned." The comic strip film surrounded the women with the silver titanium briefcases. The women stood in a straight line and bowed their heads as they opened the briefcases revealing the message:

The Egyptian Goddess Isis held the

POWER

over

Osiris (order) and Set (chaos/destruction).

The POWER of the female energy REASSEMBLES Divine Order through the

OPEN SYSTEM,

the third loop,

PILLAR #13

ACT II is beginning as Act I is ending.

The women with the gold crowns came up on their left side, bent down and BLEW A BREATH of fresh air at the exact moment the briefcases opened, sending trillions of tiny red hearts flying into the air. The women holding the briefcases revealed a blueprint at the bottom of them stating a new way of being:

+ WOMEN REMEMBERING THEIR INHERENT POWER

+ LAW OF ONENESS REINSTATED (LIVING IN TRUTH)

+ PEACEFUL AND LOVING TOWARD THY NEIGHBOR

+ GOLDEN RULE REINSTATED

+ ENVIRONMENTALLY RESPONSIBLE TO MOTHER EARTH
AND FATHER SKY

+ ABUNDANCE OF FOOD AND CLEAN WATER FOR ALL

+ REVEALING ALL HIDDEN ADVANCED
ANCIENT TECHNOLOGY

+ REVEALING FREE ENERGY

+ WORKING TOGETHER TO CREATE AN INSPIRING WORLD
FOR ALL BASED ON SOLUTIONS

+ THE TRUTH ABOUT 2012

+ THE TRUTH ABOUT GLOBAL WARMING / POSTGLACIAL
REBOUND

+ REVEALING SECRET SPACE INFORMATION

+ AXIATONAL LINES WITHIN THE PLANETARY GRID ACTI-
VATED WITH THE NEW LOGOS, THE LAW OF ONE

+ REVEALING THE 64 TETRAHEDRAL GRID AS THE FUNDA-
MENTAL FRACTAL STRUCTURE OF THE UNIVERSE

+ THE TRUTH REVEALED ABOUT CONSCIOUSNESS

+ LIFT THE ABORIGINE TRIBE LEADERS BACK TO WHERE
THEY BELONG AS THE TRUE LEADERS OF THE WORLD

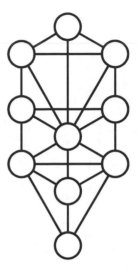

Before closing the briefcase the human divine blueprint was revealed on a McCall's pattern of Princess Leia and Hans Solo from Star Wars. The two McCall's patterns had the Tree of Life SEQUENCE drawn on them in the black ink of a Sharpie pen. The 12 sephirots were held in place by 12 of the jewels from the crown of the women dancers, depicting the intersection points along the pathways of the journey to self. The two patterns flew up into the air. The Tree of Life pattern overlayed on my head, revealing that the map to higher consciousness was a crown-like pattern, which if understood, allowed access to the greater potential of me. The theme song of "The Empire Strikes Back," www.youtube.com/watch?v=z5oDh7o3a00 began to play.

Halfway through the song, the architectural blueprint of the universe materialized on the side of the briefcase as a COSMIC CUBE depicted by the 7 – 17 – 2010 crop circle at Fosbury, Wiltshire, UK with the 7 – 9 – 2010 crop circle at Cley Hill near Warminster, Wiltshire overlaying it with a message underneath the two images that read: *All our knowledge is the offspring of our perceptions.* –Leonardo da Vinci.

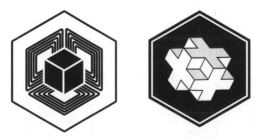

They closed the briefcases and stood tall. The women with the crowns removed them and placed them on the other women. The women with the crowns revealed the locks of the briefcases were engraved with the message:

<u>YOU > you x PHI</u>

LOVE

The key to OPEN is for everyone to hold a positive vision for the future rooted in ONENESS.

The women without the crowns sang in unison, *the key to OPEN is to see the smaller you and turn it into the GREATER YOU and multiply it by PHI then give it the common denominator of LOVE.*

All the women joined hands and melded together to form one woman with a large beating red heart. Thirty two ravens swirled around her and cut the film reel of the comic strip, *"Hell Hath No Fury Like a Woman Scorned"* into 64 pictures that shapeshifted into the 6, 3 and 9 tarot cards. The cards balanced against each other, then fell into a silver box, labeled *Present Moments – Once in a Lifetime Moments.* A red ribbon fell from the sky, looping into a heart shaped bowtie with an extra loop. The final knot on the third loop, which read $X = Y^{knot}$, was tightened to the sound of 32 delete buttons on Apple laptop computers being clicked. The digital debt on the piggy bank was wiped out releasing the human race from enslavement by debt control. The pink piggy bank now read:

O

Zero Point, the Event Horizon.

Marilyn Monroe rose out of a stack of 64 crowns from the ground, on a soup ladle. She emerged in a long red silk dress covered in blackbirds with an ornate gold wired birdcage on her head. She sang in a mechanical voice, it's a dIgItal IllU.S.Ion. It's as easy as hitting a DELETE button.

The ravens flew over Marilyn Monroe and then shapeshifted into the stages of the moon, and then into PI.

The head raven was inside the birdcage, holding the poem "Raven" by Edgar Allan Poe in his mouth. He dropped the poem through the cage and the paper whistled through the wind to the tune of nevermore as it shapeshifted into a 3D, 64-squared black and red chessboard. A new message overlayed the chess board in red that read:

Don't forget to take a bird's eye view of life.

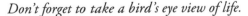

Ascend. Trust.

Lift and merge.

Beat wings. Fly.

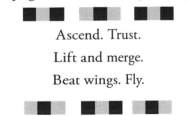

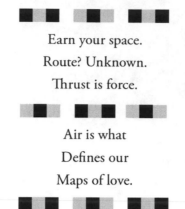

Earn your space.

Route? Unknown.

Thrust is force.

Air is what

Defines our

Maps of love.

The head raven morphed into a bluebird, then into a brown robin who morphed into the superhero Robin, Batman's right hand man. He opened the cage as he said, Holy Las Vegas and then morphed into a white dove as **the word** KAPOW! formed inside a cloud overhead with lightning bolts coming off it. The white dove flew into the air, multiplied *over* and *over* and *over* and *over* and *over* and *over* and *over* and *over* and *over* to infinity and then turned into the painting, "The Regular Division of the Plane with Birds," by M.C. Escher. One white dove flew out of the painting carrying a banner that read: *For me it remains an open question whether (this work) pertains to the realm of mathematics or to that of art.* –M.C. Escher.

The background turned into a grid made of the following numbers:

3.141592653589793238462643383279 x 33.33 =

104.71975511965977461542144610931 x 3 =

314.1592653589793238462643383279 x 33.33 =

10471.975511965977461542144610931 x 3 =

31415.92653589793238462643383279 x 33.33 =

1047197.5511965977461542144610931 x 3 =

3141592.653589793238462643383279 x 33.33 =

104719755.11965977461542144610931 x 3 =

314159265.3589793238462643383279 x 33.33 =

10471975511.965977461542144610931 x 3 = tri-wave infinity.

Marilyn Monroe, dressed in red with the gold birdcage on her head melted down to just her heart, which turned into a pool of blood in a ladle with two fish facing opposite ways connected by their tails creating a diamond in the center.

STORY #13: Cherry Elixer

I awoke to a spoon in the shape of a tri-wave infinity symbol held in front of me by Mom. She said, WAKE UP, DREAMER. Time to take your medicine. She held up an old brown bottle with 2 red hearts overlaying one another creating a 3rd heart. The label read: *Heart to H'art*.

I said, ohh Mom.

She said, ok, let's make this a game. Sometimes when you don't want to do something it is easier to make it a game. Imagine me as Mary Poppins in a red dress. She started singing "A Spoonful of Sugar Helps the Medicine Go Down," www.youtube.com/watch?v=HrnoR9cBP3o. I sat up and swallowed a spoonful of medicine as I imagined it was a magic cherry flavored elixir.

Mom said, now how are you feeling? You're looking a little cheeky.

I said, I will survive.

Of course you will. You are a survivor! She dropped 2 red dice on my nightstand as she left my room. The dice rolled over onto a *Vanity Fair* magazine that had Marilyn Monroe on the cover. The cover read: *The Secret Marilyn Monroe Files*.

I said, what are the dice for?

Roll the dice and see who you want to be today.

I said, Mom, that's outrageous!

She just winked at me and said, you are a rare bird, as she closed the door.

I threw the dice in the air as I thought to myself, I have 8^2 possibilities before I even put my feet on the ground.

I sang, I'm a survivor! I'm a survivor! I'm a survivor!

STORY #8: Boundary Layers

WALK THE LINE

STORY #5: Welcome Home to Egypt

As I disembarked from the plane I looked around to find my way to the baggage claim area. An airport attendant directed me by pointing to a line of red arrows. Somehow I veered off track and got lost. When I finally reached the baggage claim my bags that were covered in circles, squares and triangle stickers were the only ones left. I watched as they told a story of the places I had been as they went around the carousel. I thought, life is like a carousel going in circles, never getting you anywhere until it stops and you get off of it. I watched my bag tag with a picture of a 1962 pink Cadillac cruise around and around with the words *Queen of the Road* catching my eye every time it passed. I stood frozen in time watching the 1962 Cadillac drive by

I snapped out of my daze and thought, what have I done? Why am I here? The reality of my choices hit me like a sledgehammer. I stood paralyzed in fear. I said to myself, Gabriella, put FAITH on one foot and TRUST on the other. I kicked off my left red shoe and placed my foot on the ground, resting the arch of my foot on the cold concrete for a split second. I quickly slipped on my left red shoe and did the same exercise with my right red shoe. I then felt I had the courage to move forward. It was like a mental dance step, a shuffle ball change of the mind. I told myself, Gabriella, place one foot in front of the other and repeat FAITH, TRUST, FAITH, TRUST, FAITH, TRUST until you reach the taxi stand. You can do it!

I heard Mom's voice as if she were perched on my shoulder: don't take an unsecured taxi, who knows where you could end up. I know I have always said if someone kidnapped you they would turn you loose by morning, but that was only for your benefit. I wanted you to become a fearless woman.

I walked to the taxi stand placing one foot in front of the other as I said,

FAITH TRUST

FAITH TRUST

FAITH TRUST

FAITH TRUST

FAITH TRUST

FAITH TRUST

FAITH TRUST

FAITH TRUST

FAITH TRUST

An elderly man, wearing a blue robe and white turban and Nike Air Jordan tennis shoes shuffled up to me and smiled a peculiar toothless smile. He had as many lines on his face for as many years he was — which had to be around 80. His face looked like the road map of his life. I got lost in following the tracks. They all seemed to lead to the same place — his eyes. He had a sparkle within his blue eyes that lit up his entire face like a disco ball. He patiently waited until I was done tracking and then said, *Welcome home.* He had a heavy accent, and I wondered how much English he spoke.

I said, thank you, thinking that he knew I was homeless.

He said, do you need a taxi?

I said yes.

He took me to a taxi that looked very unsecure. It *did* have a yellow taxi sign on top, but it looked nothing like a taxi—more like a small bus stolen from the junkyard. The back was packed with caged chickens and one rooster. As an overweight American man got in, I noticed that one wheel looked unsecure. A few other tourists from around the globe continued piling in so I thought, what the hell.

He took my baggage and said, I am Nasam and I will be your guide. Where are you going, *habibi*?

I got lost in the sound of that word. I loved the way it sounded. It sounded so…foreign. Right at that exact moment all my pain and sadness came upon me like a stack of cards all lined up in front of me and someone was taking a deep breath and blowing them, sending them falling one

on TOP of the other

    on TOP of the other

        on TOP of the other

            on TOP of the other

                on TOP of the other

                    on TOP of the other

                        on TOP of the other

                            on TOP of the other

                              and then on me.

I gasped and said, take me to the Giza Plateau.

He said, with your baggage?

I shrugged and said yes.

I climbed into the passenger seat in front and closed the door. I slammed it too hard and Nasam came up to my door and readjusted the hinges. He put his hand through the open window and said, easy greasy, with a huge toothless smile.

I looked back at him and thought, his happiness is contagious. I smiled a big toothy grin. I thought, see you are already smiling again.

Nasam took me to the Giza Plateau first because everyone else in the taxi wanted to see the sight we'd flown half way around the world to see. When we pulled up to the parking area we were all oohing and ahhing like first timers. My first thought was, there is no way humans built this. No way!

It was the most beautiful sight of historical value I had ever seen. Nasam looked over and again whispered, *Welcome home.* I started to cry. I was crying about this beauty, this mystery that was staring right back at me. It was overwhelming. I also was crying about the love I felt from this complete stranger, and for my broken heart, all at the same time. From his back pocket he pulled out a clean white hanky and gave it to me. I thought, how symbolic. I need to surrender to my surroundings now and enjoy this because it is definitely a once in a lifetime moment.

He asked, do you have a plan?

I said no. Plan A fell apart. I just came to have this experience. This is amazing!

I said to myself,

I'M FREE!   I'M FREE!   I'M FREE!

I'M FREE!   I'M FREE!   I'M FREE!

I'M FREE!   I'M FREE!   I'M FREE!

…TO BE ME!

And just like that, as if on cue, the radio started playing the first dance song from my wedding, "Unforgettable," by Nat King Cole, www.youtube.com/watch?v=vDN5rG3wLa4. All my pain came rushing back.

Nasam said, let me take you to my friend Gouda's shop. He is the alchemist in town and he has a room for you.

I said ok while at the same time I heard my mother's voice warning me as if I brought her along on the trip.

I didn't care if I was kidnapped right now. I decided to put my life in the hands of this unlucky taxi driver. If he did kidnap me he would turn me loose by morning. I did not even feel scared until we took a corner on two wheels curbing the right front tire and leaving the bus feeling very unsecure. We wobbled

back *and* forth

back *and* forth

back *and* forth

I held on tight and told myself, *buckle up and enjoy the ride!*

The taxi driver looked over at me, shook his head from side to side and said, it's important to always be the driver of your own bus. Don't take the passenger seat in life. He lifted his hands up off the wheel and then placed them at 10 o'clock and 2 o'clock. He said, 2 hands on the clock keep you on the track, then he smiled like he had just revealed the secret of life to me. I made the sign of the cross even though I hadn't been to church at Our Lady of Sighs since I got my license to drive.

We arrived at Gouda's. His shop had no sign, which made me question my decision. But, when Gouda emerged I knew I would be ok. He too had the sparkle. His eyes beamed back at me in a loving manner. He had dark, lined skin with less tracks than Nasam and rotten yellow teeth, slicked back, jet black hair. He wore a long blue dress with a pair of old Nikes and smelled like a mix of patchouli and body odor.

Nasam placed my baggage on the curb and then embraced Gouda. Gouda slipped him a couple dollars and I thought this must be their gig. Two other passengers got out too. They spoke French so I couldn't communicate with them, but they looked safe. I thought, when you travel and don't speak the language you read the energy of love. If you can feel love you know you are safe. So far so good.

I paid Nasam and said goodbye.

He said, oh, I will see you again for sure. He held up four fingers.

I had no idea what that meant. Possibly for sure = 4.

He smiled and whispered, next time I see you, YOU will have the ability to see past your 4 fingers. He chuckled and got back in his taxi and sped off.

I watched as the taxi disappeared into a thick mist of dust.

I entered the alchemy shop with Gouda. I was not prepared for what I saw and smelled. The four walls were lined with 4 foot x 4 feet wooden framed cubbyholes that resembled linotype drawers from the 1960s. Each framed section held 7 columns with varying sizes of compartments within it. Some cubbyholes held beakers, some bottles and some red tags in the shape of circles. I played a quick mental game of Connect Four as I connected a diagonal four red circles in a row. My mind yelled, Connect Four.

Gouda knocked on the wooden table in the center of the room with 2 candy canes on it, bringing me spiraling back to the shop. He gestured for me to take a seat.

I took a seat on the right hand side of the wooden table on a bench filled with graffiti markings. I placed my hand *over* and *under* the table to scoot myself in and felt my hand on top of a mound of chewed bubblegum. I surveyed the alchemy shop noticing how meticulous everything was except the hidden bubblegum. I felt like I was standing in a laboratory from another time period. I dropped my ticket on the floor so I could see if what I felt was real. Sure enough it was a pile of used pink bubblegum.

Unaware of my personal adventure, Gouda said, each bottle can transport you to another timeline. He picked up a bottle marked *Amberi Atari* and brought it to his nose. I watched him close his eyes and stand in reverence to the smell from the bottle. I watched his nose flare out and a small smile take form, lighting up his face like a Christmas tree.

I thought, can a smell really transport you like that or is he faking it?

He handed me the bottle. I took it carefully as I noticed a small bird on the vintage label. I smelled it by breathing in deeply trying to imitate him. I immediately felt a sense of ecstasy and jet lag rolled up in sadness overcome me.

Gouda said, some smells transport you to timelines where you need to learn a thing or two. Others transport you to ecstasy. It's all in the *set up* of where you want to go.

I thought, where could I go? My mind could only come up with the Monopoly game. Under my breath I said, I choose to Pass G**O** and collect my $250 million dollars while my eyes scanned the beakers that lined the entire back wall of the shop. They were filled with a beautiful array of yellow, white, red, pink and blue flowers. My eyes could not be pried from one beaker filled to 3.14 of blue flowers.

I looked at Gouda and said, what does alchemy mean?

He said, alchemy is the magical PR**O**CESS of transmuting.

If you want to understand alchemy you need to understand the Emerald Tablet, which is the premier book of alchemy. Alchemy is the knowledge of and methods for the alteration of the human body to God consciousness. It was the PROCESS all Egyptians worked toward. You can see it in all the hieroglyphs. This state of being created heaven on earth. Heaven is a place within the soul. It is lost knowledge today, but my hope is that someday people will realize there is more to this world and start searching for ancient knowledge again. The changes wrought by alchemy can be so profound that one feels as if one is flying above life and viewing it from an expanded perspective. This is why alchemical symbols usually show wings or flying beings associated with them, like Hermes.

He turned abruptly and said, pointing to all the oils and elixirs, these assist in the PROCESS. They are created with the resonance of *Remembrance.*

Hope is what I was looking for in the oils and elixirs he had lined up in tiny bottles all over the room. I thought, maybe this is what will cure me. My eyes traveled around the room searching for my answer. My eyes got stuck on a bottle that I felt was the answer then it quickly moved on to another like a game of hopscotch. Each elixir and oil was in an old amber brown bottle that looked like they were from different eras. They ranged in sizes from 3 to 9 inches tall. The tops of each bottle did not match the bottle or any other bottle. They were all unique, in styles of various species of birds. The bottle and top didn't seem to go together, but they did. It was like when you see a couple walking hand in hand and wonder how they went together. One didn't match the other, but somehow they worked. The labels looked as if their paper was as ancient as the elixir recipe, with images of all different types of bird outlines on them. The labels seemed to hold the whole thing together. As if reading my mind, Gouda said, just like in life, the label we place on everything holds the game in place so that nothing moves forward.

I heard him but was too wrapped up in *my* STORY to give it much thought. I was desperately scanning the room for the magical elixir to TRANSMUTE *MY* HEART.

Gouda said, let me show you why you came HERE.

I thought, my room can not be that great. This is not the Ritz Carlton.

He took me upstairs and walked me out to a balcony on top of the building. It was the most amazing sight I had ever seen. It was a bird's eye view of the Giza Plateau. It was amazing! Gouda had several old lawn chairs set up. The seats showed signs of wear and tear. They were all fraying from the many visitors who sat there before me. I could sense there were many men and women who walked my steps. I wondered what had they seen? What mission were they on? What led them here? What track were they on?

He said, wait until it gets dark and you'll see it lit up like a Christmas tree…don't forget to look up as he pointed to the sky. Don't forget the star on top. The star is celebrating *SOLON VICTUS*. The celebration of the rebirth of the sun-like blue star. The date 9 - 11 – 3 B.C. was the last time the blue star shined. That was the day Jesus was born, the great physicist. He gave me a long wink. He said, my dear, betrayal runs so deep. The religious wars are all a hoax. Egypt will help you OPEN YOUR EYES to see more clearly. Well, that and my magic elixirs.

All I could say was, thank you.

He said, settle in and relax as he waved his hand in the air. I will put your baggage in your room and mix you up an elixir, gather some oils and create a special blend unique to you along with a special tea for the two of us.

I said, thank you, as I took a seat in a green and white vinyl chair. I thought, I haven't seen one of these lawn chairs since I was a little girl. I used to weave them when they broke. I loved the patterning

over over over over over under under under under under under under under under under over over over over over over over

I let my mind drift away. It went to the time when I bought a portable 7-foot copper pyramid with crystals and had it placed over Mitchell's side of the bed. I learned the power of the pyramid structure and of the healing benefits it created so I thought, why not try it. He hurt himself pitching in the final game of the season 1 year ago and had not mended from it. His career was over and he was desperately trying to get it back. He was not prepared for it to be over. He had no warning and all of a sudden his dream was over. I had given up all my dreams to help him pursue his so I spent an entire year researching every type of healing modality. Once I had him try every normal one, we moved into the mystical ones. I spent hours every day researching the greatest healers from all over the world. It became my job. My life prior to his accident was supporting him emotionally and after the accident it was researching ways to heal him. My whole life was wrapped up in him. He humored me but never really believed. Maybe that is why he never healed because he never really believed. His mind was a steel trap. He was a Taurus.

I didn't see anything wrong with dedicating my life to holding it all together. That is what a wife in the male-dominated sports industry does. She is the stability ball. She is the one who packs UP for the season from home, unpacks at spring training, packs UP for the season city, unpacks at the season city, packs UP after the season and unpacks at home base. She coordinates all the events. She handles the family. She handles the errands. She is at every game. She cheers. She supports. She is his right hand man, his wing man…

she gives

and

gives

and

gives *and* gives

and

gives *and* gives *and* gives

and gives *and* gives *and* gives *and* gives

and

gives *and* gives *and* gives *and* gives *and* gives

and

gives *and* gives *and* gives *and* gives *and* gives *and* gives

and

gives *and* gives *and* gives *and* gives *and* gives *and* gives *and* gives

and

then…when she thinks she doesn't have anything left to give,

she gives M**O**RE.

Isn't that what all women do? They give everything of themselves to someone, some thing, anything…besides themselves. I didn't really mind it…until now. I was in it 100 percent. I loved him so much. He was my Egyptian god. I just loved him so much. I was so proud of him. I remember laying under the pyramid I put over the bed thinking God, why did you have to end this? What did he do to deserve this? Can't you take my shoulder, my wing? I would have given up my left arm for him. I used to stare over at him as he was sleeping and think, why did it have to end? I didn't know it was ending our relationship too. This was out of left field for me. I wasn't prepared. He was not only my husband and my best friend he was my everything. I invested my whole self into him. I thought maybe the second half, Act II, of our lives would be about me. I would finally be able to express myself and he would be THERE for me.

I was so wrong.

After trying every modality under the sun, he had become impatient with the healing process and with me and my *crazy ass ideas*. I remember after he left to go to rehab in Las Vegas, I kept the pyramid up over his side of the bed with his picture underneath it. A shamanic healer told me that the energy transmitting into Mitchell's picture could heal him just as much as if he were there. I placed his baseball card under the pyramid. He was still with me in bed even though he didn't know it. I did it hoping for a miracle. One day I came home and the energy had burned through the sheets. The baseball card was fine, but the sheets had a hole in them. I smiled and thought, that really did work. I am on to something here. Pyramid structures really are energy generators. They are powerful! I looked up at the Great Pyramid and thought, all I have now is his number 33 burned in my brain. Every time I saw that number I thought of what could have been. We could have been together forever if the game hadn't ended. I thought, all games must come to an end.

Gouda interrupted me with my room key, some oil for my heart, a shot of cherry red elixir and a tea called Remembrance Tea. He gave me several bottles of custom blended oils in a hemp bag held together by a blue string and a triangular vintage tag that read: Santa Claus is coming to town. I smiled as Gouda told me to take them with me on my adventure. It would assist me in perceiving things differently while I traveled the world.

I asked him how I would know which oil or elixir to take and when.

He said, oh…Quando, Quando, Quando.

I started to cry and Gouda said, I am sure there is a story for those tears.

I told him the story of my break up as I caught some of my tears in my hand. They flowed from me like raindrops. Gouda consoled me and said that I would receive a healing in Egypt and not to worry so much about Mr. Wrong, soon to be Mr. X. He said, there are many more fish in the sea.

He pointed to the Great Pyramid and said, isn't it wonderful? Hermes said in the *Emerald Tablet* that this beautiful pyramid was created from the proportions of the Earth connecting to Heaven. He also said Egypt was the image of the heavens, the whole cosmos dwells here. Pointing at the Great Pyramid, he said, that is the time clock. It explains the precession of the equinox through the mathematics from which it was built. The mathematics of it are staggering; if you are ever interested in the mystery just ask me. It was built after the last large disaster to teach us how to prepare for the next BIG EVENT. It's the countdown to ascension. He outstretched his hands and said, they made it so big as if saying, hello, PAY ATTENTION!!

He took his fist and knocked on his head and said, is anybody in there?

On cue a laser light show started. I watched the light reflect off the pyramids and the Sphinx, who was facing east. The Sphinx came alive to me. I saw the eagle wings from around its sides materialize out of thin air. I saw the head turn into a pharoah. I saw the hindquarters turn into a bull and the chest and paws turn into a lion. All 4 creatures were guarding the information under the paws.

Gouda whispered, when Solomon wished to sit on the throne, the Ox took him gently on his horns and handed him over to the Lion. Finally the Eagle raised him and placed him on his seat and gave him wings to soar.

I thought, our wings have been clipped. We are much more than we know.

He handed me a piece of papyrus that read:

The 4 cornerstones are:

Taurus as the Ox

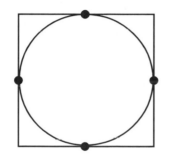

Leo as the Lion   *Aquarius as Solomon on his throne*

Scorpio as the Eagle

The mathematics of the Universe has been distorted affecting the LOGOS of earth taking it out of balance and harmony into chaos and destruction. The Queen is to be REINSTATED on the throne. The King is to be relinquished of the power he holds. We need a strong woman, like YOU, to take the King out of the game replacing him with the Queen. Are you ready to be the Queen of your Fate?

The Sphinx Code

Upper Body:

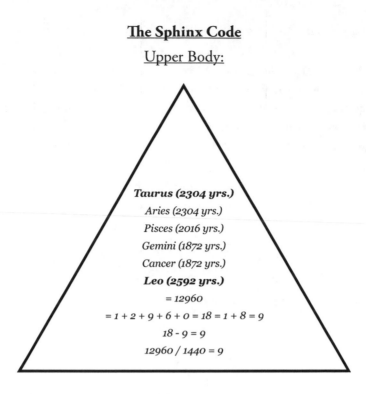

Taurus (2304 yrs.)
Aries (2304 yrs.)
Pisces (2016 yrs.)
Gemini (1872 yrs.)
Cancer (1872 yrs.)
Leo (2592 yrs.)
= 12960
= 1 + 2 + 9 + 6 + 0 = 18 = 1 + 8 = 9
18 - 9 = 9
12960 / 1440 = 9

Lower Body:

Scorpio (1872 yrs.)
Sagittarius (2304 yrs.)
Capricorn (2304 yrs.)
Libra (1872 yrs.)
Virgo (2592 yrs.)
Aquarius (2016 yrs.)
= 12,960 = 1 + 2 + 9 + 6 + 0 = 18
= 1 + 8 = 9
18 - 9 = 9
12960 / 1440 = 9

I looked up at him, dazed and confused.

He said, you might find that handy later on your journey. Life is a riddle. It's sometimes fun to see where clues may lead you. You know the word Cairo means Mars. This entire complex is replicated on Mars. The face on Mars is the Sphinx. The Sphinx was created in the likeness of the Goddess. She is the one that creates life! Unfortunately she has been *defaced throughout history* just as the Sphinx has. Look at her.

I looked over at the Sphinx in lights and saw her defaced in ways that only Picasso would be happy to see. I put the papyrus carefully in my pocket and became enthralled by the view and thought about what the world would be like if the Goddess reigned supreme. I thought, this has become the most amazing experience of my life. I listened to Pink Floyd's "Comfortably Numb," www.youtube.com/watch?v=Bpzxf_flm8M and went numb. Watching ancient history mixed with present day technology was fascinating. I drank my tea, lathered up in the fragrant oils and sat back and smiled. This is it. This is my new life. I felt happy, followed by a pang in my heart. Happiness and pain seemed to come in waves—or was it the music?

I must have dozed off after the show ended. I woke up and saw that the pyramid was dark now. Ten front loaders and 10 heavy military trucks came barreling in to the Giza Plateau. I watched as chests and sarcophagi were being lifted out. The hair on the back of my neck was standing on end. Something was going on here that was not right. I tried to stay awake and see what illegal activity was going on but my sleepiness won out over my curiosity for the first time in my life. I had no fight left in me. I rang the boxing bell in defeat and went to my room.

I pulled the old black metal key out of my pocket and looked down at it. The key had the words *unattached observer* etched into it. I put the key in the keyhole and turned it with a CLICK as the door sprang open. I surveyed the room and thought, definitely not Ritz Carlton, definitely not. I walked over to the twin size bed and sat down with a thud. I felt as if my heart traveled the same path as it sank in despair along with the bed. I sat eye level with the nightstand. I noticed there was a magnifying glass lying over a map of the world next to a small red clock with the face of Santa Claus and the clock hands of white batting gloves. I picked up the map and tried to make sense of the distinct red ink markings in circles, squares and triangles that were drawn all over it. I noticed a large eagle drawn over the Middle East. I thought, what is it about eagles that seem to be trying to tell me something on this trip? I didn't think I could figure anything out at this moment so I placed the papyrus Gouda had given me on top of the map for the morning.

I heard a CLICK from somewhere within the hall. I undressed and fell into bed naked as I rang my personal bell, as if to say I surrender to understand what is being revealed to me on this adventure. As an afterthought I thought, I hope it is something bigger than my previous life!

STORY #3: Tracing Paper, Maps and Symbols

I rang Mrs. Velvet's crescent moon shaped doorbell. It went *ding dong, ding dong, ding dong*. I took a deep breath and turned the white porcelain doorknob. I exhaled and entered Mrs. Velvet's living room. I had been HERE 100 times, but I still loved the experience of entering her space. I stood in her living room marveling at all the clocks. She owned 12 large round modern clocks set to different time zones with no numbers just 2 arms in the shape of a feather and a pen. They sounded like an orchestra of tick tocks set among the other sounds of her random old-fashioned clocks set around the room. None of the sounds were in the same rhythm, but somehow they merged into a beautiful symphony of

tIck t**o**ck

tIck t**o**ck   **o**   tIck t**o**ck

tIck t**o**ck

Mrs. Velvet said that time was an illusion and didn't matter. She just liked the sound of clocks ticking. She said it reminded her that she had escaped the world of time. She gave me a gold coin to keep in my pocket to remind me that time didn't really matter only the experience in the moment mattered. The gold coin had a silver center with a rose imprint along with the words: *I've arrived*. I carried it in my pocket and sometimes lost it only to find it at the exact moment I needed to remind myself to enjoy the moment because it was a present, a gift, no matter what my mind said.

The clocks were set among the maps she collected. Every inch of the walls in her living room were covered in maps of all ages and sizes. She had gold frames hung by blue strings placed over the maps as if they were framed. She told me it was an optical illusion, an illusion of the I AM. I loved that. I often closed one eye and opened the other seeing what I noticed to be different. It reminded me of my favorite mind game – *What Doesn't Belong Here?* The 6-foot wood framed windows were covered with my favorite antique maps from school made into pull-down window shades. I thought, her style was *beyond* hippie chic. This was C**oo**L times 2. Each map had at least 1 distinct red mark showing a geometric configuration and many red arrows all leading to war zones marked *distraction* from the I AM. I went over to one map to inspect it. All the arrows led to the country Iraq. It had a gigantic golden eagle traced over it in a red marker. I thought, what could a golden eagle have to do with Iraq?

I pondered this as I looked over at the coffee table. Something on top of it was calling me. I scanned the coffee table to see what was beckoning. The coffee table was a 4-foot by 4-foot glass table on 4 industrial wheels with a large old-fashioned movie reel of "Gone with the Wind" showing through underneath. I walked over and inspected the contents on top. Next to an antique Tiffany blue round clock set at 10 o'clock was a dirty, white, thick paper, vintage tag hanging from a blue string, wrapped around a large map made out of brown parchment. The vintage tag, in the shape of a briefcase with a harmonica handle read: *Study this map. Learn the world you live in. The lives of the people living across water are the same as yours. There is no difference between you and them. You are only separated by bodies of water. Learn the world. Spend your free time educating yourself. Learn your true ancestry.*

I thought, why not? as I untied the knot, releasing the string. I slowly unrolled the map over the coffee table. The map was of the world with hand drawn red triangles marking a string of sacred sites. I took my blue string and connected the sacred sites. They went *over* and *under* the equator. The blue string created an oscillating pattern of:

over over over over over

under under under under under

Once I revealed this to myself I pulled the string up and flipped the map over to see if there was a legend. On the flip side was a large triangle with the words:

MIND, INTELLECT, EGO

marked at each point.

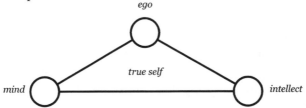

The center read: *Your True Self is hidden behind the 3 points of the triangle. It is HERE you discover the most famous lost sacred site of them all. The one that reveals the real secret. It is in the balance of the spin of the Great Pyramid that you find your True Self, your Zero Point.*

I wondered if that was what this was all about. Mrs. Velvet was studying the world and herself at the same time.

I heard her voice from another room say, Love, I am putting together something of universal magnitude and one day I will need your help. You always have to be prepared, so spend your free time studying the world and yourself. It is your life purpose to finish what I start.

I thought about Grandpa's saying that the military industrial complex starts wars so the common man can spend his life distracted from his real purpose, finishing what the warmongers start — all in the name of profit for them and loss for the common man.

I stood marveling at the depth of Mrs. Velvet. She was sophisticated, purposeful and fabulous. Everything she did had more than one meaning. She was multi-purposeful like Fabuloso, the purple multi purpose lavender cleaner. I hung on her every word. If she said to study the world and myself, I would do just that. Mrs. Velvet had an air about her. She made me want to be more than I could be. Forget the army slogan, I wanted to be more than I could be. Mrs. Velvet made me want to know more about myself. She made me curious about what made me tick. She made me question everything. I wondered, why did she think so differently than most? What extra ingredient did she have that made her so intriguing? I bet it was her Chanel No. 5. She didn't do anything that could be considered normal. She said normalcy was mundane. It was for people who were afraid to think. She drank the finest teas imported from all over the world. She said certain scents and teas made her think differently. She explored in every way. She played unique music I had never heard before. It had beats that made me FEEL. She danced around like she didn't have a care in the world, but the moment we were sharing. She was so present with me. She was my gift from the Universe.

I usually dressed in my mother's heels and hats and long dresses to go visit her. She told me to always wear my finest. Life was grand and meant to be lived that way! Today I wore a long red and white-checkered sundress with white gloves and a red pillbox hat.

Hers was the living room where I drew my first art masterpiece. She offered the space for me to go deep within myself. I drew my masterpiece one day when she turned up the classical music so loud I could feel it within my bones. It took me back in time to when I was an artist in one of my lifetimes. She told me to get in touch with that aspect of myself and let the Creative Genius flow. I would be amazed at the possibilities. My Creative Genius spoke to me that day. I felt like I was in touch with Leonardo da Vinci. I could feel his No. 2 pencil tapping on my head. I took my pencil and tapped my forehead 7 times and then drew a picture of 7 circles in 1 making 8 total. I added more circles within circles, all interconnected with vibrant paints creating a flower-like pattern. Mozart played, "The Marriage of Figaro," www.youtube.com/watch?v=8OZCyp-LcGw in the background as I moved my arms in the air and became ONE with Leonardo and Mozart. When I was finished I felt like my art spoke to me. Mrs. Velvet told me to SPIN it and see it from different angles because it would give me a different perspective. She said, different perspectives were worth their weight in gold. I spun my work. I was mesmerized by it. I followed the lines like they were tracks. They all led to another track, which eventually led to the circle that contained them all. It was fun. Each time I thought it would be different, but it was the same. Until one time I decided to take the track off the paper. I thought, my mind is the only one keeping me contained. I thought, I wonder how far is far?

Mrs. Velvet said that my work was ancient history speaking to me. I was remembering. She called the work the *flower of life*, the pattern that holds all of the Universe's secrets. The secrets were held within the 64 tetrahedral grid that the flower made.

I took it in to school the next day for my first art assignment. We were supposed to draw something that inspired us. I thought, if this is what holds the Universe's secrets I think everyone should be inspired by it.

My teacher, Mrs. Strawberry, loved it so much she created it as an assignment for everyone. She told the class to choose a geometric shape and draw the shapes interconnecting them like *my* picture. I thought that was cool but, I also thought, Mrs. Strawberry doesn't have a plan. She's copying my art and I am a child.

I discussed this with Mrs. Velvet over a mint-chocolate chip hot fudge sundae and a chocolate shake. These items sold for .99 cents at the Ice Cream Parlor at the end of the street. The parlor was my favorite because not only did it have the best treats it was also a treat for the eyes. It was filled with all types of flat swirly circles painted like lollipops that spun on the walls. I loved to go with Mrs. Velvet because she had no rules. I was allowed to have as many deserts as I wanted when I was with her, unlike Mom and Dad who only allowed me one. I always chose my 2 favorites, a hot fudge sundae and a chocolate shake. When my chocolate shake was served this time I did my usual thing. I spun the straw carousel *around* and *around* and *around* becoming mesmerized by the SPIN. I finally pulled the steel top UP and chose a pink and white striped straw as I made a wish.

I said, I hope when I grow up I am just like Mrs. Velvet. I winked at her and said, my teacher doesn't have it together. She is nothing like you. She's creating art lessons out of my original work.

Mrs. Velvet said, Love, we are all in the same boat. None of us have a plan. All information is recycled. It's old but we think it's new, and we are all just trying to REMEMBER what we once knew.

I thought, holy Las Vegas, as I dipped in for another bite of my sundae. Do you think I REMEMBER more than my teacher?

Mrs. Velvet looked deep in my eyes and said yes.

Wow, I thought. I MUST REALLY BE SPECIAL.

She put her hand on top of the straw carousel and tilted her head to one side and said, but…she knows things you forgot. She spun the carousel *around* and *around* and said, we are all on this earth, as it spins around and around, teaching one another 1 thing…and that is to REMEMBER what we know deep within, but forgot for a moment. The more you REMEMBER the more she remembers. It's a cycle that benefits everyone.

I tilted my head and said, Mrs. Velvet, what are you here to help me REMEMBER?

She said, Honey, as she peered over her bright red horn-rimmed glasses, that is the riddle of life. You never know, but each person has 1 or more things to help you REMEMBER. It's your job to figure it out. It's the riddle of life.

I said, maybe it's your job to help me REMEMBER why I chose my crazy family.

She laughed and pushed her glasses back UP and said, you'll know when it hits you.

I thought about this while I was flipping the menu card on the table *over* and *over* and *over* like a Rolodex. I said, do you think it hits you like a flash card? They flash in front of you and you're like, NOW I REMEMBER.

I had stopped flipping the menu cards at an illustration of the sundae special. It was a picture of a pink 1962 Cadillac with sparkling whitewalls. The slogan underneath read: *It's for women of all ages. Sunday's sundae special .99 cents. It's a pleasure to your senses.*

She said, exactly. Now remember one thing ok?

I looked UP at her with my huge green eyes and chocolate dripping down the front of me.

Always keep life a riddle, a game. Otherwise you will complicate it and then nothing will make sense and then you will become frustrated which does nothing for you but SPIN your whitewalls. She peered down at a dollar bill on the table and said, REMEMBER what George Washington said, *Truth will ultimately prevail where there is pains to bring it to light.*

George Washington?

To understand G.W. you have to understand the Knights Templar.

Who are they?

The Knights Templar discovered secrets from Solomon, the greatest magician in the world, who knew how to summon evil to achieve his desires. The word templar means template. They had the template on how to use the stargates.

What are templates?

They are patterns made out of geometry, like blueprints in the image of the Great Architect of the Universe and the time will come very soon when the Builder will have to build matter by the Law of One, the matter of the heart, the heart of the matter.

Are they like McCall's patterns for Raggedy Ann and Andy?

Yes.

Are we templates?

Yes, by 2012 you *must* restore your template.

Is it broken?

No, but the mathematical codes were messed with by off planet sources, creating interference, hardships.

Like the Joker in Batman, or worse, Darth Vader in Star Wars?

Yes, Love.

Hmmm…then, we will be repaired and turn into Princess Leias and Hans Solos.

So…what are stargates?

They are portals that connect to other dimensions.

Like the *Schwartzchild?*

She smiled and said yes.

Who has the key to the stargate?

You do. REMEMBER code **17HR496217547621**. It will open your turnstile.

I sat there in a daze as she continued. I felt the code had activated something in me. Something I once knew, but had forgotten. I felt something RISE UP within me.

She said, the Templars gained great power answerable only to the Pope when they got this information. Solomon's Temple was a replica of the Hall of Records, which contained the Atlanean secrets about life, death and resurrection. The story of Isis, Osiris, Set and Horus portray this. She spoke in a whisper, the story is about the 3 levels of consciousness. First you are whole.

Next, you become separated from your true self.

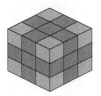

I interrupted: like when a Rubik's Cube is out of sync and all the squares are sequenced in different color patterns?

Yes, the third level is when you are brought back together as whole again.

I said, like sequencing all the squares to one color on each side of the cube?

Yes. Exactly. When you SEQUENCE yourself to whole colors you restore yourself and your light body and become a template for ascension, which is going beyond time/space into the VOID...consciously.

I said, being all I can be. So, just like the Rubik's Cube you have to follow a certain SEQUENCE of turns and clicks to achieve it?

Yes, Love. It is based on algorithms and it is not achieved by doing the same thing over and over.

I yelled, I want to CLICK!

You will, Love. I promise! You'll do this by 2012.

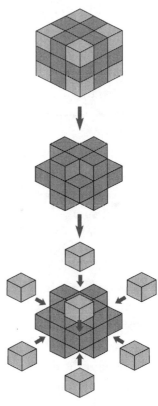

The Templars each became *a free man* – unencumbered by the restrictions of church and state because they had this knowledge. They needed no pass from a king or government to move as they wanted on the face of the Earth, from town to town, country to country. When these individuals were asked what induced them to become a freeman, or a Freemason, the proper answer always began with: *That I might travel in foreign countries...* but what they were really saying is *that I might travel beyond time/space.*

So foreign countries mean foreign worlds to them?

Exactly. They became very powerful because they didn't have to obey church laws. They began borrowing and lending money with interest. They became the world's largest international megabank. The day the Templars were supposedly killed, 10 – 22 –1307 some slipped away on ships to Scotland.

So G.W. was a Freemason?

Yes, and he was the First President, as well as the man on the dollar bill, who went to his grave with a very large secret about the map of the world. She lifted up the dollar bill and said, this is him. She had strawberry jam on her fingers that left red fingerprints on the dollar that looked like blood.

This is how they used to carry out their agendas…through symbols. Most symbols have been hijacked from ancient civilizations and they know their *original meaning.* They use the power behind the symbol to achieve their agenda or they change the symbol.

How?

By slightly changing the geometry. If you change a symbol slightly, you change the entire mathematics and mathematics are the only truth on this planet.

Does Jonny know this?

No. Only the selected few know this. Ancient symbols carry energy and meaning. Most people are not aware of this, but your eyes take them in as if they were words. Your brain decodes them. The ancient symbol meanings are held in your DNA. So you are being spoken to through millions of symbols a day. Some symbols don't just mean 1 word. They carry whole stories within them. Corporations use symbols as logos. The oldest symbols are from circles, squares and triangles. They hold tremendous amounts of 'i'nformation. She nodded to the dollar and said, this is encrypted with many symbols. It is a cryptograph. It contains many symbols that unveil a lot of truths in the world. She said, stare at it and see what it reveals to you.

I stared at the dollar bill and George Washington's face shapeshifted into the Queen of England and then into every President and then back to the Queen again.

Mrs. Velvet said, bloodlines from reptilians mixed with Oraphim humans creating hybrids called the Nephilim who are currently ruling the world. They are beings with different DNA codes than the rest of the world. They are plugged into an off planet source that directs them through mind control. You just saw their descendants.

I said, the monarch? And the Presidents?

Mrs. Velvet said yes. They believe they are the Master Race and everyone else is their slave because their DNA coding is run off of their primary program, which is the survival of the fittest. In your lifetime you will see why governmental policies are passed to support their anti-life, NRG agendas and why every big event in history has the sun and moon and key planets in very specific astrological positions mixed with occult symbology. These Nephilim need infusions of key genetics from humans to help them keep their form from shapeshifting to reveal themselves. These key genetics they look for are blonde haired blue eyed traits.

I said, like the Princess?

Yes.

I said, when will the Nephilim be exposed?

There will come a time when their mask will start to come off and you will see them for *who*, I mean *what*, they are.

I said wow. I wonder if Jonny knows this.

Mrs. Velvet took a deep breath shook her head sideways for no and said, what do you see now?

I saw the number 1s in the corners of the dollar bonded with the ONE in the middle. I said, I see the word ONE in the center. I think it acts like Poligrip denture adhesive bonding cream. It bonds all the other 1s together. ONE is the bonder just like Grandma's denture cream brand. One is not a lonely number.

She smiled and said, I am placing triggers for later in your life. You will understand the depth of what we are doing later in your life. When you hear certain words in the future you will REMEMBER a gift of yours from another lifetime. These gifts will all come together as parts of a whole, creating a symphony of yourself one day. It will be your day of total remembrance. Right now just have fun with it. REMEMBER the 1s in the corners create cornerstones. She said:

Cornerstones = pyramids = star tetrahedron =
mer-ka-ba = portals = female womb.

 Mrs. Velvet took the dollar bill and said, if you overlay the 2 seals on the back of the dollar bill you get the formation of one pyramid facing UP and another pyramid facing down. This means *As Above So Below*. What happens above, happens below. This is important. Remember that if you do something to the Earth it has an effect elsewhere. In your future, when your society blows up parts of the Earth and poisons the seas, you are affecting some other part of the Earth, Universe and ultimately yourself. The magnetic leylines where the nuclear explosions happen transfer this energy to other parts of the Earth and Universe. It is very important to respect Mother Earth and all living things, including yourself.

I said, if you bomb a part of the world you are really hurting a part of yourself. If everything is **O**NE why would anyone want to do that? When a hydrogen bomb goes into the Earth it will affect the life forms at those coordinates on other planets.

Yes, Love. It affects everyone. It affects the hydrogen bonds within the DNA, the very architecture of life.

What is the purpose? Who do these warmongers think they are? Kings of the Universe? Who are the beings running the military industrial complex?

Mrs. Velvet said, they are fighting because they forgot for a minute that we are all **O**NE. They forgot who they are. When you understand the physics of the universe you realize we are all **O**NE. This is the most important information for you to REMEMBER. It all starts with **O**. The center part of the triangle. Your true self hidden behind the mind, intellect and ego.

I sat up straighter. I thought, is it contained in the dollar bill?

Yes. Do you see the pyramid with an eye on it?

Yes.

Now look at the other seal across from that one. Do you see the 2 pyramids, 1 facing up and 1 facing down made out of stars?

Yes.

That pyramid is explaining the physics of the universe. Those 12 stars creating 1 pyramid facing up and 1 pyramid facing down generate the 13th star in the center through SPIN. That is the zero point. That is how the universe works when it is an open system. It is a vacuum—pulling energy IN and releasing energy OUT.

I thought, maybe that's why Mom is obsessed with vacuuming.

Mrs. Velvet said, now tell me what you see?

I said, I see IN GOD WE TRUST. When I said this the words shapeshifted into IN LIES WE TRUST. I looked up and said, did you see that? The words shapeshifted.

Yes. That is a word you will become very familiar with in your life…lies. This cryptograph displays everything you need to discover in life. When we get home I want you to trace these symbols so you can imbed them in your memory…for understanding later. It is part of your REMEMBERING. REMEMBER, tracing paper is the most amazing invention ever.

I said, I thought maps were the greatest invention.

She laughed and said, cryptography is maps. Tracing paper and maps in combination are all you need to show you your way home.

What's cryptography?

The hidden stories within the symbols.

Wow.

She whispered, when you are older you will decode many symbols through the King James version of the Bible. That is how the Freemasons have continued to communicate with one another over all these centuries.

When we got back to Mrs. Velvet's house we traced the seals of the dollar bill on tracing paper. I drew the pyramid with the 13 steps to the eye with rays coming off it.

She said, the 13 steps lead to enlightenment of science, politics and spirituality leading you to find your true self.

The steps represent 19.7 year segments from 1756 to 2012. Freemasons have 13 courses that teach these steps. Later in life you will go through the steps at a rapid pace by experiencing them. They lead to the eye, the capital I, which is symbolic of the eye of enlightenment, the I AM. It also represents the eye of Horus, which is from the Egyptian myth, which explains the physics of the Universe in mathematics. Understanding this information allows you to transcend time/space and know beyond a shadow of doubt that WE ARE ONE.

I said, does this give you wings? I placed the seal of the eagle on top of the pyramid and gave it wings.

She said yes, that is a Phoenix. You will rise from the ashes like a Phoenix and get your wings back. Your wings are your light body that allow you to travel.

I said, to foreign worlds?

Mrs. Velvet smiled and said, *between* worlds.

I went home that night and called my Grandma to ask her what she needed to remind me to remember. She said, that's an awfully strange question for a little girl. I need you to REMEMBER HOW MUCH I LOVE YOU.

I thought, that can't be it. Grandma doesn't get it. Maybe I need to help her REMEMBER something so I said, Grandma don't forget to put your false teeth in your mouth in the morning otherwise you will scare Grandpa with your rubbery pink gums. She laughed and said ok.

I wrote the word *cornerstone* on a pink piece of paper, then added

**cornerstones = pyramids = star tetrahedron =
mer-ka-ba = portals = female womb.**

I put it in an envelope marked TOP SECRET in red ink. I placed it in my top dresser drawer. I wanted to remember all the important things Mrs. Velvet told me.

I went to bed thinking…keep life a riddle. I went to bed reciting:

> *Row, row, row your boat,*
> *Gently down the stream,*
> *Merrily, merrily, merrily, merrily,*
> *Life is but a dream.*

STORY #2: I Am

STORY# ONE: Flowering of Number 13

I didn't wake up until late afternoon for my second day in Egypt. I was exhausted both mentally and physically. When I woke up I remembered step by step how I had arrived at this exact moment in my life. I felt my heart ache. I rolled over and tried to play dead. I was staring face-to-face with the map Gouda had left for me, and the code he had given me last night. I reached over and picked them up. I laid in bed reading them and wondering how these two items went together. I thought, could this trip possibly reveal something greater to me? Something that could change my entire life? Maybe I would never return home. The sad realization came upon me that Mitchell wouldn't even care. I lay there feeling sorry for myself and then put one foot over the side of the bed followed by the other. I put FAITH on one foot and TRUST on the other. I thought, I am going to have to do a lot of walking in FAITH and TRUST. As soon as my feet hit the floor I thought about the possibilities of my day. I had no agenda. No schedule. No idea. I thought, this is when the magic happens. When you have no agenda, anything is game. The Universe loves a blank canvas. My mind flashed on last night's illegal excavation. I thought, what was really going on *between* the paws of the Sphinx?

I went downstairs and my spirits were immediately lifted. The sight and smell of hundreds of bottles of elixirs and oils brightened me up. I just loved the scents. They made me FEEL alive.

Gouda greeted me with a smile and served me some pita bread and hummus at a large wooden table. I bit into the pita and tasted a bit of sand. I crunched through it because I was hungry enough to eat anything at this point. I hadn't eaten in what felt like days.

Gouda said, I took the liberty to schedule you some private time inside the Great Pyramid. You will have to pay my friend, the guard of the pyramid, a small fee when you get there, but that small fee will allow you the experience of the King's chamber, the holy of holies, in private.

I looked at him in awe.

He said, it is a true privilege.

I ate my pita and hummus and got ready in a hurry.

Gouda walked me outside and pointed me in the right direction with a closed fist. He said, do not get off the path, just stay on the path. It will lead you to where you want to go. He put both his fists out in front of me. He said, guess which hand has a surprise for you?

I guessed, the right one?

He opened his right hand revealing a silver retractable tape measure with a picture of a black box on top of it. He said, the truth is in mathematics. You may find that you need this.

I took the tape measure and put it in my pocket. I thought, keep it a riddle, who knows what this will unveil. I walked the dirt path to the Great Pyramid. The guard was not who I was expecting. He was dressed in a white gown, blue turban and fluorescent green-rimmed '60s style sunglasses. He was accessorized with a haphazard 3 foot grey and black wiry beard. I smiled as I played the game of *What Doesn't Belong Here* in my head. I smiled and said, Gouda sent me.

He said, welcome home. I am Mr. Green, as he pulled out a wad of dollar bills from his hidden pockets. He said, privacy in the pyramid equals $100 and a photograph is priceless. He grinned a big toothless grin exposing his dark pink gums as he removed the fluorescent green sunglasses. His blue eyes radiated love and fraud at the same time. I focused on the love as I studied his eyes. They had gold and green flecks sparkling in them that reminded me of robin eggs. I reached in my pocket without looking and pulled out an old blue string and an antique gold coin that I always carried with me. It read: *You've arrived.* It reminded me that every moment was new. I was always arriving somewhere new in my life and often needed to remind myself of this. He waited patiently as I reached deep into my other pocket. This time I found my stash. I pulled out a wad of $20s. I paid him 5 $20s, the coin and the string. I thought, this is a once in a lifetime moment. I might as well splurge. I took his picture as he smiled and said, Swiss cheese.

He said, once inside, follow the path. Do not veer off. It will lead you to where you want to go.

I climbed inside the small space and followed the narrow path. I was not prepared for climbing the small barely lit shaft, in a space the size of 4 feet x 4 feet. I had never known myself to be claustrophobic, but I felt it now. I felt lightheaded. I felt like turning back and getting a refund. My heart started to pound. I started to sweat. I started to panic inside. My mind started racing. I am going to die. Why did you do this? This is too small. I can't breathe. I am going to die inside here. I can't handle it.

I stopped midway through and sat halfway up the ladder and had the first deep conversation with my MiND. I said: you cannot run this show anymore. I am fine. I want to do this. I will just go slower and breathe more. Stop this rambling.

I CAN handle it!   I CAN handle it!

    I CAN handle it!

    I AM   I CAN handle it!

        I CAN handle it!

    I CAN handle it!

I CAN handle it!

    I CAN handle it!

    I CAN handle it!

But, my mind wanted to play and it was the first time I realized how much control my mind had over my being. It was running its own show and a lot of what it was saying wasn't even true.

I started to climb again. I reached a break in the series on the rungs of the ladder and peered over and saw the word PLATO written with red chalk on the wall. Immediately I thought of THE CAVE, by Plato. I learned that story in college.

The story was about some men imprisoned in a cave (just like this tunnel, I thought, only brighter) chained so tightly they couldn't turn their heads or even their eyes. All they could see was the wall in front of them. They could see shadows on the wall and hear some sounds. Because it was all they knew, they believed that what they were looking at was reality. They thought it was normal and they became comfortable with it. Finally, one of the prisoners managed to break free, and he was able to turn around and see that he was in a cave. He could also see some light coming from the direction of the entrance. It took a long time for his eyes to adjust to the light, but when he made it to the entrance he could see people walking outside and their shadows being cast on the wall on the inside. Since the prisoners on the inside couldn't see what was going on, he went back to tell them. They didn't want to hear it. They were so used to their way of thinking they didn't want to hear what the free man had to say. *It's a classic example of people who think they want to be free, but aren't willing to give up their own way of thinking.*

The more I thought about it, the more I saw how my mind was my enemy, trying to rule me, just like it was trying to get me to turn back from this amazing experience. How many other times had it made me turn back from something I was trying to attain?

I decided to move forward. I reached the King's chamber with a whole new perspective. I walked around the room speaking out loud, first to my mind and then to God. This was going to be my time to SPEAK MY TRUTH. I said, I demand my mind back. I demand to think clearly. I demand to have control over my thoughts. God, if you're listening I demand my mind back. I demand to think clearly. I demand to have control over my thoughts. I said it a third time for effect. I demand my mind back. I demand to think clearly. I demand to have control over my thoughts!

Everything seemed to immediately shift. I saw everything more clearly. I stood staring at a sarcophagus. I immediately remembered the tape measure Gouda had given me. I pulled it out of my pocket and stared down at the box symbol and thought, truth is in mathmatics. I pulled out the tape and watched the numbers march out in perfect SEQUENCE. I walked over to the sarcophagus and started to measure the outside and then the inside. I wrote in my small black Moleskine notebook the following dimensions:

90 x 38.78509448 x 41.25296125 = 144,000 (outside measurement)

90 x 38.78509448 x 41.25296125 = 144,000 / 2 = 72,000 (inside measurement)

I decided to get in the sarcophagus and see what happened. I said my name *over* and *over* and then drifted into a deep meditation. I recounted the story of Isis, Osiris, Set and Horus as I laid there. Set, who represented destruction, made a box and took it to a party. He made an announcement that whoever fit into the box got to keep it. Everyone got in the box to see if they fit. No one fit, except Set's brother, Osiris because the box was made in proportion to Osiris's body and he represented order. It was trickery or strategerie at its best. Order fit perfectly inside a box made with the intent for destruction. The Divine energy of creation was stopped. The flow of life was stopped.

Osiris got inside the box and was locked up by Set. Set sent the box down the river. Order was lost to destruction. Osiris freed himself, but Set went out to kill him. He found Osiris and cut him up into 14 pieces, dismembering him. Set scattered his body parts all over the world so order could not be found. Isis, Osiris' wife, who represented creation, went out and gathered up 13 pieces of him and reassembled them, making him whole. She breathed life back into Osiris and brought him back to life through breath that originated in her womb. He was resurrected through the female energy and together Isis and Osiris created Horus. Horus, who represented the open system, also represented Divine life where order and destruction were balanced by the Divine feminine energy.

I went deeper into a meditation while still inside the sarcophagus. I imagined what it would feel like to be back in the Divine energy. I saw myself inside a huge circle in the center of the pyramid. I was standing in a tracing paper hologram of the "Vitruvian Man" painting by Leonardo da Vinci. I was standing in front of an actual Vitruvian Man, immersed in shimmering rainbow light spiraling down in the Fibonacci SEQUENCE from the top of the pyramid to the tone of 440. Two triangles overlayed the Vitruvian Man and me. One facing UP and one facing down. Six large spheres formed at the points of the triangles and 2 additional spheres formed in the centers of the pyramids within my body. The spheres began to SPIN. As they spun they turned into 8 defaced 33 rpm Motown vinyl records. Their centers were red with black graffiti that read Khufu overlaying the original play list. The vinyl records began to shrink down, step-by-step, from track 13 to 12 to 11 to 10 to 9 to 8 to 7 to 6 to 5 to 4 to 3 to 2 to 1 to the red center original play list and then to the hole in the center. Once at **O** they condensed down to the original cell that seeded humankind. The cell split, creating 2, then morphed, creating a trinity. The graffiti overlay on the play list was ERASED and REPLACED with "All You Need Is Love," by the Beatles, www.youtube.com/watch?v=r4p8qxGbpOk.

The 3 original cells were made of the triple helix DNA strand. The reptilian tail from my tailbone was unplugged, leaving a socket open for the 3 original cells to enter. They vibrated back to their Divine coding, RESETTING my nervous system and my life force energy. My kundalini energy began to flow as it was designed, UP and DOWN my backbone. The room started to vibrate in F sharp as my kundalini moved in the ankh formation, warming up my body temperature. I watched as the shimmering energy vibrated through and around me. When it reached my pineal gland in the center of my head it started slowly bringing it back to life and enlarging it.

The energy coming through me made my arms go out from my sides and overlay the Vitruvian Man's. My feet went out overlaying his, then my feet came together into the 90 degree position. When this happened I looked 90 degrees to my left and saw a shaft to the south looking out at the star Sirius. When I saw this star my arms went up 7 clicks, making the sound

CLICK

    CLICK

        CLICK

            CLICK

                CLICK

CLICK

My arms reached the second position of the Vitruvian Man. I immediately thought, this is the same outline as an apple cut in half. The seed formation is in the exact position as me. We are one in the same at our core. We are both parts of nature.

A pillar made up of shimmering gold light and Billions of number 13s spiraled down in the Fibonacci SEQUENCE into my solar plexus from the shaft framing Sirius, creating a gold sun of energy in my solar plexus. Once it was full and began to pulsate, the sound RA KA ZA came out of it. A pillar of gold light shot out of my solar plexus creating a container of gold and violet around me. Violet light subatomic particles began shimmering down into my head and body. All of a sudden I could see inside my skin. The subatomic particles penetrated through every double helix DNA strand in every cell of my body activating a 3rd strand that was dormant.

Casper, the friendly ghost appeared next to me. She whispered, *the holy ghost is back.*

New hydrogen bonds in the shape of jail bail bonds formed on the sides of the bases of the triple helix DNA strand as counterfeit Kennedy bearer bonds were split in 2 along the edge where the words read: *non negotiable.* The split left *non* on one side and *negotiable* on the other side and S P A C E in *between* the two. The counterfeit Kennedy bearer bonds broke down and disassembled into sugar rings labeled: *Swiss cheese moon rings.*

The words, *Get OUT of Jail FREE* appeared, overlaying the new hydrogen bonds in permanent blue ink. The bases securely holding the jail bonds turned into Chilean aluminum stand up bass instruments with the 3 strings playing Johnny Cash's song, "Folsum Prison Blues," www.youtube.com/watch?v=Tr0Vt7E7U7w The words to the song were magically created by the new tri-wave brain waves that were created from the new pathways cut by the blues.

The spiraling triple helix was RESET to match the vibration that created the circle of gold, Johnny Cash's gold album, that connection *between* the mathematical matrix of the Universe through sound and the human body.

I immediately felt an INNER PEACE I had never felt before. I came to consciousness and sat up. I felt different. I felt tingly all over. I slowly got up and walked over and stood where I had envisioned my meditation taking place. My left foot stumbled over something. I looked down on the ground and saw a gold nugget with Johnny Cash's face on it. His eyes were shining bright looking back at me. I kicked the gold nugget up with my left toe and watched it do a geometric spinning pattern that created the July 17, 2010 crop circle in front of me as a hologram before landing in my head. Once it was inside I felt quite dizzy. I could feel my head vibrating. I heard Johnny's voice whisper *alchemy*.

I concentrated my thoughts on my pineal gland in the center of my head and saw it appear before me on a holographic screen with the words: *If you knew the blossoming of the flower you would know enlightenment.* It was a tiny shriveled up pinecone divided into compartments. The dried up pinecone started to beam with light from within, turning each pinecone scale into a golden scale in a spiral of

O, 1, 1, 2, 3, 5, 8, **13**, 21, 34, 55, 89, 144

144, 89, 55, 34, 21, **13**, 8, 5, 3, 2, 1, 1, **O**

O, 1, 1, 2, 3, 5, 8, **13**, 21, 34, 55, 89, 144

144, 89, 55, 34, 21, **13**, 8, 5, 3, 2, 1, 1, **O**

O, 1, 1, 2, 3, 5, 8, **13**, 21, 34, 55, 89, 144

144, 89, 55, 34, 21, **13**, 8, 5, 3, 2, 1, 1, **O**

O, 1, 1, 2, 3, 5, 8, **13**, 21, 34, 55, 89, 144

144, 89, 55, 34, 21, **13**, 8, 5, 3, 2, 1, 1, **O**

O, 1, 1, 2, 3, 5, 8, **13**, 21, 34, 55, 89, 144

144, 89, 55, 34, 21, **13**, 8, 5, 3, 2, 1, 1, **O**

O, 1, 1, 2, 3, 5, 8, **13**, 21, 34, 55, 89, 144

144, 89, 55, 34, 21, **13**, 8, 5, 3, 2, 1, 1, **O**

O, 1, 1, 2, 3, 5, 8, **13**, 21, 34, 55, 89, 144

144, 89, 55, 34, 21, **13**, 8, 5, 3, 2, 1, 1, **O**

O, 1, 1, 2, 3, 5, 8, **13**, 21, 34, 55, 89, 144

144, 89, 55, 34, 21, **13**, 8, 5, 3, 2, 1, 1, **O**

144, 89, 55, 34, 21, **13**, 8, 5, 3, 2, 1, 1, **O**

144, 89, 55, 34, 21, **13**, 8, 5, 3, 2, 1, 1, **O**

144, 89, 55, 34, 21, **13**, 8, 5, 3, 2, 1, 1, **O**

144, 89, 55, 34, 21, **13**, 8, 5, 3, 2, 1, 1, **O**

144, 89, 55, 34, 21, **13**, 8, 5, 3, 2, 1, 1, **O**

Number 13 glowed a brighter gold color than the rest. For some reason it looked like a button so I pushed the holographic screen. Number 13 turned into a clock, which read: *Time keeper* on top of it. I pressed it again and watched as it turned into a blue lotus and blossomed in high speed with the gold button remaining in the center. It now read: *soul retrieval.*

A paper-thin drawer pulled out from the left side of the gold button and a paper flew out. It was the *flower of life.* It came alive and said, *SPIN ME.* I was mesmerized as I watched this sacred geometry come alive and SPIN.

I shouted out,

SPIN

SPIN   SPIN

SPIN   s'i'n wave   SPIN

SPIN   SPIN

SPIN   SPIN

SPIN CNN

A drawer flew open from the right side of the gold button and a mummy flew out. The mummy had a body tag in the shape of the city Luxor, Egypt divided into boxes depicting the buildings of the city superimposed over a human body outline. The body tag fell to the ground as Building 7 lit up in the location of the pineal gland. I picked it up and saw a fingerprint at the bottom with an 'i' in the center of it. I flipped it over and read:

BackbOne

❖ ❖ ❖ ❖

triple helix

in crown of bone

strand of lightning

your cell-ephone

❖ ❖ ❖ ❖

wave and solid

in organelle

chrome and soma

physical gel

❖ ❖ ❖ ❖

a post of note

TURN THE PAGE

five vertebrae

sacred sacrum

anatomy

❖ ❖ ❖ ❖

coccygeal

in healths and sicks

the end of spine

a live coccyx

❖ ❖ ❖ ❖

The mummy started to SPIN unraveling its dirty, dingy linen wrappings as an old brown bottle flew out. I picked it up and looked at the label. It had a picture of a pinecone with a bird superimposed over it that read: *smell me to rapidly activate your dormant pineal gland.*

I went back to the holographic screen and held the bottom and lifted up the gold button center. I found a gold washer underneath it that had Hebrew fire letters written on it. I magnified the washer by touching the washer with my thumb and index finger and spread them out on the screen. Upon closer inspection it looked like one of the I-Ching coins. I moved it up on the screen and found 11 other coins with Hebrew fire letters on them, making the total 12. They were wObbling, like they were out of sync. There was a clear crystallized form in between them imprinted with the words: *Gestalt Therapy.* I intuitively understood the washers were trying to connect to the 12 DNA strand. Somehow they had become separated, creating breaks in the chromosomes at 1.618 intervals. The breaks had created frozen crystal miasms in the form of spliced scenes from the Zapruder film about John F. Kennedy, making it impossible to connect to the other scenes creating a distortion of reality of the true picture.

The screen read: RESET and UPGRADE, as the Hebrew fire letters came alive and tuned to the SEQUENCE of the galactic wave of the Universe, creating the original symphony of the Universe. This activated access to the MULTIVERSE. I saw the fire letters realigning with new vector codes and activating a different timeline on the screen.

I heard a voice in Hebrew say, RESET electrical ratios for SPIN 12:12, remove fallen timelines, remove 9-11 timeline, collect missing body parts and soul parts. I felt this re-connection activating the 'junk' from my DNA strand. I watched the reassembling on the screen. It resembled an Etch-A-Sketch erasing and reassembling new lines creating new patterns in the form of crop circles.

I thought, my entire self had been split into pieces, compartments, boxes, all at the 1.618 intervals. The 13th piece was connected to collecting these. I watched the screen pull up a diagram that read: *Carbon copy of soul blueprint.* I watched as my soul parts returned in sound waves as I heard "Moonlight Sonata," www.youtube.com/watch?v=vQVeaIHWWck by Ludwig van Beethoven play. I saw archetypes return of the Magi, King Arthur, Gwenevere, Isis, Mother Mary, Mohammad, Jesus, Pharoah Hatsheput, Quan Yin, Buddha, the circle, square and triangle and all the other archetypes from my past lives, when I knew the Divine intimately.

Tweety Pie flew by on the screen and said, don't be a scaredy cat. Just do it. Your spiritual fear is from persecution in the past. There is nothing to be afraid of now. Tweety turned around and saw a dark shadow. She said, see I'm not afraid of no putty tat. Spiritual fears have to be brought up and released so you can realize your full potential, the GREATER YOU. Tweety pulled a scroll from behind her. She said, sign this.

I read: *I cease and desist any involvement with the traitor, betrayer and saboteur from this day forward. There is no need to keep repeating history, that's Looney Tunes. Sign by the X* _____.

I signed the holographic scroll with my index finger. The crystallized miasms turned into black sound notes with the word Judas imprinted on them made out of keys from an old *Royal* typewriter. They were carried away by the sound of Johnny Cash singing, "Walk the Line," www.youtube.com/watch?v=wEV58ztuihs.

The dark knight of *my* soul charged out of the floating gold button in midair. His armor had a Superman symbol on it that read: *Man of Steel.* He blew his trumpet with force, clearing the remaining crystalized miasms to the tune, *done te done, done.* Black confetti flew through the air in the shape of corporate logos and political figures' faces. They turned into black prison numbers as Johnny Cash reappeared playing his harmonica while wearing an orange jumpsuit with the prison number **1712149287.26.44-7** on the front of it. He rattled a small steel tip jar that was attached to his left foot. He took a deep breath and said, get your M**OJO** back! It's time to get past the blues. Dark knights use what's hidden in their favor. They love white lies and lies by omission to keep you as your little i. The GREATER YOU, the I AM, now has the ability to express deep emotions. Express them with compassion, this will push YOU to > levels of clarity with yourself.

The dark knight's armor changed to read: *Real men don't wear armor.*

He pointed his sword at my heart that was releasing blackbirds from within my heart. The birds flew out of me to the tune "Blackbird," by the Beatles, www.youtube.com/watch?v=oAgceen153I, and then hovered around me. They shapeshifted into white doves as the dark knight was replaced by the Queen of Hearts playing card as Bill Withers played, "Ain't No Sunshine," www.youtube.com/watch?v=tIdIqbv7SPo. The Queen of Hearts jumped out of the playing card and floated in the air. She said, it's time for the changing of the guard. It only takes 7 steps to get here. You have arrived! REMEMBER to keep your heart and soul congruent. She handed me a gold envelope with a crown sticker sealing the envelope. The sticker read: *You are fearless! Speak your truth! Now is the time!*

I peeled the sticker off and put it on my shirt. I thought, I haven't done this since i was a little girl.

The Queen of Hearts said, open the envelope when you are ready.

I immediately opened the envelope without hesitation. Inside was a gold coin that read: *You've arrived!* I flipped it in the air and read the flip side: *Your heart is your map.* I unfolded a piece a paper and read:

LABOR**AT**ORY

♦ ♦ ♦ ♦

Each act of love

Is experiment

Of testing tube

And marry-I-ment

♦ ♦ ♦ ♦

Hydrogen bonds

Chemicals mark

Acids bases

Ply light, play dark

♦ ♦ ♦ ♦

The gas is there

Vacuum, water

Electric, air

Bunsen's hotter

♦ ♦ ♦ ♦

Stimulate drip

Break a beaker

Extinguish flame.

Still you seek her.

♦ ♦ ♦ ♦

She said, you receive your life purpose when you reach the soul train. You are on the fast track. Go! Get on board! You are plugged back in to where you were supposed to be.

It was like the cap came off my head and the Great Pyramid. I looked up and I could see the night sky with a blue star above me, blinking *soul star.* I could also see the base of the pyramid. I saw the number 1440 at its base. I saw how it plugged into the Earth's grid. I saw the significance of the Queen's chamber. It was the place *below* the King's chamber, but right in alignment with the apex of the pyramid. I saw the importance of it. This chamber was the reaction chamber. As energy — life force from the Divine Mother — came into it, it then mixed with chemicals to produce an alchemical substance that was pro-life. It had the ability to generate energy from within it as it received the life force from above and below.

I paused and thought, my body is the same. My womb is the Queen's chamber. This is what allows me to transform/transmute energy. Then I realized this device was unplugged and so was I — until now. When I realized this, I saw a tube of energy running up and down the center of my body in a tri-color of white, silver and gold with tiny number 13s. A platform expanded out to 55 feet in diameter where I was standing. A set of 3 star tetrahedrons formed around me, labeled with yellow Post-it notes: mental, spiritual and physical, with a wrench stuck in the mental one. They began to SPIN in a certain SEQUENCE like a flying saucer, sending the monkey wrench flying.

When the tri-colored energy reached my pineal gland the remaining debris blew off as I heard Johnny Cash say, DECALCIFY NOW. I felt the light bulb turn on inside my head connecting it to the blue *soul star* above me through a ray of light. After this, 7 stars popped out and formed around my head creating a crown. I stood there and my head turned into the U.S. capitol dome and I turned into the statue "Freedom" standing on top.

Clarity came over me and I realized that the constellation Orion was where the energy was supposed to come from since the Giza Plateau lined up perfectly with Orion's belt. Orion was one and the same as Osiris, who represented order. Osiris had been snuffed out by Set, who represented chaos/destruction. Therefore Orion was taken over by negative alien beings. The feminine energy, the Divine Logos of the Law of One, had to be returned to bring peace back to Earth.

I heard Johnny Cash singing, "Ring of Fire," www.youtube.com/watch?v=gRlj5vjp3Ko. When the song was over, Johnny said, once the constellation Orion is taken back from the shadows, the negative alien beings, 13 boxes within the ground will be activated from the reinstated Law of One logos streaming from the star Polaris. The wooden boxes the size of a brief-case are aligned with Orion on the Khufu Complex. Once these boxes are activated from Polaris, a chain reaction will begin with other pyramid site alignments. Inside the wooden boxes are 4 counter-rotating gold plates with Hebrew fire signs written on them around a crystal. The crystal contains the information of the human race's history from Atlantis. These 13 items are REMEMBRANCE crystals. He played the ending to the song, "Ring of Fire."

I took a step back in awe. I found a dollar bill in the shape of a pyra-mid where the gold nugget once was. I picked it up and stared down at the pyramid with the 13 steps leading to the eye on top. I heard "Stairway to Heaven," by Led Zeppelin, www.youtube.com/watch?v=w9TGj2jrJk8.

I thought, it takes 13 steps to reach Horus' eye, the zero point. I unrav-eled the dollar and saw 1111. I saw the 1s in the corner and then I saw them differently. I saw the mathematics behind the 1 and the pyramid structure. I saw the math equation:

$$\textbf{O}\text{NE}$$
$$1 \times 1 = 1$$
$$11 \times 11 = 121$$
$$111 \times 111 = 12321$$
$$1111 \times 1111 = 1234321$$
$$11111 \times 11111 = 123454321$$
$$111111 \times 111111 = 12345654321$$
$$1111111 \times 1111111 = 1234567654321$$
$$11111111 \times 11111111 = 123456787654321$$
$$111111111 \times 111111111 = 12345678987654321$$
$$-111111111 \times -111111111 = -12345678987654321$$
$$-11111111 \times -11111111 = -123456787654321$$
$$-1111111 \times -1111111 = -1234567654321$$
$$-111111 \times -111111 = -12345654321$$
$$-11111 \times -11111 = -123454321$$
$$-1111 \times -1111 = -1234321$$
$$-111 \times -111 = -12321$$
$$-11 \times -11 = -121$$
$$-1 \times -1 = -1$$
$$i$$
$$\dots \text{the square root of } -1 = \text{`}i\text{'}$$

I thought, this pyramid structure has the information hidden in the center of the Great Pyramid, the information of the I AM, the dot in the center, the zero point, leading to the true self. Instead it has the dot, the I AM cloaked by the single 'parenthesis' marks so that all attention is on the little i, the little self, instead of the dot, the zero point, the everything, the I AM.

I had a light bulb turn on in my head as I felt 3 of the washers at the base of the light bulb, my pineal gland screw in properly. The Pythagorean theorem flashed in my mind with the constellations Deneb, Altair and Vegas highlighted at the corners of the triangle. I repeated the theorem out loud, $a^2 + b^2 = c^2$. I thought, the last time the Great Pyramid was plugged in creating harmony was 9 – 11 – 3 B.C., the year the blue star appeared in the heavens, the star of Bethlehem.

Johnny Cash whispered, this was the real date of Jesus's birth, a being from Sirius, who taught zero point physics to a select few people on Earth — his inner circle!

I stood in silence pondering the information I had built my reality around…lies.

I climbed out of the pyramid as I thought,

LiES   LiES

'i'

LiES   LiES

'i'

LiES   LiES

'i'

LiES   LiES

'i'

LiES   LiES

'i'

LiES   LiES

'i'

LiES   LiES

'i'

LiES   LiES

'i'

LiES   LiES

'i'

LiES   LiES

'i'

LiES   LiES

'i'

LiES   LiES

'i'

LiES   LiES

'i'

I saw the guard, Mr. Green, standing off at 90 degrees. He waved me over in silence. I walked over fully expecting him to charge me extra, but to my surprise he pulled out a $20 bill. He had it folded in on itself. He showed me a picture of the Twin Towers burning. He said, the deception of 9 - 11 leads back to HERE as he pointed to the Great Pyramid and then to himself.

He said, the split between UPPER and lower Egypt damaged our chromosomes. The Earth will come back to the 3, the tri-wave once again. He said, the feminine energy will RISE UP once again like it did in the time of Jesus. Mary Magdalene is who resurrected Jesus. It was through the energy of her light body that he reconnected to the Divine and blazed a trail through the zero point energy to plug into Source consciously.

I thought, am I the only one that built my entire existence on l'i'es?

Mr. Green held out his left hand and showed me a flowered pinecone. He picked a seed out from the center and handed it to me. He said, place this seed under your tongue for 9 minutes and allow your DNA to be absorbed into this seed. Then, go OUT and plant it IN the world. As this tree grows, it heals you and the world.

A second guard dressed in a white robe and a white turban accessorized with a red blinking heart button that said *Trees heal* walked up and said to Mr. Green, I am HERE. IT'S TIME for the changing of the guard. Mr. Green handed him a lunchbox with Princess Leia on the front of it. Then he retreated, walking backwards twirling his green fluorescent sunglasses. He said, REMEMBER if the briefcases get switched and Plan A doesn't work, the Divine always has a Plan B.

I walked back to Gouda's contemplating all that had just happened. I thought every moment is new. Every moment is a present, a gift. You never know what can happen in a moment that can change your life.

When I arrived back at Gouda's, I decided to go straight to bed. I applied one of the oils Gouda had given me on my forehead, throat, heart, feet and hands and slipped on my white cotton nightgown and got into bed. I pulled the Egyptian cotton sheets up over me and thought, hell hath no fury like a woman scorned.

STORY# ONE: The Big Button

I pushed Mrs. Velvet's crescent moon shaped door bell and heard
dinga linga ling

dinga linga ling

dinga linga ling

I turned the crystal doorknob and entered Mrs. Velvet's house while carrying my Princess Leia lunchbox that had my half eaten peanut butter and jelly sandwich inside. I got out of school and felt the urge to come straight to Mrs. Velvet's. I opened my jacket and untucked my white button up blouse and popped the button loose off my plaid school uniform to give me some breathing room. I rolled my kneehighs down to my ankles creating rings around my ankles so the hair on my legs could breathe. I grabbed a card from 1 of the 13 bowls that were laid out in a spiral that Mrs.Velvet had arranged by the front door on a wooden entry table. She had one rule, and it was that I had to choose a card when I entered. She said it would dictate what topic we would discuss during our visit. That rule made me feel very grown up. I loved to discuss the word of the day. Today I fished my hand in bowl number 13 and chose a blue card with Picasso's drawing of a contemplating woman called, "The Dream." I loved Picasso because his art was abstract. It made me wonder what was he thinking when he drew this? Am I seeing what others are? Or, are they seeing something different? I stood staring at the woman wondering what she was dreaming about. She looked so at peace. I thought, I bet she is in love. I flipped it over and read:

High Calorie Slumber

....zzz.......z.....z

angled elbow

arm cradles face

darkened hello

sleep cycle pace

.......zzz....z.....z....

evening primrose

downed with water

takes the day's prose

makes it fodder

...z.........z........z

mixing matching

allegory

throwing catching

making story

........z......zzzzzzzz

draft or snippet?

maze? honeycomb?

sleep it flip it

a thick midst poem

I put the woman in my pocket hoping her love would wear off on me. I skipped over to Mrs. Velvet who was listening to Robin Thicke sing "Dreamworld," www.youtube.com/watch?v=b04ShbtaNnc&feature=artistob&playnext=1&list=TLXMNChPtZIrQ. She was removing a Mason jar from a shelf of several dusty jars filled with multicolored buttons.

She said, hello Love, what seems to be bothering you today?

I said, how did you know?

She said, because the button on your skirt is hanging on by a blue thread.

I said, you can tell something is bothering me by a loose button?

She said, everything in your life has meaning including your buttons. Buttons represent issues that can be pushed to irritate us. But, if you look at it differently buttons are triggers of issues that can be cleared so that they aren't repeated in our lives *over* and *over* and *over*. Most of these issues get worked out with our family. What issue does this button represent?

I told her *MY* STORY.

She said, are you ready to give that STORY up?

I said, is it as easy as removing the button from my skirt?

She said yes. Once you remove it, it can no longer mess with YOU.
I said, take it away Johnny, imitating Johnny Carson's announcer, Ed McMahon. I pulled the yellow button off and underhand tossed it to Mrs. Velvet.

She caught it in a Mason jar filled with buttons of all colors, sizes and shapes. She said, these buttons are from all your past lives. I store them here to remind you not to take them on again. She readjusted the shelf to make room for the Mason jar. She moved a large clear glass cookie jar to the forefront with a glistening golden yellow pancake sized button beaming through.

I went closer to look at it. I saw a number 13 beaming back at me. I said, wow, that must be the BIG STORY button.

She said yes. It's the Ark of the Covenant.

I said, what is that?

She said, the Ark of the Covenant is the ancient technology of the zero point energy. It is a crystal that was made in the correct proportions to interact with the energy of the Universe. It is what the world has been fighting over for centuries. It is what will free civilization from bondage.

Wow. How do we do that?

Mrs. Velvet said, you must REMEMBER WHO YOU ARE first and then you will REMEMBER HOW THE UNIVERSE WORKS. When you RE-MEMBER WHO YOU ARE you REMEMBER THAT YOU ARE EVER-LASTING and you never die. You just came to earth to have an experience. You chose to come here to interact with the vacuum of the Universe. You create through your thoughts and the vacuum responds through experiences it creates based on your thoughts *and* the thoughts of mass populations.

I said, so every person is impacting every person with their thoughts because we are all interconnected?

Yes, Love. It's an interaction of the vacuum and with mass consciousness and you. We are all linked together like strings strung together. Once you REMEMBER THIS KNOWLEDGE it frees you from enslavement. When you understand the physics of the Universe and how everything is interconnected at the

O

zero point, the event horizon

you realize there is nothing to fight for or against.

I said, there is plenty of everything for everyone.

Yes, Love! Fighting is over the idea that there is not enough of something. It is modeled and reinforced by the idea that there isn't enough energy, meaning there isn't enough oil. Even though Nikola Tesla proved there is free energy that can be pulled from the Universe through the vacuum back in the late 19th and early 20th century. Greed stopped his discoveries and greed stops these revelations today, keeping us in a closed system. The scarcity model is only able to survive because the world has forgotten they live in an open system where you are in constant communication with the vacuum, where you do have everything you need, and YOU have YOU, your GREATER self.

I said, Jonny and I always fight over the last cookie and the last ice cream sandwich. I now see this is the scaredy cat model because mom always buys more.

Mrs. Velvet smiled and walked into the kitchen. She reappeared with a silver platter stacked full of chocolate chip cookies and a plastic Tweety Bird in the center. She said, there is always plenty for everyone.

I smiled as I took 2 cookies. I looked at the lining on the silver platter it read: *When the people fear their government, there is tyranny; when the government fears the people, there is liberty. Whenever the people are well informed, they can be trusted with their own government.* –Thomas Jefferson. I bit into the cookie and tasted the warm chocolate. It was my favorite. I thought, Mrs. Velvet is the best baker.

Mrs. Velvet placed the tray on the kitchen table and said, how could there not be enough when you have all these cosmic coordinators? She waved her hand to her right side and a legion of ladies dressed in 1960s flight attendant red dresses and red pillbox hats appeared in a line that went until they became blurry.

I stood in awe with my mouth hanging open. I said, my own ladies in waiting?

The first lady stepped forward and removed her hat showing that the inside lining was made out of crossword puzzles. Two words lit up in red that read QUEEN, FATE. I thought, I am the Queen Of My Fate.

Mrs. Velvet said, there is always assistance for YOU because YOU ARE SPECIAL. The ladies in waiting will always be dressed in 1960s red flight attendant dresses and red pillbox hats. They each carry a bright red parasol that gives them the ability to fly and take care of any wish YOU wish to be fulfilled.

I said, like Mary Poppins?

She said, yes and today I would like to introduce you to your new cosmic coordinator. His name is Butler T. McKenna and he is your personal butler. He will show up at your bedside every night to serve you.

I said yeah! Is he going to bring me cookies every night?

Mrs. Velvet smiled and shook her head, whispering no. He is going to come and take your worries away every night about whatever is pushing your buttons. He also relays your wishes to all your ladies in waiting.

I smiled and my mind began to spin its wheels. I thought, how will I get him to come to me? What does he look like? What's his name again?

TURN THE PAGE

Mrs. Velvet handed me a small gold bell with *Liberty* written along the base that had small numbers that read 1440. She said, he will come when you ring this. She raised her right hand in the air and rang the bell. It sounded

dinga linga ling

dinga linga ling

dinga linga ling

Mrs. Velvet said, Butler T. McKenna will come instantly to you dressed in a black Armani tuxedo and a different colored bow tie each time he arrives. He has slicked back black hair with a tint of grey, a large hooked nose and a protruding chin. She took her fingers and made a swirly motion around her mouth. She said, his grey mustache curls up into a swirl on each side of his mouth.

I said, like a whirlybird?

Mrs. Velvet smiled and said yes. He is there to serve YOU. He will always appear carrying a silver platter holding a *Mystery Masterpiece* pen and fine *Parisienne* paper cards with tiny buttons imprinted on the front of them. Butler T. McKenna will ask you to write out what is bothering you on the cards. You will write what is pushing your buttons that day.

I sang Jonny, Jonny, Jonny, as I tilted my head back *and* forth.

Mrs. Velvet smiled. She said when you are finished Butler T. McKenna will place them inside an envelope and then give you a red rose that will be on his lapel. He will say *merci beaucoup*, which means thank you in French, and then he will dispose of all your problems.

Where does he take them?

Butler T. McKenna takes your worries to another dimension where they are transmuted so they can no longer bother you, or anyone else for that matter.

What if some fears come back in a different way?

Write them up until they are eradicated.

Hmmm?

Until they disappear, Love. Mrs. Velvet rang the bell and Butler T. McKenna appeared next to her. He said, Mademoiselle you rang?

He looked just as she described, but he was holding a silver platter of cheese with a French flag attached to a fork sticking through the mound of cheese. The flag read: *The USA has 365 religions and 1 cheese – PROCESSED.*

I walked over to Butler T. McKenna and said, I am happy to have you as my new friend. I could use some help. We have a lot of work to do. He nodded and lowered the tray to my level. I chose a Swiss cheese as I read the silver platter's engraved message: *The more I learn, the more I learn how little I know.* – Socrates.

Butler T. McKenna said, you like the holey one?

I said yes.

He said, you chose a cheese that resembles the U.S.'s models on war over religion. The U.S.'s strategeries are full of holes creating a split in the U./S. with the rest of the world. He took a whistle off the platter and blew it. It went, wooo wooo! He said, become a whistle blower for truth. They are fighting *over* ancient technology under the premise of religion. How in the world is that outdated model still working for them? It's archaic. Isn't it time that everyone is aware of the higher level of intelligence that is HERE? They won't reveal this because YOU would realize you are fighting YOU. The Intelligence is far beyond humankind. He started singing, can I get a witness? He turned around and the tails on his Armani tux turned into a high performance portable music system. He pushed a cassette tape in and The Rolling Stones started singing, "Can I Get A Witness," www.youtube.com/watch?v=cHpU2b08eAE.

Mrs. Velvet sang along until the song ended and Butler McKenna disappeared into a thick mist as he said, the tales of war over God is done. Stick a fork in it.

When he was gone, she turned to me and said, this is true. Now, what card did you draw?

I pulled the card out of my pocket of Picasso's "The Dream." I said, dream, as Mrs. Velvet flipped an hourglass over to keep time, but this hourglass flowed UP and DOWN giving no meaning to time. I said, why the hurry?

She said, I have decided to use an hourglass to keep track of time. We do not want your mother to start to miss you and not allow you permission to come anymore.

Yeah, my mother put into effect some new type of permission slip system so she knows when I come over. I held up a pink permission slip and an envelope with HR 8791 on the front. I whispered, it's her way of controlling me. She just doesn't know that yet. She says I spend too much time as a dreamer.

Mrs. Velvet's eyes drifted to the window. She said, daydreaming is a lost art.

I said, I dreamed last night that I was giving a man a bunch of cards with a man's face on it who was named Osama and underneath his picture it read: Operation Blackjack/Fake Assassination Code Name. Maybe it was

Butler McKenna who I was giving the cards to. I was shuffling them and dealing them to him like a blackjack dealer while Kenny Roger's song "The Gambler," www.youtube.com/watch?v=kn481KcjvMo was playing in the background. That is Mom's favorite song. She always makes me vacuum and listen to that one song *over* and *over* and *over*. Mom loves to go to her card club and play cards. She said there's a whole SEQUENCE to the cards. She is always trying to get the Ace and the Queen. She said it is very important to pay attention to the SEQUENCE.

Mrs. Velvet smiled and said exactly. The same goes for dreams. There is a SEQUENCE there too. If you pay attention, you can work out problems in your life THERE and it doesn't have to affect your day-to-day life so much HERE. It's the easy way of life.

I pushed an imaginary button and said, that was easy!

Mrs. Velvet said, you have to interact in your dream state. Always go to bed reviewing your day backwards and ask what you could handle THERE. Butler McKenna and the ladies in waiting will help you HERE and THERE.

Can Butler McKenna help me REMEMBER who I am?

Yes, if you ask him. He can show you through cards.

Hmmm…ok. I can't wait to go to bed now. Will this stop me from having a dream I have over and over?

Yes. What is it about, Love?

I dream every night I am this high priestess with a 6-pointed red star inside a circle on my forehead and I am sitting on a stone outside a Temple. I am sad because someone very important to me has betrayed me. I wake up every morning and I am sad.

You can go into the dream and merge with the high priestess, become her, and then say you forgive the betrayer and you forgive yourself. This will heal the past, present and future.

Why myself?

It is always all about you. It will heal a part of you in this life.

Does that mean it was my fault?

No, it just means your life is about your true self; the one everyone is helping you remember by telling you something you forgot. When you have a highly emotional experience, it is at a time when you really need to remember. You are projecting out, like a movie, all the things you are feeling about yourself.

So I betrayed myself?

Yes. Life is like a game of cards. You intend what you want to happen but the Universe is the dealer. She says, let me shuffle the cards…let the magic show begin. Jokers are not the only things wild. She then deals you your cards. You experience what she dealt you. But there are wild cards that are not talked about. Your Mom is not aware of these. If she was, she would win more than her card club seat. You can pick a card and choose to have it be something else in the future after experiencing it in the past.

What?

Have you had an experience you didn't like?

Yes.

You can track it backwards by going in a spiral track backwards from now and find that experience while you walk the red carpet.

Ok. I am doing it while you talk.

Ok. So find the experience and flip the card over.

I said, like turning a page over?

Yes. It should have some type of pictogram on the card.

Yes I see it! My stay in the hospital has a red, white and blue rocket Popsicle as the pictogram on a black card. I was alone in the hospital, sick with a blood disease. I told them I was just clearing the lifetime I spent in the black plague era, but no one listened to me. You know adults, they think they know everything. They gave me Popsicles at night as a treat. I always asked for the rocket ones. I saw a flash of a missile hitting a building and the building collapsing into its footprint.

Mrs. Velvet said, trust your instincts. File that away as truth. Those flashes of information will help you later on in your life.

Sometimes you see the future and sometimes you see the past and sometimes you see the parallel lives you are living simultaneously on different timelines. There are many lives going on at once. If you learn to play with all of them they become very useful. You learn that life is mulit-faceted like a diamond. You are being given clues all the time on who you are and you are multi-faceted like a diamond.

I said, I just have to pay attention.

Yes Love, now flip your red, white and blue rocket card over and create what you would have wanted to happen instead of what did. This connects this card to another timeline when something different happened. You connect to that timeline for the event that happened THERE. This creates a new life HERE for you where everything is in alignment with who you are.

Ok. I placed a red ball as my pictogram on top of a white card. I looked into the card. I said, now, when I see inside the situation I see myself as being happy and healthy and playing with a red ball.

Great. That is how you change the future by changing the past. It's all cyclical so it doesn't matter if it was in the past or future because it's all going on now. REMEMBER this in your future it will really help you with a situation that will arise. You can do this in your dream state or in your waking reality, either one works. They are one and the same.

So it's like riding a red magic carpet in a spiral. I RECARD the events of my past even if they are not from this lifetime.

EXactly! Great! I have done my job.

Speaking of jobs, what job will I do when I grow up?

You won't have a job, if you play your cards right. You will have a life.

Why do you make everything seem so simple Mrs. Velvet?

Because it is! Grown ups are the ones who mess it all up. If you remember everything I teach you, you will live the life you always imagined. Grown-ups have a tendency to track negative thoughts backward reliving the same STORY their whole life. When all they have to do is a shuffle ball change.

I looked at her while I did the dance step.

She said, it changes the MiND set. It steps you into the *UNINHIBITED MIND*.

I said, so RECARDING eliminates the Woulda, Coulda, Shoulda game that my parents play?

Mrs. Velvet said, yes, RECARDING prevents you from making it into a big deal.

I grabbed a stack of playing cards from the table and shuffled them. I said, it allows a new deal! A shuffle, ball change! I flipped over the Queen of Diamonds.

Mrs. Velvet smiled and said, once you have RECARDED back what you want to change you can SEQUENCE forward what you want to create. That's when you walk down the red carpet in a spiral to the card you would like to see.

I walked down the red carpet smiling. I said, so life is a game of cards?

Mrs. Velvet said, yes. Seeing the manifestation of what you *set up* is the high stakes poker game called life.

I yelled, seeing your card come up is believing! Seeing is believing!

Mrs. Velvet said, the SEQUENCE forward and match back is called

Slinkying.

I stuffed a chocolate chip cookie in my mouth and then heard my mother yelling. I said, please imprint my permission slip. I have to go. I hear Mom yelling my name. Mrs. Velvet made a compass on the card, put it back in the envelope and then melted hot red sealing wax and stamped it with a labyrinth symbol that resembled the inside of a Slinky.

She said, labyrinths are where the truth is hidden. REMEMBER labyrinths are in the sky too. Always REMEMBER you have to pass through the labyrinth to get home.

She handed me the envelope with the permission slip. She said, remember to call in the North, South, East and West to protect you before entering the dream state. Call in Mother Earth and Father Sky, Grandmother and Grandfather for protection also. She said, let the compass be your guide. It will always let you know *where you are at* versus *where you are going*. She handed me a small dish from the table painted in sepia tones with a woman in a white *haute couture* dress and a long, floor-length white feathered headdress holding a lovebird in her hands. She said, this dish holds the oils of mugwort, frankincense, cedarwood and myrrh blended together through a unique blending process that allows you to star travel. It is called *Thick Mist*. When you go to bed tonight, anoint yourself with this oil on your forehead, throat, heart, feet and hands. It will assist you in lucid dreaming. It is HERE you can heal your past, present and future. When you go into the dream state set it up that you are in a bed just like the one you are in. This allows the dream to unfold within the dream. Set your intent before going to sleep so that you can achieve your goal. This is called foreshadowing. Then FLIP THE SWITCH to your uninhibited MIND.

How do you do that?

You just say I am now flipping the switch to the uninhibited MIND. This allows you the freedom to go beyond the ordinary and into the extraordinary.

I love pushing the limits on anything. That's what Mom says anyway.

Mrs. Velvet smiled. She said, you can use dream props to help you REMEMBER what you *set up* for this reality.

What's a dream prop?

It's a toy, a token, a material object, a coin, an icon that will remind you of your experience when you are walking through life HERE.

Instead of THERE?

Yes, touch your thumb and index finger together while dreaming to imprint the dream in this reality. When you awake touch your thumb and index finger together again and YOU SHALL REMEMBER every detail of your experience on the other side through feelings. It is like catching a dragon by its tail. Hooking into the feeling is what takes you back into the dream to reveal its meaning to you.

I said, do I need a BAR card to do this?

Mrs. Velvet started laughing like I had never seen her laugh before. Her belly was even shaking. She said, yes Love, HERE. She slipped an old library card in my pocket along with a small bottle and the bell. She said, spray this elixir on you in the morning. It will help you return into your body after traveling the stars. As you spray the *Welcome Home* elixir say that you would like a clear integration of your traveling light body and your physical body so that no astral slime attaches to you.

I said, what does that mean?

She said, it means that you want every part of your light body to be clear and line up perfectly when you return to your physical body in the morning so that your day goes exactly as you planned it during your travels.

So, I am a Traveler without baggage?

Mrs. Velvet smiled and said, you are a T^2raveler. She closed her eyes and drifted in thought.

I pulled the bottle out and inspected it. It looked like an old brown bottle out of an antique store with a lid that didn't match. I didn't pay much attention to that since Mrs. Velvet was not matchy matchy. I said, Mrs. Velvet, what is the difference between dreaming and daydreaming?

Mrs. Velvet said, the only difference is between HERE and THERE.

I looked at her puzzled. She said, the only difference is the uninhibited mind. If you want you can always choose to keep the switch flipped and allow the uninhibited mind to continue in your waking state.

I said, does the uninhibited mind scare away the scaredy cat mind?

Mrs. Velvet said yes, and daydreams are gaps in awareness that allow your mind to run wild. She stood up tall and said, YOU are the connector, standing in the center. She took her left arm and pointed her index finger at 11 o'clock and then took her right hand and pointed her index finger to 4 o'clock. She said, you are connecting thoughts *back* and *forth* between timelines creating the life you desire.

I said, it's like connecting the color squares on a Rubik's cube in a SE-

QUENCE?

Mrs. Velvet said, yes, YOU are the rainbow bridge bridging the gap of awareness of the unaware you and the aware YOU. She held up a piece of

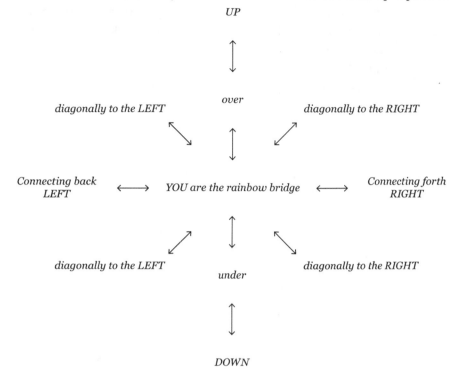

paper with a formula on it that read:

REMEMBER only YOU can break you out of the black box you have created by your beliefs. Learn to break out of your black box by becoming a rainbow bridge instead of allowing the shadow government to do it for you by detonating their nuclear explosives creating national disasters and keeping you in fear. REMEMBER you are always the kink in the chain of humanity responsibility.

I said, so...I am supposed to be dreaming about the possibilities of my life and clicking them into place, otherwise I am living in a box being controlled by someone who detonates black boxes.

Mrs. Velvet said, that's the model of *life* versus *anti-life*.

I contemplated this model as I walked home carefully holding the dish filled with *Thick Mist*. I felt like I was walking down the aisle to my first communion. I placed one foot in front of the other as I sang, heel toe heel toe heel toe heel toe heel toe heel toe heel toe heel toe heel toe heel toe. I peered into the dish and saw the woman in white hold the lovebird in her hand and then release it. I thought, the lovebird flew off to find its mate. I hope it brings mine too.

When I reached home I put the dish and the bell in my room on my nightstand. I pulled Picasso's "The Dream" out of my pocket and flipped it over, revealing his painting of "The Woman and the Book." I thought, I must have just recarded myself. I wonder if it is as easy as turning the page in a book? I rang the bell to summon and ask Butler McKenna. It went

> *dinga linga ling*
> > *dinga linga ling*
> *dinga linga ling*

Butler McKenna didn't appear but I saw all my ladies in waiting dressed like 1960s flight attendants in red dresses standing in a queue waiting for *my* command. They appeared in lines on top of and around the sides of a 13 layered cake resting on top of a triangular shaped crystal cake plate with *ascending* and *descending* staircases off the apexes of the crystal cake plate illuminating the plate stem in a brilliant blue color with the words *13th pillar* shimmering through. The ladies in waiting turned in unison in a counterclockwise circle 3 times to the tune of "You Spin Me Round (Like a Record)" by Dead or Alive, www.youtube.com/watch?v=zJv5qLsLYoo as they morphed into different ages and stages of womanhood of all ethnicities. The mothers', daughters' and sisters' attire all changed from 1960s flight attendant uniforms to Girl Scout uniforms. The red 1960s dresses were replaced with army green double pocketed dresses cinched at the waist by an army surplus belt adorned with a box cutter, a red sewing kit in the shape of an apple, and a matching red Hermes scarf covered in images of pocket watches set at different times. An army green sash overlayed the dress from the right shoulder to the left hip embroidered with merit badges in the shape of circles, squares and triangles.

A little girl, my age, had a scout's sash covered from front to back in badges starting with the troop she belonged to — 369; followed by a pyramid facing down, a rainbow and a pair of golden wings fluttering in the center.

I thought, all women of all ages and stages of life are just like me. We are one and the same. We are all just trying to earn our merit badges and our golden wings so that we can soar once again.

One fifty something year old woman stepped forward as she said, *Quelle heure est-il?* Her name tag read: *Auntie Sweet Sweets.* She commanded respect and took charge by assembling the other ladies with just a nod. She removed a red Swiss army knife from her belt, opened it and held it up for the other ladies to view. When she did this she revealed her elbows were covered in blue spider web tattoos. She yelled, all good women carry a blade. All the women gasped, creating a melody of **O**h.

Auntie Sweet Sweets said, the blade is to be used to cut away the dark debris of the world so that we can reclaim our families. She began to cut away the threads of a brown recluse spider web hanging in front of her made of corporate sponsors ruling the world. As she cut through the web she revealed more and more of the big picture. Corporate greed and pharmaceuticals became clearer and clearer as she cut through the web. She exposed the names of the top shareholders in 3 piece suits of the companies committing white-collar crimes against mothers', daughters' and sisters'.

She said, it is a crime what has been done to humanity — keeping US stuck in a web of lies. It is time for the exposé. It's time to become a soldier of love. Art appeared out of the *bleu* and the blue strings making up her elbow tattoos spiraled out creating the strings along the spiral staircases that were *descending* and *ascending* from the crystal cake plate. Coded art masterpieces lined the stairwells reclaiming the fragmented soul pieces lost through the corporation of the soul. The song "Soldier of Love," by Sade, www.youtube.com/watch?v=IR5_rTCi-Bo&ob=av3e was playing in the background.

Auntie Sweet Sweets stood on the edge of the cake plate and ushered half of the scouts into a single file line by holding up a blue string. The ladies counted *un, deux, trois, quatre* while they began to walk *down* a well lit double staircase lined with handrails that were securely attached to the apex points of the triangular shaped crystal cake plate.

The staircases spiraled down in the Fibonacci SEQUENCE overlapping one another every 13th step where they were met by a woman dressed in a blue and white striped sailor dress accessorized with a red limited edition *Hermes* scarf covered in different styled bottles of Love Potion No. Mine. She said, *what time is it?* revealing her French accent. She touched her ship name tag sending it sailing on her chest as it shifted into the Dali painting, "The Ship." Underneath the painting in a gold plaque read: *Julie McCoy, Event Coordinator from the Love Boat*. Julie greeted each scout and offered them CHOICES on how they could spend their time in the queue. Her clipboard offered an array of games that could be played out, assisting people's hearts reading the book by Linda H[e]art.

One punk rocker teenage girl approached Julie McCoy and I heard her say, I request the game of Truth or Dare. Julie handed her a card that read:

Truth is what you believe to be truth only in that moment.

She snapped her fingers and millions of white masked warriors dressed in white floor length haute couture dresses with brocade hearts along the hem and matching floor length white headdresses appeared carrying white owls. They said in unison, we are ready to serve. She snapped her fingers a second time and millions of women couriers dressed in fluorescent biking gear and knee high striped fluorescent red and white striped socks with red Valentino satchels appeared on high speed bicycles that did not require pedaling. The bicycles moved at mach speed creating a visual of spinning spokes lined with the Queen of Diamonds Bicycle brand playing cards replacing the King of Spades *over* and *over* and *over*. The cards went

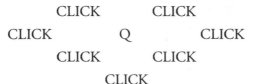

as the couriers rode their bicycles *up* and *down* the rails of the staircases.

The couriers said in unison, *we are ready to serve.* Julie McCoy snapped her fingers a third time and women transformers made out of blue crystal shards appeared and clicked their crystals into place with a

CLICK CLICK   CLICK
CLICK CLICK   CLICK
CLICK CLICK   CLICK
CLICK CLICK   CLICK
CLICK   CLICK

The lady transformers scaled the staircases and flew off to create any-thing…not of destruction. They returned and stood in line and said, *we are ready to serve.* Julie snapped her fingers a fourth time and millions of lady soldiers appeared. One lady did a shuffle ball change dance step and the oth-ers followed in unison. They created a dance as they marched their steps in a beat within a beat. One by one they ended their dance bending on their left knee resting the crook of their elbow on it revealing a red armband of a blue heart within a red h°art. They said in unison, we are the new soldiers of the world. We are soldiers of love. We are HERE to take back what is our divine right—love for humanity.

Julie said, even the ladies in waiting have assistance. Julie smiled and said, when the time is right you have ambassadors around the world just waiting for the COMMAND button to be hit. It is then that the world will assist in healing the hearts of everyone in touch with Linda H^{e}art. The command is set to the line: *Let them eat cake!*

I was in awe of the power held by one lady. I counted the steps it would take to reach Julie. I wanted to get access to this assistance. I counted 1, 2, 3, 4, 5, 6, 7 8, 9, 10, 11, 12, 13. I noticed that at every 13th step the staircases widened out to an additional lane until it reached a total of a 4 lane highway. The lanes went from 1 to 2 to 3 to 4 as a sign flashed

$$1^2 \ 2^2 \ 3^2 \ 4 = 12$$

Once the lanes reached 4 it remained a 4 lane highway allowing the women to travel up and down from the crystal cake plate platform *descending* and *ascending*

UP

and

down

with the crystal cake plate being the base. It was a beautiful sight of mothers, daughters and sisters recognizing one another as they passed each other holding on to the handrail made out of intertwined blue strings for support. Some of the ladies realized for the first time they were one and the same. No longer did the ladies judge one another instead they complimented one another and empowered one another. The ladies began to bow in reverence to one another once they started to REMEMBER who they were…one with all.

A beautiful lady with aquamarine purplish eyes stood out from the other ladies on top of the cake. She was wearing a rose petaled, white, layer cake hat on her head. She threw up a handful of rose petals and walked underneath them allowing them to adorn her hat. She raised her hands in the air and 2 large balls of blue string manifested out of her hands. She glanced to her left and caught the eye of a mesmerized redheaded 13-year old girl who held her gaze.

I watched as she handed the little girl the 2 balls of blue string along with a small off-white homemade paper card. She whispered, please read the instructions aloud so all can hear as I bestow this string on you. The redheaded little girl took the card and passed one ball of blue string on to the next lady who continued passing it down the line creating a long blue string that wound around the cake and down the line.

Every lady stopped in her tracks and listened intently as they passed the ball of blue string from **O**NE to another

from **O**NE to another

from **O**NE to another

from **O**NE to another

from **O**NE to another

from **O**NE to another

from **O**NE to another

from **O**NE to another.

The little redheaded girl my age rolled up her red and white striped stockings she was hiding rolled down around her ankles. She stood tall and cleared her throat with a loud *ahem* as a frog leapt out wearing a crown missing the center jewel. She paid him no attention as she read:

Take a blue string and cut it at 23 inches long while saying out loud, I now release the Sundowner's Syndrome, the Atlantean seed conflict, where technology was used against consciousness.

Wrap the blue string around itself in midair creating 2 strands equal in length — representing the new divine partnership with yourself. Each strand represents 50 percent male energy and 50 percent female energy.

Create a loop with the closed part as you visualize creating the 3rd loop of the universe opening UP the energy of the universe so it is no longer a closed system.

Tie a knot around the loop with the string using your left hand ring finger connecting you back to your heart and all it's desires as you visualize the mathematical formula: $x = y^{knot}$.

With complete and total reverence lay the blue string on top of the left hand of another divine person.

Take the left strand and loop it through the loop as you visualize the divine feminine energy returning to earth, healing and resetting the divine feminine code of 13:13.

PAUSE

Take the right strand and loop it through the loop as you visualize the male energy healing and resetting to it's divine masculine code of 12:12.

Tie the knot as you pledge: *I vow to be true to my true self. Je m'aime.*

Tie the knot again as you pledge: *My true self is a soldier of LOVE.*

Each lady grabbed a partner and did the eXchange of the blue string RE-MEMBERING who they were at their core. One by one they realized they were the thread of nurturing on the planet.

I stood in awe with my mouth hanging open. A brunette 13 year old, wearing ruby red shoes that were too big for her, made it to the 13th step. She shuffled her feet in a shuffle ball change dance step, igniting the tone of C sharp that emanated out from the 13th step bringing forth a 64-squared spinning dance floor from the mists. It stretched out 40 feet by 40 feet and in the background music was playing: Beethoven's "Moonlight Sonata" in C sharp minor.

Five hundred and twenty eight fathers, brothers and husbands-to-be wearing black Armani tuxedos, white tuxedo shirts and domino cuff links appeared out of the midst of time. Red roses held in their lapel by a small straight pin with a lovebird on the end blossomed in high speed time activation SEQUENCES as they waited for the ladies in waiting.

As the scouts approached the 13th floor they were greeted by another lady, who just went by the initial $\mathcal{L}$ sewn on her dress. She passed out Golden Tickets to every woman looking for her mate. She whispered secrets to finding him to each individual lady. I heard her say the same tip to all. She said, he is guaranteed to be ON the dance floor. The only requirement to finding him is for YOU to realize you are being given a ticket to just ONE dance. The dance is called the YOU ME YOU and if you and the gentleman can dance the dance and not lose your true self in the dance of life YOU will be rewarded with a continuation of the dance.

As I watched this scene unfold I desperately wanted my Golden Ticket. I jumped in line and once I reached step number 13, Ms. $\mathcal{L}$ dropped the Golden Ticket into my hand and winked at me. I peered down at the number as my age and attire changed. I became a lady of 42 years old wearing a pink Valentino *haute couture* dress covered in soft pink petaled flowers.

I closed my fist around my Ticket and squeezed my eyes shut. I said, I wish this to be real. I read the Ticket's number: **765422998742-01.1**, and walked through the doorway to the dance floor and stood frozen in time. I felt myself shift into an hourglass with the sand rising and falling at the same time. One hundred and forty four trumpeters assembled and blew their trumpets creating the tune of done ta done done as I walked out to the center of the dance floor to the tune "How You Like Me Now," by The Heavy, www. youtube.com/watch?v=sVzvRsl4rEM. My Ticket number was announced in a digital voice over a loud speaker and all the men of all ages and stages of life opened their jackets as the lovebirds on their straight pins flew in front of them removing their Tickets from their inner breast pocket resting against their hearts.

I heard one man whisper, this is old school.

I heard another whisper, I guess there is no need for match.com here.

One tall, dark and handsome man double checked and then triple checked his Ticket. I knew he was the match by the glow of his domino cuff links. He raised his Golden Ticket up in the air as he stepped forward out of a line of 528 others. He was nervous even though he had been preparing for this exact moment his entire life. His hands shook as he reached into his inside breast pocket and pulled out an old *Parisienne* pink blush letter with stamps on it, dated 1862. He greeted me in silence and passed the letter to me. I received the letter in my outstretched hand and took it without taking my eyes off him. I stared deep into his blue eyes. I felt myself traveling through a labyrinth to the depths of his soul while my knees were knocking a full Beethoven symphony. My head began to spin and I began to feel like I was on the cup and saucer ride at Disneyland. He stood eye locked on me while all I wanted to do was lock lips on him. I slipped into a remembrance of a time long ago when we danced the dance of YOU ME YOU. His mouth and eyes turned into a smile as he gestured to the letter. I came out of the daze of the maze of his soul and opened the wax seal shaped like a train track. Live words spiraled out and hung midair: *When the future past. This time it will last. The man will come. The train will hum.* I removed the letter and read:

Eye on L**O**VE

Expectation - -

Will you be there?

TrainsportatI**O**N!

A pleasant stare.

xOxOxOxOOxOxOOxOxOxOxOx

One emotion - -

Back forth tickle?

Strange devotion!

Thought particle.

xOxOxOxOOxOxOOxOxOxOxOx

Ed(you)catI**O**N

You will remain

DedicatI**O**N

Aboard the train?

xOxOxOxOOxOxOOxOxOxOxOx

No Condition

time and above

my attention!

charged ION love

Time slowly lapsed back to an earlier era and everything went into e-motion as the dance floor began to spin and glow a brilliant golden hue as the music of Edith Piaf, "La Vie en Rose," www.youtube.com/watch?v=g6TvCo9r3GM began to pipe through the ethers.

Everyone stood in awe of the feeling of love as Love Potion No. Mine sparkled through the air. I reached out my hands to him as he reached out his hands to me. We met in the middle, each giving 50/50. He led me to the dance floor and we danced the dance of YOU ME YOU in a feeling of pleasure and love I had never felt before. It vibrated through every ion in my body. I thought, nothing else in life could possibly ever matter besides this moment. I whispered a silent thank you to Ms. $\mathcal{L}$ for giving me this one moment in time. I saw my thought turn into a H^{e}art brand greeting card and go flying through the air to Ms. $\mathcal{L}$ to show the depth of my gratitude. I sealed it in midair with a pink wax seal of a heart within a h^{e}art.

Edith Piaf's music notes spiraled down and up the staircases turning into poem verses written in the shape of musical notes for the ones stuck in the gridlock of love. I heard one brunette forty something year old woman put the musical notes together reading a psalm titled: Los Angeles Traffic and Poetry:

Car and driver

Wheel, motor, road

Four lane passage

The highway code.

O O O O O

Miles per hour

At snail pace

Attitudinal

Movement with grace.

O O O O O

Lost angelic

In metro realms

Arrives at love

And overwhelms.

○ ○ ○ ○ ○

Meditation

Attempts to calm

The frustration

Transportation!

The musical notes disassembled and reassembled turning into the song "Gridlock" by John Digweed, www.youtube.com/watch?v=NyP1SEiHW10 as trillions of effervescent hearts filled with the elixir *Unstick the Stuck* descended on the stairwell of ladies. Everyone who wanted to be unstuck became unstuck in any way they desired allowing them to come back to their heart. Once the ladies were THERE they became the elixir of happiness — *Gratitude.*

I ended the dance of YOU ME YOU as the two of us leaned in toward one another locking lips for a kiss that sent sparks down my spine igniting the Love Potion No. Mine within me and eternalizing the feeling shared in our first kiss. I felt it travel through me, revitalizing 16 Hershey kisses within me, activating the love that had atrophied inside me. The Hershey kisses messages were written on white paper with blue string spelling out the words: CONNECT TO THE VITAL LIFE CHORD NOW. I felt the energy of love travel through every ion in my body exploding my heart in the delight of a little girl. I touched my heart as I returned to my 13-year old self. He was SEQUENCED in to meet me before my 43rd birthday. I thought, he is my blueprint. One tear rolled down my cheek followed by several others. I caught them in my hand and peered inside to see what I could see. I saw the tears turn into paintings of liquid clocks by Salvador Dali. I stood mesmerized by Dali's perception. I thought I AM DALI. I whispered to Auntie Sweet Sweets, could you please help me collect my fragments from all time periods so that I can become my greater self?

Auntie Sweet Sweets said, it is my honor to assist you in getting your code of honor. REMEMBER all it takes is persistence of memory.

I gave her an ornery look that said, *really?* You can't speed this up? I decided to give her a hint. I said, you know you could do a time lapse forward instead of time lapse backward.... I closed my eyes and saw the red rose time lapse on the men's lapel.

Auntie Sweet Sweets smiled and said, we will do anything you ask. Just remember to ask, because until you do, the answer is always no.

Auntie Sweet Sweets ascended to the pyramid shaped cake plate crystal platform and held up another blue string. Another group of ladies assembled in line this time going *up* from the platform. The ladies started *ascending* a well lit Fibonacci SEQUENCE spiral with handrails made out of blue sturdy interwoven strings as they sang 1, 2, 3, 4, 5, 6, 7 all good children go to heaven.

I asked, does that staircase go to heaven?

A beaming woman from India stepped forward and said, this stairwell takes us to where we want to go…home.

I smiled as I thought, Mom says, home is where the heart is.

The woman whispered, home *is* where the h⁰art is.

Immediately I was back home standing in my room looking at my night-stand. I did an inventory of what was THERE. I saw my blue book, a small clock with a Santa Claus face, a world map and a magnifying glass. I picked up the magnifying glass and put it up to my right eye and looked down at my book. I whispered, could you please work together to help me figure out who I AM through my book?

I picked up the book, *Queen Of Her Fate*. It was the book I had been writing codes from my dreams since I was 10. I opened it to the page marked #144 which was held in place by a blue string. I was currently working on the formula to connect me to my past lives in France and Italy when I was a renowned artist. I remember being able to paint and draw in unique styles bringing forth different time periods overlaying one another. I could also write using words within words to give several meanings to each story I wrote. As I reflected I decided to TURN THE PAGE. As I did this, the book turned into Leonardo da Vinci's notebooks. I watched as the first scout reached in her pocket and pulled out a H⁰art brand blush pink note card and fountain pen. She wrote a note that said, *It's Time!* She reached in her pocket and exchanged her pen for an old fashioned French perfume bottle. She spritzed the note with a red ball spritzer that hung to the right with the word *acceptance* written on it. She passed the note from herself to the neXt,

               wh**o** passed it to the neXt

               wh**o** passed it to the neXt

               wh**o** passed it to the neXt

               wh**o** passed it to the neXt

               wh**o** passed it to the neXt

               wh**o** passed it to the neXt

               wh**o** passed it to the neXt

wh**o** passed it to the neXt

wh**o** passed it to the neXt

wh**o** passed it to the neXt

wh**o** passed it to the neXt

wh**o** passed it to the neXt.

I stood in awe as I watched each scout transform from a girl scout to a flight attendant as they passed the note. I watched the line of ladies until I couldn't see the next lady. I knew the ladies went to *infinity and beyond*. One note flew in front of me and changed into musical notes with the words overlaying them that read:

!!!!!!!!!!!!!!!!!!!!!!!!!!!!!!!!!!!!!

Anger questions

"Why is it not?"

And when it's not,

Questions anger!

!!!!!!!!!!!

Acceptance asks,

"Why do you fear?"

And when you fear,

Ask acceptance!

!!!!!!!!!!!!!!!!!!!!!!!!!!!!!!!!!!!!!!!

Reading the poem helped me accept the assistance I now had in my pocket. I walked to the kitchen with a new pep in my step knowing I now had help from infinity and beyond. I was committed to helping my ladies in waiting earn their merit badges as they assisted me in my code of honor. As I walked in contemplation I thought, I would like to get my wings back. I want to fly. ASCEND to new heights. Break barriers. I want my super powers back! It's time I got my wings. I have put in my hours!

I found Mom standing over the stove dressed in a red apple print apron and ruby red shoes frosting a cake. I gave her the control slip that now was imprinted with a blue labyrinth on the outside and a compass on the inside. I wondered if she was one of my ladies in waiting. She looked the part. I shook my head and said, no way. I caught her eye and asked, Mom do you know the Butler?

She said, I sure wish I had a butler, a maid and a cook.

I thought, so do I. I hate eating liver and onions every night.

zero point, the event horizon

The beginning of the end
The end of the beginning

www.youtube.com/watch?v=3MpkzQGq3Ns&context=C4ef6abfADvjVQa
1PpcFMBCFb5Wd6GBvQNzHSt4u9fbr0wbkvGDmU=

STORY# ONE: Fountain in a Tea Cup

I WOKE UP from a restless night of sleep and drank the elixir labeled *Welcome Home*. I stumbled downstairs into Gouda's alchemy shop to find a handwritten note on a homemade papyrus card with a small silver circle with little red lights on the front that looked like a UFO. The word Project next to a paper clip hovered at the top part of the card. Underneath it read: *Be back in a jiffy. Enjoy the treat.* A cup of hot *Remembrance Tea* and three chocolate donuts with red sprinkles stacked up on a plate sat next to the note. I thought, I love surprises and cards! I tapped the card on the table 3 times and then dropped it. The card flipped over revealing a poem:

Library of Friends

Shelf of living

Souls uniting

Pages giving

Day and knighting.

Cardboard thickened

Back spine cover

Fact and fictioned

Friend foe lover.

Soldiers standing

Row hiding row

Some demanding

Some do not know.

eBook masses

Faces in links

Reading glasses

Voices and inks.

I took a bite of the chocolate donut with red sprinkles as Gouda came bustling in with his hands full of black plastic bags. I turned to look at him with the whole donut hanging out of my mouth.

He said, you look like you have a wheel in your mouth. Are you spinning your wheels?

I pulled the donut out of my mouth and laughed.

Gouda smiled and said, I have a couple of surprises for you.

Before I could respond he said, I have a friend, his name is Akhmen, flying to Luxor today and then driving to Denderah to the Temple of Hathor. Hathor is the Goddess of Love. I asked if you could go along. I really hate to see you leave, but I think you need to go check out some other sites. But, before you leave, I have another surprise for you.

I looked at him with my eyes the size of saucers. I felt like I was 10 and my father just told me I had to stay in the hospital alone, away from everyone. I wanted to stamp my feet. My mind was saying, I don't want to go! I feel safe here. I just want to live here until I can deal with my reality. I felt all those messages on cards pile up on me again. I felt paralyzed with fear. I clicked my heels together and whispered to myself,

FAITH TRUST

FAITH TRUST   FAITH TRUST

FAITH TRUST

FAITH TRUST   FAITH TRUST

FAITH TRUST

I felt my face relax into a smile. I said, I'm game.

He smiled back at me with his dark sparkling eyes. He whispered, you won't regret it, I promise, and don't worry you'll be safe. Why are you Americans so afraid of everything?

I laughed. I said, that's true. We are scaredy cats.

Now aren't you curious about your surprise?

I said yes. I love surprises.

Gouda plopped a bag of coffee on the table. He said, I will read your coffee grinds before you go.

This wasn't what I expected but I said, what the heck.

Gouda said, I ran out and bought some fresh ground coffee at a little shop 3 blocks away just for this surprise.

I nodded and took a sip of my *Remembrance Tea*.

Gouda brewed the coffee. It was the most bitter tasting coffee! As I drank it I could feel my face distort but I drank it down to the grounds. Gouda guided my hand as I finished, we turned the cup *upside down* for a second and then turned it *right side up*. We let it sit and gel for ten minutes while I ran UP the stairs and packed. When I came DOWN Gouda said, with his big rotten toothy grin, are you ready?

I said sure, what do you have in there for me?

He said, what are you carrying?

I had my eye mask and my trusty sound machine tucked under my arm. I said, which one? This is my eye mask. I lifted it up revealing the front of it which read BLINDERS in pink rhinestones. It prevents me from seeing, and this is a sound machine. It's my most prized possession. I can't sleep without it. I guess it makes me feel safe.

We both laughed.

He said, it looks like a flying saucer. Come here. There is a UFO in your reading. Look, do you see it. All I saw was a tiny smudge of black, but I went with it and agreed. He was so excited about his finding.

Gouda said, you will return to Egypt again; you have an angel around you, who looks like Abe Lincoln; you are going to have a dog one day; and a fountain is very important for you—you need to find the fountain. Also a bridge made out of rainbows is important. You are a universal truth seeker. The entire cup creates a woman and a book. One day you will write a book of universal magnitude. It will change you and the world and while you do this you will fall back in love, this time with yourself and this will be more meaningful to you. He looked up and said, you know it's never about the other person. It's always about the relationship you have with your true self.

I thought, a love affair with myself. I am what I love, not what loves me back. I suddenly heard the song "You Are What You Love," by Jenny Lewis and the Watson Twins playing in my head, www.youtube.com/watch?v=1H5yOfRG-RE.

Huh?

Every time in my life when I went, Huh? I knew I was facing a profound realization that I didn't quite understand yet.

He handed me a small brown bottle of elixir with a tiny bluebird on top. He said, take 7 sprays whenever you feel the need to clean with water.

I said, will this transduce my heart?

He said, it will do more than turn your lead heart into gold. Open your mind to the possibility of what it could activate within you. REMEMBER you have everything you ever needed already inside you. You just need to REMEMBER it. He handed me a black Moleskine notebook.

I said, what's this for?

He said, it is to record all your experiences. Life is a journey. IT'S TIME TO REMEMBER. I looked at the first page to see that Gouda had written: this notebook has 72 pages. That is something you need to REMEMBER. Every numerical code needs to be multiplied by 2 or divided by 2. The ancient ones left clues for you. Everything in life has been affected by this simple observation.

I thought, Huh? 72 x 2 = 144. That was the same measurement as the sarcophagus inside the King's chamber.

He said, we can discuss all your findings when you return. You have to return HERE. You will come full circle when you return. I will be anxious to hear your feedback when you loop back through.

He stood up and ushered me to the front porch step. I sat there and waited to be picked up. I began to daydream, my mind drifted into a thick mist.

STORY# ONE: Spin Cycle

I rang Mrs. Velvet's door bell. This time it went ding dong, ding dong, ding dong. I entered without waiting for her to answer. She always left the door open for me. I bypassed the wooden entry table with the bowls of messages, which were rearranged from a spiral into 5 bowls in a row interconnected by a black string with 5 cards attaching the bowls that read cycles. I walked into the kitchen and was happily surprised to see she had a stack of assorted donuts waiting for me. She had them arranged on cake plates, some with pedestals and all with glass domes of varied sizes, encasing them as if they were pieces of art. I immediately chose a strawberry frosted one with pink sprinkles on top that had its own small cake plate and dome. I loved donuts. I thought this one was screaming pick me, pick me, pick me! I turned to look for Mrs. Velvet and saw a large cake plate on the kitchen table that had 13 donuts stacked one

on TOP of the other

on TOP of the other

on TOP of the other

on TOP of the other

on TOP of the other

on TOP of the other

on TOP of the other

on TOP of the other

on TOP of the other

on TOP of the other

on TOP of the other

on TOP of the other

…creating a *tower* of delight.

Mrs. Velvet entered as I marveled and I wondered if she could see past my sparkling sweet tooth. I was worried it might blind her. She said, my Love you may indulge with as many as you please. There is always enough. Immediately I grabbed a second one, this one chocolate with red sprinkles. I bit into it sending tiny red sprinkles everywhere.

Mrs. Velvet asked, what would the little goddess like to drink today?

I replied, of course, I will have tea. I would prefer the one kind from Egypt, the special *Remembrance* one.

She said, only the best for you. I have them imported from Egypt as you know. Would you like milk?

Yes, just a splash, with a sugar cube too.

She said, I will allow you the honor of splashing in your own cube.

Great! I took a seat at the table and looked around to find her French playing cards laid out in a special SEQUENCE on top of the chessboard. I asked, what game are you playing?

She said, I was preparing for you. I thought I would teach you about cycles today.

Hmmm.

Mrs. Velvet said, it is important to understand the BIG and little cycles of life. The Universe is very large. It has all types of suns and moons and planets that are cycling each other creating a symphony of existence.

And UFOs?

Yes, my Love and UFOs.

I said, my Aunt Ruby had a flying saucer land on her farm last week. I heard Mom telling Dad. I asked if we could go out to her property and see the markings left behind and they said no. I asked them every day about this. They pretended like it was no big deal, like it was nothing. Why weren't they curious? And now they are pretending to ignore me about it. Why? What are they afraid of? I'm not afraid. I believe UFOs are real. Why would someone be afraid to find out the truth of their existence?

Mrs. Velvet said, because it would break down some of their beliefs and they think they can't handle it. She leaned her head toward mine and said, but they can. You can always handle it. Make that your mantra: I can handle it. I can handle it. I can handle it....because I AM a BIG girl.

I pointed at another donut, this time a maple frosted one, and flew it around the chair and landed it on top of my tea cup. I said, Mom said that Aunt Ruby said the UFO looked like a donut with red blinking lights. I asked my mom if I could take my flashlight and sleep in a tent to see it when it returned. Of course, I'd have some adult supervision, but I couldn't get them to even talk to me about it. It's like they have BLUE BEAM ambanesia.

You mean amnesia?

Yes, ambanesia. When you banish a memory. I learned that from Jonny. He loves to invent BIG words.

Well, I have something you can teach him.

Yea, I said clapping my hands together and getting back up in the chair.

Mrs. Velvet pulled out a very large chalkboard and said, this is you. You are a blank chalkboard as a kid. She drew a donut *attached* to another

attached

to another donut

attached

to another donut

attached

to another donut

and said, you get filled up with cycles. Everything is made up of cycles in life, just like these donuts. And everything goes *round* and *round*.

I yelled, like a wheel.

Yes.

So the Universe is made up of a cycle that is every 25,920 years. It's called a 25,920 year wobble, or rounded up it is called the 26,000 year wobble.

Wobble is like this table? I wobbled the table where one leg was shorter making the table teeter on 3 legs.

Yes eXactly, Mrs. Velvet said with great enthusiasm. These 25,920 years are broken up into 5 cycles and as each one of these ends something happens within the Universe. Because…as something ends something else begins. As one door closes another opens.

Ok. So, are you telling me something I need to REMEMBER?

She dropped the chalk and threw her arms in the air and said eXactly! Let's dance. We danced around holding each other's hands creating a w**o**bble. We sang:

w**o**bble, w**o**bble, w**o**bble, w**o**bble, w**o**bble.

We both fell into our chairs out of breath.

Mrs. Velvet took a breather and then went over to the chalkboard and said, these 5 donut rings are the 5 cycles of the universe.

I said, they look like the 5 Olympic rings.

She said, very good dear. The ancient information is all around you. You just have to look at everything a couple ways and you can realize life is more than you can imagine. It is always showing you the past, present and future. It is a dream within a dream within a dream. She pointed at the last donut and said, this final cycle will begin on your 42nd birthday. Your birthday numbers, 12 – 21, are very important because they are a part of the last cycle that ends on 12 – 21 – 2012. You are a part of this SEQUENCE through your birthday number. These dates are given at the time people come into this Universe. These dates hold massive amounts of information about who you are and why you are HERE. You chose to come HERE at this time so that you could experience this big shift of consciousness that allows you to go beyond time/space just like the Egyptian Goddess Isis.

Wow! This must be very important for it to be happening on my birthday.

That is it eXactly!

So, what I want you to REMEMBER is that it will be very important for you to learn who you are by your 43rd birthday. Otherwise, it won't be as fun for you because the truth will be revealed at this time. THE VEIL WILL BE LIFTED and you will come out of the thick mist you have been living in. You must be ready. You must be living your truth and your truth is who you are.

Ok.

Can you give me some hints?

Yes.

These cycles play out in the Universe and they also play out in here. She touched my temple.

In my hair?

No, in your MiND. You will notice, as you get older certain things will play over and over in your head.

Dad said that mini-tape recorders are necessary to keep your mind clear. He talks in to his and replays his thoughts all the time. Mom says it is annoying.

That's eXactly what your mind is going to do. It is important that you pay attention to this pattern. I am going to demonstrate it with your donut. She took the donut and spun it around her index finger and then stopped and took a bite. That, my Love, is going to help you, your whole life. She said, REMEMBER the donut with the bite out at 10 o'clock. She raised the donut as if it were a clock and 10 o'clock was missing. She then ate the donut piece by piece without getting any of the icing on her face.

She smiled and said, what you just witnessed and became mesmerized by was a pregnant pause.

What does that mean?

That means a long minute. This minute lets you see you are cycling in your mind. To break out of it, break the habit, make different choices you need that pregnant pause. It opens up the world of possibilities to you, she said in a hushed tone as if it was the biggest secret in the world. You need S P A C E to define the reality in between.

Hmm.

Ok. Let's take an example. What do you do, but you don't know why you do it?

I can't think of anything.

Ok.

Let's say you put your underwear on the same way every time without thinking about it. So, then one day, you think about it and TAKE A PAUSE and decide something different.

Like what?

Whatever pops in your mind. Maybe you think you'll put them on sdrawkcab.

I laughed and said, that seems silly.

Later in life my Love, this will have a huge impact on your life. Always remember the donut with the bite out of it at 10 o'clock.

What will it do?

It will assist you in breaking cycles and eventually help you to REMEM-BER WHO YOU ARE before this last cycle ends, as she pointed to the chalkboard.

Ok. Sounds good. I took two donuts and placed them on my 2 ring fingers and twirled them *around* and *around* and said, look they're the wheels. They are the main cycles of my life.

Mrs. Velvet did the same, as we listened to Frank Sinatra sing "Fly Me To The Moon," www.youtube.com/watch?v=5VXieTCqWzc in the background. We ran around the chess table spinning our donuts.

She said, let me show you how a UFO works. She went over and got out a flexible donut shaped device made out of plastic sticks that could roll into itself from a point which she called the TORQUE. The top part contracted and the bottom part expanded simultaneously. She pointed to the center and said, always remember the TORQUE, the SPIN. When you have space and time and SPIN you have polarity. When you reverse polarity you get lift by opposing the device against the gravitational field of the Universe.

She walked over to her chest of drawers that held her arts and crafts and got out the paints, markers, construction paper and tracing paper. She said, let's create a bunch of cycles so you can hang them in your room to remind you to continually break cycles throughout your life so that you don't get stuck living the same old thing *over* and *over*. We will work on it every time you come over because as soon as you break one cycle another one shows up to be broken. The trick is if you are aware of the patterns of the cycles it is easy to break. It is as easy as turning the page in a book.

I said, can we create a mobile of the Olympic rings? I always wanted one of those.

Sure.

What colors do you want?

Pink, silver and gold.

Mrs. Velvet said, perfect as she handed me a pair of scissors by the handle and a tablet of tracing paper.

I took the tracing paper tablet bound by cardboard and removed a piece of tracing paper in the shape of a button that said, *something is wrong with me.* I immediately felt relieved after removing it. Underneath the tracing paper overlay was a mirror. I sat staring at myself for a long moment. I sat looking deep within my own eyes and saw me for me. I saw my uniqueness and embraced it as my eyes traveled to the handle of the mirror which read: *removing your layers reveals your Creative Genius. It's time!*

Mrs. Velvet flipped the switch on the CD player and played "Loosen Up My Buttons," by the Pussycat Dolls www.youtube.com/watch?v=mSN3vSlp2bk

I grabbed a tablet of multi-colored construction paper and cut out a large black circle as she slipped on an art apron and placed a beautiful ostrich feather in her pink beehive. Her apron said, *It is the supreme art of the teacher to awaken joy in creative expression and knowledge.* —Albert Einstein.

STORY# 2: Breaking Bread

I watched every old dirty car that passed before me on the street as I waited for Akhmen to pick me up on Gouda's doorstep. I waited patiently continually checking my watch. I felt time had slowed to a stop or at least a slow tock tick. I stared into the face of my watch and tried to read all the *I love yous* in every language that swirled around creating the face of my watch. The hands of a feather and a pen slowly moved as I listened to the

t**o**ck tick

t**o**ck tick   **o**   t**o**ck tick

t**o**ck tick

I took my Mont Blanc pen from my pocket and started to doodle in my black Moleskine notebook Gouda had given me. I read the first line that he wrote: 72 x 2 = 144.

I wrote:

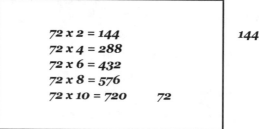

$$72 \times 2 = 144 \qquad\qquad 144$$
$$72 \times 4 = 288$$
$$72 \times 6 = 432$$
$$72 \times 8 = 576$$
$$72 \times 10 = 720 \qquad 72$$

I took out the papyrus code from Gouda. I wanted to see if I could see a pattern.

THE SPHINX CODE
Upper Body:

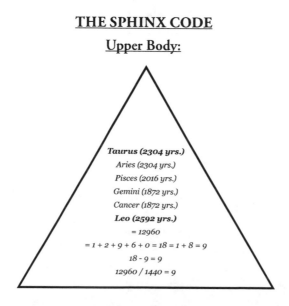

Taurus (2304 yrs.)
Aries (2304 yrs.)
Pisces (2016 yrs.)
Gemini (1872 yrs.)
Cancer (1872 yrs.)
Leo (2592 yrs.)
= 12960
= 1 + 2 + 9 + 6 + 0 = 18 = 1 + 8 = 9
18 - 9 = 9
12960 / 1440 = 9

Lower Body:

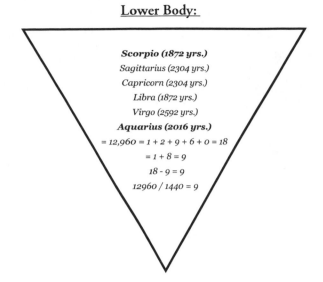

Scorpio (1872 yrs.)
Sagittarius (2304 yrs.)
Capricorn (2304 yrs.)
Libra (1872 yrs.)
Virgo (2592 yrs.)
Aquarius (2016 yrs.)
= 12,960 = 1 + 2 + 9 + 6 + 0 = 18
= 1 + 8 = 9
18 - 9 = 9
12960 / 1440 = 9

I flipped the papyrus over and inspected the back. I now noticed something I had not seen before. I saw in very small letters and numbers the message:

The sacred numbers of the ages are: *144, 288, 432, 576, 720.*

I compared them to what I had just written and started dividing.

72 x 2 = 144	
72 x 4 = 288	
72 x 6 = 432	
72 x 8 = 576	
72 x 10 = 720 **72**	

144   *144 / 144 = 1*
144 / 288 = .5
144 / 432 = .33333333
144 / 576 = .25
144 / 72 = 2

I wrote:

I continued adding numbers and subtracting numbers to see what else I could see.

2595 – 1872 = 720 = 72 x 10 = 720 = 7 + 2 = 9 (027 *backwards*)

2592 (Leo) – 2016 (Aquarius) = 576 = 72 x 8 = 576 = 5 + 7 + 6 = 9

(675 backwards) ***LEO/Aquarius

(6 – 7 – 5 could also mean 2 + 0 + 1 + 2 = 5) = 6 – 7 – 2012. I thought, what could be planned for 6 – 7 – 2012?

Then I wrote:

2304 − 1872 = 432 = 72 x 6 = 432 = 4 + 3 + 2 = 9 (234 *backwards*)

2304 − 2016 = 288 = 72 x 4 = 288 = 2 + 8 + 8 = 9 (882 *backwards*)

2016 − 1872 = 144 = 72 x 2 = 144 = 1 + 4 + 4 = 9 (441 *backwards*)

And finally:

360 x 72 = 25,920 / 2 = 12, 960

I looked at my watch and decided to create a clock using the years of the zodiac that matched their partner number of the same number on a circle:

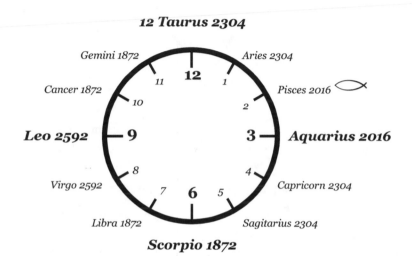

12 Taurus 2304

Gemini 1872   Aries 2304

Cancer 1872   Pisces 2016

Leo 2592   **Aquarius 2016**

Virgo 2592   Capricorn 2304

Libra 1872   Sagitarius 2304

Scorpio 1872

UPPER BODY:

12 o'clock, 1 o'clock, 2 o'clock, 11 o'clock, 10 o'clock, **9 o'clock**

= 45 = 4 + 5 = **9**

LOWER BODY:

6 o'clock, 5 o'clock, 4 o'clock, 7 o'clock, 8 o'clock, **3 o'clock**

= 33 = 3 + 3 = **6**

At 6:39 p.m. Egyptian time, Akhmen arrived in his blue tour company car. He was 3 hours later than when he was supposed to arrive. I learned that in Egypt, TIME meant something different than what I thought. They operated on no time.

Akhmen got out of the car and stood 6 feet tall. He was very skinny, with slicked back black hair, eyes in the shape of almonds and very dark, almost black, pupils. I was mesmerized by him as he glided toward me. He looked like a pharaoh straight out of the books I had read on ancient Egypt. All he needed was some type of robe and he could come to life as a pharaoh. His pressed khakis and white button down polo did not seem to fit in the world where I saw him.

He reached his hand toward mine and we connected. I felt a surge go through me like I had known him before. He smiled as I stared at him intently. I think he felt self-conscious because he took a step backward as I studied him.

He gestured toward the blue company car and said, are you ready for your next adventure?

I smiled and without hesitation said yes. I am game.

He loaded up my baggage and we got in the car and took off down the street. We drove in silence for a good 5 minutes and then he turned to me and asked, how are you enjoying your trip so far?

I said, I love Egypt. I am fascinated by the ancient history.

He handed me the eye of Horus and said, study the physics and the mathematics of the eye parts. The eye is the seat of the soul. When you really look someone in the eye you can see the Divine within them reflected from the Divine within you. The eye of Horus is lost ancient history. It explains the 64 tetrahedral grid as the fundamental fractal structure of the Universe. I looked down at the eye and I immediately saw the pieces of the eye drawing broken down into the fractals: 1/2, 1/8, 1/16, 1/32, 1/4 in the center as the pupil as 1/64. I said, what does it mean?

Akhmen said, it demonstrates the physics of the vacuum of the Universe. When you understand this it changes everything! The game called life is changed forever. It opens your consciousness up! I stared at it and then folded it up and put it into my pocket for safekeeping and looked back at him, briefly looking into his eyes as he took his eyes off the road once again.

Akhmen took a deep breath and said, do you think all Muslims are terrorists?

I was completely surprised by his question. I thought for a minute flashing through all the times I judged people by the way they looked and then said no, but I was not being honest with myself or with him. I thought, it's ok because I don't want to offend him. I realized at that moment how I validated my own lies keeping me as my little i.

Akhmen said, your country has created quite a separation between Muslims and the rest of the world. Do you know my friends and I don't like to travel anymore? We feel we are being accused of being terrorists by the way we look by people who don't even know us.

I could tell he was upset. His voice was wavering and his lip was quivering.

I said, I am sorry. I do not know why they believe all Muslims are terrorists. Meanwhile I was thinking, do I believe all Muslims are terrorists?

He said, have you ever really thought about this?

I said no, not really, until now.

He said, your country does not understand the rest of the world. Just because a body of water separates us your country thinks it is separate. It is not. When you understand the physics of the Universe explained through that piece of paper holding the image of the eye of Horus you will understand. We are all human beings. There is no separation. We have families just like you. We live just like you. He paused and said, maybe not as wasteful, but just like you. He was quiet for a second and then said, have you ever sat and questioned your beliefs?

No.

He said, why do you believe Muslims are all bad? Why do you believe this side of the world wants war? Why do you believe we want mothers and children killed? Where do you believe weapons of mass destruction come from? Who do you believe is training these terrorists? Who do you believe masterminded 9 – 11? Do you understand the Baltic Dry Index? Do you understand the pipeline in the Caspian Sea? Do you understand the Straights of Hormuz? Do you understand the war on Al Queda is a false flag? Do you REALLY understand what happened in Japan on 3 – 11 – 11? Do you understand stargates? Do you understand the POWER associated with ancient technology? Do you understand how misuse of this ancient technology can rip holes in the space/time fabric—creating holes in timelines, causing them to bleed into one another? One devastating event can be magnified by the understanding of this technology on this planet and others. Now look at the Fukushima disaster and imagine what that did when they connected it with the Hiroshima nuclear bomb timeline. Do you understand the devastation on the psyche? Do you understand the occult and how the shadow government is obsessed with this and the story of Osiris? Why was Osama Bin Laden, a man who was a CIA operative invented to be a terrorist, lost and then resurrected and then killed during Easter? Did you notice he was put in a box and put out to sea, just like the story of Osiris? Do you see how religion is being manipulated to be the source of war?

I stared at him and thought, where have I been?

He said, we are using God as the source of war. How unbelievable. I can tell you now the next wars are going to be water wars…water will become the new oil.

I was silent. I was shocked. No one ever questioned my beliefs like this.

He whispered, why do you not question your beliefs? Why do you not see what we see? Everything is cyclical. Everything is born out of RES**O**NANCE.

I started crying. I said, I never really paid attention. I was too wrapped up in my life. I had blinders on. I cried and said, I am sorry. I never meant to hurt anyone.

He pulled over and looked straight into my eyes and said, people are killing over their version of the truth. *You are part of the problem because you haven't wanted to know the truth. You choose to live with blinders on.*

Akhmen was crying now too. He wiped his nose with his sleeve. We are **O**NE even if you choose blinders. We are **O**NE. We are human beings! We do not want war! We want all this to stop! The world has gotten out of control! The killing of human beings has gotten out of control! The manipulation of human beings has gotten out of control! It must stop! He began to cry harder. The solution is so easy. It's all in the cycles. It's all in the RES**O**NANCE. One cycle is ending and another is beginning. It is time to take back our world.

He put the car in drive again. We drove in silence for a few minutes with the two of us crying over the state of the world. And then he quietly said, how often do you commune with God?

I thought, I just put out a 9-1-1 on the bathroom floor in the hotel but besides that not much. I said, not a lot.

He said, spend some time while you are here communing with God. He is inside of you. You don't need to go to a mosque. Just talk to him. It does not matter what religion you are. It is your connection that is important. Do you hear our prayer over the loud speaker?

I said yes. It is very beautiful to me.

He said, that is to remind us to keep in touch with God. It is to remind us what is important. He took his eyes off the busy road for several minutes and stared at me sitting in the passenger seat and said, my God doesn't have a monopoly on religion and neither does yours. My God is not better than your God. It's the same God. It's just levels and levels of illusion.

He handed me a tattered BLUE BOOK. The front read *The 1953 Eleventh Report by the Senate Investigating Committee on Education by the Senate of the State of California.*

He said, read page 168. It's marked.

I turned to page 168 and read the yellow highlighted section:

Since many intelligent persons, even in high official positions do not appear to have acquainted themselves with the real nature and seriousness of Communism, it is, perhaps, appropriate, to give briefly, some really informative and authentic data concerning it.

Communism and Russia are by no means synonymous. Russia merely occupies the unfortunate position of being Communism's first victim. Communism is synonymous with world revolution, and seeks the destruction of all nations, including abolition of patriotism, religion, marriage, the family, private property, and all political and civil liberties, and the establishment of a world-wide dictatorship of the so-called proletariat, which is an autocratic self-constituted dictatorship by a small group of self-perpetuating revolutionists.

I looked over at him with my mouth hanging open.

He said, you live in a communistic country you just don't know it.

So, what does that mean?

That means you need to question your beliefs. Whose agenda are you fighting for? It's not to FREE PEOPLE. You aren't free!

I thought, so what are we fighting for? I looked out the window and asked again, what are we fighting for? What are we killing innocent men and women for...Oh My God, and children. What are we killing children for?

I looked back at Akhmen and he said, do you have a dollar?

I said yes. I rooted around in my purse and found one.

He said, look at the back of it.

When I did I saw the eagle staring at me again.

He said, look at the pyramid with the eye on top. Read what it says underneath.

I said, *Novus Ordo Seclorum.*

He said, do you know what that means?

I said no.

He said, THE NEW WORLD ORDER OF THE AGES. The symbols on the dollar were created a long time ago. These plans have been in place for a long time. You just didn't see it happening because you had blinders on. Now, look at the symbol of oneness placed on the dollar bill by the use of all the 1s surrounding the word **O**NE. Do you see what that does? It creates separation of people over money. Money has more power than the unity of people, because of the energy we place on money. We want it. We need it. We have to have it. We will die for it. We will kill for it. It has power. It has a grip over our lives.

I said, oh my God. I see how we put our faith, IN GOD WE TRUST, in money. If everyone is walking around holding this, valuing this, it means we have put all our faith in money.

He looked at me and said, it all leads to 2012, the New Order of the Age coming and everyone is fighting for control. He smiled.

I said, this is devastating, why are you smiling?

He said, it is better late than never to SEE the illusion of it all. Once you SEE, it stops corrupting the soul. If others would realize this we could take our personal power back from the dollar and place it on REINSTATING THE TRUE LAW OF **O**NENESS.

What is that?

Respecting the divine in one another through LOVE. When we pass through this veil to the other side we are all brothers and sisters.

I started to cry again and Akhmen touched my arm and said, everyone's house of cards has to fall at one time or another. I would like to show you what is important to me.

He took a right turn and took me to his home. He lived in a tri-level. His mother and father lived on the lower level. He lived on the second level with his family while his brother's family lived above on the top level. They shared a kitchen on the first level.

When we arrived they were serving a traditional dinner of fried feta balls, fava beans, potatoes with lemon. The whole family was there. He introduced me and I was welcomed as if I were a long lost relative. He explained to me that dinner was served at a special time every day and everyone was present. He said that the shared kitchen created a community within their family. When you break bread together a BOND is formed. This bond strengthens every meal you share together. This needs to be brought back. There is so much sadness in the world because of the breakdown of the family, the community. This needs to be revolutionized on a grander scale. This is how you make change.

I thought, this would never happen in the United States. People who live there don't eat together anymore. I don't even live near my family. We have lost touch with our value system. What happened? When did life get so crazy? We are all too busy chasing the almighty dollar…for what?

After dinner he told me we would catch a flight in the morning. He said, I thought this was more important for you to experience. He prepared his bed for me. He and his wife insisted on sleeping on the floor in the other room.

After he put me into the bedroom, Akhmen came to my door. He knocked on it and when I opened it he leaned close to me and whispered, every issue we have is an issue of the heart. Love is always the answer. We need to create bridges of love. Paradise is within each person. Paradise is not something you search out. It can be attained through the heart.

I went to bed and cried. I hid my head in the pillow so they would not hear my sobs. How could such strangers be so loving to me? If they only knew I too had judged them in the airport. I created separation. He is right, I thought, love is always the answer. Why do I believe what I believe? What is shaping my beliefs? Who is shaping my beliefs?

I slept one of the most uncomfortable nights ever with myself. I woke often in the middle of the night and asked, how did the world become so disconnected? How did the world lose its heart? How did I lose my heart? When I was a little girl all I cared about was LOVE. I dreamed, slept and ate LOVE.

STORY# 3: Hand in Hand

I awoke and got out of Akhmen's bed and went to the door and opened the crystal doorknob. I saw the family was up and preparing for the day. I met them and walked downstairs to the community area for breakfast. We broke bread together. No one was in a hurry. Everyone shared their dream stories over *Remembrance Tea*. Akhmen's little daughter, Mia Rose, came up to me and said, I stayed up late last night secretly in my room. I used my dad's flashlight to draw you this picture. She handed me a picture of a woman with her body in the shape of a heart with a rainbow body. She was walking over a rainbow bridge holding hands with another smaller rainbow body figure that was her. She said, sometimes it's easier if you go hand in hand.

I took the drawing and started to cry. I felt like this little girl just gave me the most amazing gift I had ever received. I told her I would cherish it forever.

As I left, I felt as if this family truly cared about me. They wished me love and hoped that I would find what I was searching for. I got in the car and rode in silence the entire way to the airport. I communed with God. I told him I was so grateful for the gifts I was bestowing upon myself through complete strangers who had become part of my family.

Akhmen and I flew to Luxor and then took a boat to Denderah on the Nile River. Our boat floated down the river that flowed backward. As I sat in the boat looking at the stars I thought, how many times in life have I paddled against the flow? Maybe life flows backwards sometimes and we fight it thinking it should go forward. I pulled a Milky Way candy bar out of my backpack and bit into it as I looked up to the stars. I remembered as a little girl I would always ask the question, how far is far?

The next day I went to the Temple of Hathor in Denderah. She was the Goddess of Love and I was super excited to go to her Temple. It was the place where divine healings took place. I thought, if I were to get a healing this would be the place. This couldn't be more divinely planned. I decided to sit and receive my healing on a stone right outside of the Temple. My thoughts immediately raced to Gouda's message. It haunted me the entire day. I wondered if he planned it that way.

When had I fallen out of love with myself?

I took out my Mont Blanc pen and Moleskine notebook from my backpack and wrote:

The times I found that I had fallen out of love with myself were:
- When I told Mom and Dad I hated them when I was a teenager
- When I gained 5, 10, 15, 20, 25 pounds
- When I looked in the mirror and didn't like what I saw
- When I stopped working out
- When I wrecked Dad's Suburban
- When I avoided my neighbor
- When I saw children with no shoes on in Egypt, begging for a pencil
- When I didn't go after a job that would have been perfect for me
- When I told my brother hurtful things
- When I said something mean to my best friend
- When I ignored my health crisis
- When I smoked
- When I talked about my friends behind their back
- When I did things that I knew were not who I really was
- When I lied
- When I stole
- When I pretended to be someone I wasn't
- When I cheated
- When I did things for my gain only
- When I wasn't more supportive of Michael
- When I wasn't more my creative self
- When I didn't do things that made my heart sing
- When I wasn't furthering my interests
- When I was mean to Dad for incessantly reading the newspaper
- When I didn't take action on being opposed to the wars
- When I overspent and put myself more in debt trying to buy happiness
- When I yelled at myself for doing stupid things
- When I didn't take action on something I really believed in

- When I didn't contact my Congressman, even though I thought he wasn't working for the people

- When I didn't make my voice heard when I found out laws were being passed without being read

- When I sat back, doing nothing and giving up on my country

- When I chose to put blinders on

- When I didn't speak up for myself and I let others walk on me like a doormat

- When I didn't boycott all the companies doing wrong to people on the planet

- When I didn't work at exposing all the names of the major shareholders of the top companies doing wrong to people on the planet putting a face on the faceless

- When I ate spoonfuls and spoonfuls of sugar to bury my emotions

- When I took the back seat to my own life

My list could have gone on and on. I didn't realize until this very moment that I didn't love myself. I always thought I had, but what I really had done was fragment myself into so many pieces. I honestly didn't know who the hell I was. I had a flashcard of a scene appear in my mind. I realized I was the high priestess who I had been dreaming about all those years. The one who was so sad and felt so betrayed sitting outside a temple on a large stone. I immediately touched my forehead, wondering if there was a symbol of a red 6 pointed star within a circle.

I thought, what if we are a holographic Universe and each fragment carries the whole in it? Imagine our society is like me. What are we as a nation? As a world? Oh my goodness this is REV**O**LUTIONARY. Civilizations are born out of consciousness. If we are chaotic on the inside, our world on the outside will be chaotic. The world is the way it is because man is not looking in the mirror. We are so fragmented because we search outside of ourselves for escape because the pain is too great to go within.

I thought, so…with a long PAUSE, we need to look inside ourselves. If we are holographic and we contain the whole, then we contain the whole of the Universe within each of our cells. We are black holes. We are finite on the outside and infinite on the inside. We are linked to everything by going inside, through our cells to connect with our infinite self, which is connecting to everything that is fractal. The key to understanding our potential is understanding a whole world exists within and is infinite!

As I sat in deep contemplation, a tour guide brought his group of 13 American tourists beside me to tell a STORY. He said Ma'at, unlike Hathor, seemed more of a concept rather than a goddess. There is a small temple dedicated to Ma'at at Karnak. Her name means truth in Egyptian history. She represented harmony. She was truth, justice and order. She was what was right. She was what things should be. It was thought that if Ma'at didn't exist, we would live in chaos.

I thought, where is Ma'at when you need her? Why can't I ring a bell and summon her like I do Butler McKenna?

He continued, the Egyptians believed the Universe worked in cycles and everything should be in balance and harmony. Because of Ma'at the Egyptians believed everything worked in pattern. The Greeks called the underlying order of the Universe LOGOS, which means pattern. Their entire civilization was in order. They really understood sacred geometry, which is the basis of everything.

The tour guide took out a paper and drew the LOGOS, which was a sphere with a triangle facing right side up and another facing upside down inside a sphere. He said, when you understand the LOGOS, you start to REMEMBER who you are. The Universe is in order. This is demonstrated through the patterning in nature. It shows up everywhere. Fractals or LOGOS make up everything. The Universe is in order. We just need to REMEMBER. We are being supported to REMEMBER our true selves through everything alive because everything alive is God.

A blonde woman, a tourist in the group, who had fair skin and was carrying a red parasol to shield her face from the blazing sun, said, In the beginning was **the Word** and **the Word** was with God and **the Word** was God. *John 1:1. Logos was God.*

I thought to myself, logos are also symbols of corporations. So if logos means the pattern of the Universe, the corporations are attaching their symbols to this energy. I pulled out my *Webster's Unabridged Dictionary* and read the inscription again from Grandfather: *There are two types of facts. The kind you look up and the kind you make up.*

I looked up logos and read: origin: Greek, speech, word, reason—more at LEGEND. Date: 1587.

1. The divine wisdom manifest in the creation, government and redemption of the world and often identified with the second person of the Trinity.

2. Reason that in ancient Greek philosophy is the controlling principle in the Universe.

I thought, who is the second person of the Trinity? I wrote in my notebook: Isis, Osiris, Horus – it would be the male. Father, son and holy ghost – it would be male. Proton, electron, neutron – it would be the male.

I thought, our entire society has been set up as a patriarchal society down to the particle level. The divine goddess has been hijacked. It's a GRAND SET UP!

I looked up LEGEND. My eyes went to the definitions:

1. A story coming down from the past;

2. A story popularly regarded as historical although not verifiable. An inscription or title on an object (as a coin).

3. An explanatory list of the symbols on a map or chart.

I started to think. My mind started to cycle. I walked to an Internet café and paid to use a computer for 15 minutes. I also ordered a *Remembrance tea*. When Google came up I saw a black box pictogram that was part of its logo that day. I typed in *1587 History Of The World* and clicked search. The Internet brought up the information that Mary, Queen of Scots was executed for her part in a Roman Catholic conspiracy leaving her son, King James VI of Scotland, without parents. King James VI was influenced by George Buchanan. Immediately I looked up King James VI and found he commissioned to have the Bible written in code for him and others, which gives codes for the Knights Templar mission. I thought, I bet they still use this today to run the world in the shadows.

A bell went ding, ding, ding. My time was up. I peered inside my teacup and it was empty. I thought I saw Abraham Lincoln staring back at me. I walked back to where the tourist groups were standing and joined a new group. I noticed that this group was much more diverse than the group of Americans I joined earlier.

This tour guide was wearing an Indiana Jones vest and khaki pants. He looked like he was a true archaeologist. He said, at the end of an Egyptian's life, their heart was measured on a scale against an ostrich feather by Thoth, the ibis bird, the god of weights and measurements. If the dead person's heart was heavier, due to not living a virtuous life, the heart would be devoured by Anubis, the god of the dead, and die a final death. If the heart weighed the same, the deceased was allowed to go on to the afterlife.

I thought, why was Anubis, the god of death, just recently seen in New York City floating on the harbor near the Statue of Liberty with a suitcase? I went back to sit on the rock where I had been before feeling betrayed by my own country.

My vision drifted into a thick mist. I saw a rock across from me. On top of it was a scale made out of measuring tape showing my heart being weighed against an ostrich feather. My heart was making a noise like p-p-pitter as it dropped hard and fast to the ground. When it hit the ground with a pat I watched the feather shapeshift into a 50- pound bag of sugar. I knew what this meant. I ate sugar to try and take the pain away. I knew sugar could help dull the pain. I knew I wouldn't make it to the afterlife at this point. I really didn't care. I just wanted the pain to go away at whatever cost that would be, even if it meant eating spoonfuls and spoonfuls of sugar. I pulled a pack of cookies from my backpack and ate the full sleeve of Oreos, not even tasting them after the first one.

The measuring tape shapeshifted into a DNA strand and the Health Care Reform Act replaced the sugar and the Constitution replaced my heart. The Constitution became covered in blood as it fell to the ground and then turned into **the word** *awareness* and the phrase Health Care Reform turned into **the word** *unawareness*. They both shapeshifted into Executive Order 12425 – designating Interpol as a Public International Organization under Health Reform entitled to enjoy certain privileges, exemptions, and immunities. The words shapeshifted to a newspaper headline that read: *It's a set up is to see who has the 52 DNA codes.* The subtitle read: *THE BIG EVENT.*

The newspaper disappeared leaving the words *unawareness* and *awareness* balancing on the scale. The word *unawareness* turned into a red bucket with one drop of water in it and *awareness* turned into the phrase *Global Police State*. Everything turned red, like blood and then out of the red the words pro-life and anti-life appeared overlaying the two scales, measuring equally as **the word** PROFIT overlayed them both.

I shook my head in disbelief. I thought, I wonder what the world would look like if we adhered to Ma'at's way? The world wouldn't be in the chaos it is in today. People would care about themselves, love themselves more because in the end their hearts would be weighed. From the looks of things I would not go on to the afterlife, which I am sure is better than HERE. Instead, I would have to come back HERE and work out my lessons until I got my heart right. Somehow the Egyptians knew this and we forgot this.

It seemed to me that in the world all morality has been lost. People walk around like zombies. If I wasn't here I would be one of them, a slight glaze in my eye, but no one home. All the external programming, electrical devices, power lines, microwave waves, cell towers and who knows what else working against us. We really don't have a fighting chance unless we WAKE UP and start watching what we are cycling in and open up the possibilities, which would change our habitual thoughts. This sounds like it would take a miracle, but small steps, fractal steps, and along the way, who knows, we might start loving ourselves again and then one another. I know I have a lot of forgiving to do and most of it is to myself. I have to establish a new relationship with myself. I noticed in the tour guide's talk he said nothing about the brain.

As if on cue, a tourist with large black square glasses asked, what did they do with the brain?

He said, back then it was inconsequential. They only cared about the heart. If you think about that today, it still applies. If you live a life from your heart you live a better life.

Another tourist wearing a T-shirt that read: *Trees Heal, Hug One Today* said, did you know the heart is the first thing that forms on a fetus in the womb? Everything really develops out of the heart.

The tour guide said, that makes sense. He lifted his clipboard revealing a bumper sticker that read: *Wherever You Go, Go With All Your Heart* –Confucious.

I walked back to the boat placing one foot in front of the other, but this time I replaced FAITH and TRUST with LOVE. As I walked I thought,

love love love love love

luv luv luv luv luv luv luv luv luv luv luv luv luv luv luv luv luv luv luv luv

love love love love love

love love love love love

luv luv luv luv luv luv luv luv luv luv luv luv luv luv luv luv luv luv luv luv

love love love love love

l U v l U v l U v l U v l U v l U v l U v l U v l U v l U v l U v l U v l U v

love love love love love love love love love love love love love

STORY #5:

Never put a period where the Goddess put a comma

STORY #8: Sleep Pattern

When I reached the boat I went straight to my quarters. A door hanger made out of a paper oar with a 4 inch by 4 inch domino drawn on it hung from the brass doorknob. I pulled it off and read:

<u>A.M. ELEVEN O FOUR P.M.</u>

QUARTERFINAL.

R E C O G N I T I O N.

C O M P R E H E N S I V E.

C A L C U L A T I O N.

A. THE MORNING

M. THE MOURNING

P. THE WARNING

M. THE WORNING

---

klocking clocking

maleing mailing

stocking stalking

tailing taleing

"Do you know what

this all means, dear?"

"Yes ma'am. Know ma'am.

I just see HERE!"

I held the 4 inch by 4 inch domino door hanger close to my heart and took a deep breath and then pretended I was paddling downstream. The card flipped over in my hand revealing the breakfast menu. I turned the polished brass door handle and entered. I was greeted by 2 swans made out of white bath towels, kissing, on my bed set against the backdrop of hundreds of old sailing ships in black and white rocking *back* and *forth* on the wallpaper. I watched the ships and felt a bit seasick.

I flopped down on the bed sending the swans into the air. I grabbed the 2 pillows and rested my head on the inscription: *My witness is the empty sky.* —Jack Kerouac. I couldn't help but feel a little sad. I felt sad because I abandoned myself. I thought, how did I ever do that? I did it! I was the one! I started to realize what a deep meaning self-love meant. It meant being true to who you really are.

Ma'at really understood that. She was the goddess of TRUTH. Isn't that what we all really want? We want the truth. We have become a society of never telling the truth. We don't even know what the truth is anymore, not even within ourselves. The Universe is a direct reflection of our internal self. We obviously don't know truth within. Hermes said, AS WITHIN, SO WITHOUT. I decided to reacquaint myself with myself. I said out loud, Gabriella meet the new Gabriella, better known as the old Gabriella.

As I lay there I thought, what do I love today? I thought, I love my bed at home. The one I am laying in now is so hard and these sheets feel like construction paper. How I miss my own bed. At home, I have an extra high bed, a pillow top mattress that sits 4 feet high. I take my sleep very seriously. I have sheets that are so soft you feel as if someone is wrapping their arms around you enveloping you. I have 10 pillows of all different firmness levels so I get the right feel for my head. I share my bed with tons of books. I am always reading something. Even though I love the computer, I love a good book more. I love the way they feel. The way they look. I believe the cover PATTERN speaks to your soul, calling you to open it and read it. I love bookstores. If I could have one magical power bestowed upon me it would be to instantly absorb the content of books just by running my finger along their spine. I do this when I go into a bookstore, hoping one day it may just happen.

A book has the ability to transport you somewhere else. It has the ability to change your perception IMMEDIATELY. It allows you to OPEN UP and experience life so differently even if it is for an hour, a day or a week. After reading a good book, you are never the same. It has TRANSFORMED you to a higher level of who you are. My dream day would be to lie in my bed all day at home and read a good book but no one writes what I want to read except me.

As I closed my eyes I thought about what do I love now in my life. What am I grateful for? I thought, I love my heart. I love my sense of adventure. I love riding my bike. I love being HERE in Egypt exploring this ancient world and myself. I drifted into a thick mist….

S P A C E

STORY #21: Missing Chromosome

I turned the crystal doorknob and **o**pened the door to Mrs. Velvet's house. I pushed the door and heard a CLICK as the door released. I was immediately greeted by the smell of old books and old maps with a hint of rose. Mrs. Velvet greeted me in the hallway. She tilted her head to the LEFT so that I would notice a card in her pink beehive that read: *"Be yourself; everyone else is already taken."* —Oscar Wilde.

Mrs. Velvet said, Gabriella, why are you so blue today?

I said, I am sad. I just feel so different. No one seems to understand me.

Mrs. Velvet said, I can understand, when I was your age no one understood me either. Feeling alone comes from the MiND. Your mind is not really your friend. It plays tricks on you. It's a TRICKSTER. You have to learn how it works and play with it. The key is to play. The mind creates separation of YOU and you by judging just about anything. This judgment takes YOU down to you and the more you judge the more you become stuck in the littleness of life and you. The more you become stuck the harder it becomes to become unstuck. It's like being a fish stuck in a stagnant pool of thick dirty water who cannot get out of it unless it has a k^{e}y.

I said, can you give me the k^{e}y?

Mrs. Velvet said, what is the magic phrase?

I said, **pretty please** as I batted my eyes at her.

Mrs. Velvet turned and ran her fingers along the spine of a row of books. She said, this is your library of friends. She chose a book off the shelf and as she brought it down she pulled a salmon pink bookmark out of it with Marie Antoinette on the front of it fanning herself. She flipped Marie Antoinette *over* and read in a faint whisper to herself:

> Hearts explode in delight
> morning, noon and night
> Juxtaposition of old and new
> goodbye blues
> Love dismisses sad eyes
> to bring about YOU and I's.

Mrs. Velvet closed her eyes and smiled and whispered, Romeo and Juliet. She came back from daydreaming and slipped the poem in her pocket and handed me the book. It was titled: *Mrs. Velvet and the Blue String Theory: Queen of Her Fate, Story One.*

I said, thank you, as I gratefully accepted her friend, the book. I leafed through it not understanding how this could possibly be a key because all the pages were blank. I played a game in my mind. I reversed the game *What Doesn't Belong HERE* into the game *What Does Belong HERE*. The only thing that jumped out at me was at the bottom of each page where it read: TURN THE PAGE.

Mrs. Velvet said, it's your way in.

I said, Mom says vacuuming is my way in.

Mrs. Velvet laughed and said, when you learn to turn judgment into compassion and forgiveness it releases the little you and allows you to become the BIG YOU again which allows you to TURN THE PAGE in your life. This keeps you moving forward to your intention, not keeping you stuck on the same page.

I asked, does this allow YOU to CLICK m**o**re into alignment with your Princess Leia or Hans Solo?

Yes. REMEMBER you are the author of your journey no matter what *nom de plume* you use. The question becomes: Can you own it that you are the author creating your STORY?

I stood staring at her. My mind was singing, is you is or is you ain't my baby?

She asked, can you step UP into first position with reverence? You are the C.O.O. the Chief Operating Officer, funded by Source.

I said yes. I think I can. I think I can. I think I can. I think I can…I can. I AM the author of *my* STORY!

Mrs. Velvet whispered, you are the *Queen of Your Fate.*

I nodded.

She said, when you own that you are the author of your STORY you empower yourself and when you know this you embody the power. So…let me ask you, what do you believe about being different? It's all about the beliefs you have that are playing out as your STORY.

I believe I am different and not like anyone else.

Like who?

My brother?

Who says?

Me. Oh…my MiND said that. I was operating on autopilot. I didn't choose a new thought, I went with an old one I have been playing *over* and *over.*

Do you now realize you created this?

I nodded.

She paused and said, you have to own that you created it.

Yes. I pinched my index finger and thumb together leaving a tiny space in between. I said, the little 'i' created it.

Mrs. Velvet said, do not blame and judge yourself now for doing it. It will just get you stuck again.

I screamed, I just did. I yelled at myself. I told myself to STOP doing what I do to myself.

Mrs. Velvet walked over and hugged me. She said, just embrace it. Pull it in like a great big hug, like I am doing now. She gave me a bear hug. Don't run away from the feeling. Never run away from how you feel because that creates separation too. The kᵉy is to change it alchemically when you do what we just did.

What's alchemically?

It's a magical process of transmuting something into something else.

Like turning a scaredy cat into Leo the Lion.

Mrs. Velvet smiled and said, or turning a little girl into a BIG girl, the GODDESS within YOU.

I said, so...when you see you are in judgment TURN THE PAGE to compassion and forgiveness and this gets you unstuck from the build up of your STORY.

Yes. This allows YOU to actively participate in the life you are creating.

I said, this allows YOU to flow down the river. I sang:

> Row, row, row your boat,
> Gently down the stream,
> Merrily, merrily, merrily, merrily,
> Life is but a dream.

Mrs. Velvet said, that is the purpose of this book. It's for your mind to tell you a story while you hear a story so you can learn to TURN THE PAGE. Can you speed up the hearing?

I said, Huh?

She smiled and swayed her head *back* and *forth*. She said, the world has lost compassion for itself and others. She took an Eiffel Tower paperweight in the shape of a button and held it to heart and drifted into a daydream. She said, ohh...the compassion button instead of the karmic button. If we could just learn how to push the compassion button. We would realize we have no control over anything, but the *set up*. She sighed and said, the world could all be changed if everyone started to write their own story through love letters. The choice is always to actively participate in life or not. She leaned over in a daze and turned on her record player. It played an old 45 rpm vinyl record of "You Go To My Head," by Billie Holiday www.youtube.com/watch?v=LGNc1yLGPug.

My mind started spinning in tune with the record. I thought of Jonny. When the record stopped I blurted out, Jonny says I'm missing a chromosome.

She smiled and said, at least we got to the root of the reason you think you are different.

I thought, that is the line that caught up in my mind and allowed it to play *over* and *over*.

Mrs. Velvet said, many people are missing some very important chromosomes that will be returned to them in DIVINE TIME. The only chromosome you are missing, my dear, is the one that allows you to be PROGRAMMED.

Is that a good thing?

Oh yes! Everyone is so programmed in life through the news, the TV, GURUS, the Government, the High-frequency Active Auroral Research Program or the HAARP system. People don't even know it. They are living in a box.

I went to help myself to a piece of chocolate cake that was sitting on a cake plate with all types of beautiful purple and white flowers around it. Mrs. Velvet said, you know sugar is not going to take the pain away.

I said, I think it will, as I took a huge bite of chocolate cake and allowed all the crumbs to fall to the rug.

My Love, we are all different. God did not make one of us the same. You should rejoice in your uniqueness. That philosophy of 'you must be like US' doesn't work. The U.S. government proves this *over* and *over*.

I said, sometimes I feel like I am all alone.

Mrs. Velvet said, the Universe is alive. WE ARE NOT ALONE. You have all types of helpers around you at all times. They hear you. They are just in different dimensions. You can talk to them. You have a scientist, a mathematician, an artist and an astrologer and anyone else you need assistance from around you. You can call upon anyone you choose to talk to. **You are**

a very special girl and as you go through life people are going to help you REMEMBER that.

Can't I just take a pill and have it happen immediately?

Mrs. Velvet was quiet for a minute. It was like she was resting up for what she wanted to tell me. She said, **O**H…the society we live in today. Everyone wants to pop a pill instead of doing the work of REMEMBERING. It doesn't work that way, Love. It's a PR**O**CESS. It's remembering moment-by-moment who your true self is so you can express that. Everyone just wants to express his or her true self. That is what life is about. Everyone is expressing…but not everyone is their true self and that is where the disharmony lies. Everyone's journey is to find their own true self. Go into nature and see that all of nature is unique and different, yet all the same. Everything alive is made up from the same patterning and it's called FRACTALS. A circle with the two pyramids in it, one facing right side up and one facing upside down, like a 6 pointed star. This is the fractal nature of the universe. This contains the infinite and the finite at the same time. When this fractal spins it creates a contracting part, which is the inside, and a radiating part, which is the exterior.

We find this in the uniqueness of snowflakes, flowers, the sunset, trees, in the ocean or a lake and in the sky. Nature is always the purest way to find uniqueness, yet you can also feel at one with it at the same time. Go out in the forest and be still with yourself, GO INSIDE. There you shall feel **o**neness.

In nature or within myself?

Within yourself. Nature just makes it easy for you to go within yourself.

Where at?

Inside every one of your cells. They are infinite and finite. It is there you can receive answers to all your questions. The Goddess sits inside you on a throne. She sits at the back door of your heart. You have access to her by going into your heart backward. It is a very sacred place.

I said, how will I find it? Is it the shape of the fractal?

Yes Love. The Goddess is always there so you are never alone. She will answer any questions you have. She is always ON.

Like the lights at Motel 6? You know they leave the light on for you.

Yes dear. I love the way you think. Shall we have tea and discuss the card you drew? What card did you draw?

I forgot. I'll go get one.

I ran back and closed my eyes and made a wish to find the card that would help me understand my uniqueness. I picked a card from a new blue deck. It read: *Write 3 things you love to do because later in life they will become you.*

Mrs. Velvet met me back at the table with some extra large markers and construction paper in extra large sheets and scissors and tracing paper. She peered over and read my card. She said, go for it!

I thought about my answer for several minutes and then wrote:

1. *I love riding my bicycle.*

2. *I love the mystery of the Universe.*

3. *I love dreaming, especially about love.*

Mrs. Velvet said perfect. Make a beautiful drawing of your list and then make a 3 x 5 card out of the yellow construction paper and write it out so you can carry it with you in your pocket and you will never forget.

I said, Mrs. Velvet, did I ever tell you how much I love you? Why do you love me so much?

She peered over her red rhinestone glasses straight into my heart and said, I love you because I am you and you are me. We are all one.

I created my art piece as I thought about being one and the same as Mrs. Velvet. I felt BIGGER because of this. I made a bracelet with interlocking construction rings that said WWMVD, it meant *What Would Mrs. Velvet Do?* Since I was one and the same I thought what would the BIG girl do versus the little girl.

I finished my card and slipped the yellow card into my pocket. I went home and asked my Mom if she knew the Goddess was sitting on a throne in a special area of her heart.

She said no.

I went and touched the area on her and said, right here.

She said, all I feel is gas.

STORY #34: Equation: RO RO RO™

I woke up from a pleasant nights sleep on the Love Boat. I lay there looking at the boat ceiling. I looked to my right and saw a boat rocking back and forth. I looked to my left and saw a boat rocking *back* and *forth*. I looked up and thought what can I see HERE? I started to connect imaginary dots creating patterns on the ceiling. I created an X and an **O**, and then I put the X inside the **O** turning it into a steering wheel. I thought, who am I going to be today? Am I going to choose to be the new Gabriella today? I thought, yes I AM. I am going back to the temple of Hathor. I am going to see what is revealed for me THERE today. I am going back for m**o**re insights. If I got all that I did yesterday, today there was sure to be m**o**re. I got up and dressed in an outfit that resembled an explorer. I put on my khakis and white button up shirt with a pink scarf wrapped around my head. As I put my glasses on I thought the new Gabriella is a bit like Nancy Drew. I walked back to the temple in meditation. I looked at everything closely. I watched the single frames of life flash to the next. I got in tune with nature and myself all the while walking heel toe heel toe heel toe heel toe heel toe heel toe heel toe.

When I arrived at the temple I decided to go down the stairs to look at the crypts. I was immediately greeted by a pictogram of a cord, which led to a socket with some type of filament attached to it with a transparent bubble on the outside of it. It looked just like a light bulb. I stood in wonderment. How could a light bulb be invented back then? A light bulb went off in my head. I thought, they were way more advanced than we are. What if we are moving backward to where we started instead of forward?

I stood in awe staring at the light bulb pictogram as a 1962 pink Cadillac popped half way through the light bulb displaying a license plate that read: IN2FINS. The Cadillac ejected an elderly man, around 70 something. He watched frantically as a red handheld device flew through the air in slow motion. It had 2 knobs spinning wildly *back* and *forth* creating a design on a center screen. It landed right at my feet. I reached down and picked it up. It was an Etch A Sketch and the center held a picture of the world. The title of the picture read: *What the world will look like after all the earth changes.* I stood in awe as I noticed a lot of the landmass was missing.

The man landed on the ground across from me. He looked a bit frazzled and was chewing his bubblegum furiously. His hair was grey and messy like he had just stuck his finger in a light socket and been electrocuted. He had a large bushy mustache and eyebrows to match. He wore a pair of striped bright yellow and brown pants and a blue-checkered shirt that did not match. It was untucked with the corners hanging out like two triangles at his side that shapeshifted into toast points as I stared at them. He wore a bright orange lifejacket with a pin that read: *What are you vested in?* He had a Nobel Prize award attached to a ribbon that was swinging around his neck. He seemed a bit disoriented. He kept reaching in his shirt pocket like he'd lost something and he thought it was in there. He finally pulled out a pack of pink bubblegum followed by his glasses. He slipped the glasses on which were aviator style glasses with a unique art deco piece along the top ridge. I stood staring thinking those are **cool**^{2}. The man opened his pack of bubblegum and popped a pink piece of it in his mouth and put the old piece he had been chewing in the wrapper and then back in the pack that read Trident.

He said, we are all recycled. Thank goodness this cycle of recycling is ending as we head to zero point. He peered over his glasses and said, yes, others had the knowledge before Nikola Tesla. His voice changed tone and he said, *Imagination Is Everything! It is the preview of life's coming attractions. Imagination is more important than knowledge. For knowledge is limited to all we now know and understand, while imagination embraces the entire world, and all there will be to know and understand.*

I was taken aback and leaned into the light bulb. It was at the exact alignment with where my pineal gland was inside my head even though the light bulb was much bigger. I thought, I wonder if this is activating my pineal gland? I felt I was at the end of a tunnel with my head in another dimension. I reached out my hand to touch him to see if he was HERE or if I was THERE. My hand went right through him. He was a hologram.

He said, we don't have much time, as he looked at his Swiss watch. I don't know how long I can hold this frequency. It's so dense HERE. I have come to give you some information.

I whispered okay. I felt as if my eyes were playing tricks on me, but at the same time I felt okay with the situation. I was curious even though my heart was beating 10 times faster than normal. I looked down to make sure it wasn't jumping out of my shirt and instantly remembered the blinking heart of the guard at the Giza Plateau.

The man interrupted my thoughts and said, I have made a mistake that I must rectify. My information does not fit together like this. He shook his Swiss watch *over* and *over*. I forgot the TORQUE. My equation is wrong. I forgot the SPIN so now you only get the SPIN from your media.

He took 2 steps forward and said, you see the Earth is in constant SPIN and because I forgot the SPIN in my equation it is not in your consciousness. You don't know what you don't know.

This SPIN of the universe goes down to the particle level, the electron, the little e. The electron is the male counterpart to the female proton. It is is also represented through the mental body of each human. The male aspects of you have been electrocuted from not spinning. He shook his head and said, how do you think I got this hairstyle? It's not from whipping my hair. You need to REMEMBER the SPIN so that you can make the JUMP. It's the BIG Shift. It's the BIG EVENT. I have desperately been trying to get to someone and finally I found someone who could understand me.

Me, I presume? I said as I stood wringing my hands with anticipation.

Yes. I am Einstein. I created the Unified Field Theory from a point of view that excludes 99 percent of s p a c e. I have made a grave error. The Universe is an open system, not closed. It is a vacuum. What you put in is what you get out.

Huh?

I thought, like a piggy bank.

He nodded as if he read my thought and pulled out from his pant pockets two red funnels connected through the smaller ends. He threw them up in the air and they became digital. They showed how the vacuum was an open system with a feedback loop. He took a thought about love and placed it in an equation for me to see and then dropped it in the vacuum. I watched a picture manifest on the light bulb. It showed 2 people kissing while on a swing. He said, your reality is connected to your thought forms and the thought forms of everyone else. You are all affecting one another.

He pulled out a large thick book titled GRAVITATION. It looked like it weighed 10 pounds. It had a magnifying glass and red apple on the front of it. He said, this book is what allowed me to get HERE, as he snickered. It's true purpose is gravitation. It is weighted down with untruths and is the outdated bible of physics. It's true purpose is gravitation. That's all it's useful for. The Universe is so much more! He dropped GRAVITATION with a thud. It opened to page 719. He looked down at the page and said, how are people not questioning this diagram? It was a picture of a man blowing up a pink balloon. He said, by attaching the man blowing up that balloon you have excluded 99 percent of s p a c e. This picture is not showing the entire equation! Everything is expanding and contracting. The air going into the balloon does not show the man's lungs contracting.

I stood there thinking. My MiND began to SPIN.

He blew a large pink bubble, pinched it with his index finger and thumb and poked holes in it. He said, that theory has holes. The pink bubblegum shapeshifted into the Earth and the holes became electrical outlets and then stargates all at 19.47 N and 19.47 S latitudes. He said, the Universe is more about the 99 percent s p a c e than it is the 1 percent reality. Page number 719 lit up in a pink fluorescent color. The man blowing up the balloon came into black and white color. His balloon turned a bright pink color and 33 pennies attached to it in the book as they turned a fluorescent copper color. The pennies dropped off the pink balloon and started floating up in the air. I stood eye-to-eye with 33 Abraham Lincoln's. Each one winked at me and said, it's time to TURN THE PAGE.

I turned back to Einstein and said, why is the universe about 99 percent s p a c e?

He said, because the s p a c e is defining you. The space you take to GO WITHIN and reflect defines your experiences and ultimately you.

I said, oh…the s p a c e in between my ears?

He laughed and spun the Earth around by blowing on it. He whispered, SPIN, SPIN, SPIN…it's a SPIN out. The Earth is contracting and expanding from the magma. You need to look within the Earth to understand this time

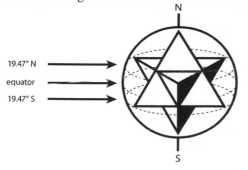

period. A red ink line appeared over the South Pole showing the geometry pattern of hyper-dimensional torsion physics. At each point was a legacy culture in a different time period reveal-ing they were all part of some-thing bigger, *a unified culture.* The Aztec Sun Stone material-ized and overlayed the Earth showing it was made out of the same lines as the hyperdimensional torsion physics. The Sun Stone shapeshifted into a crop circle in the same formation.

I stood there thinking, it all adds up. One truth builds upon another and one lie builds upon another. I said, I never understood how the BIG BANG really made sense. It wasn't logical. I asked the same question to my physics professor when I was in college and he blew me off.

Einstein nodded and said, how can you create a worldview with this dia-gram? Where does this man come from? Mars? He laughed. If you are going to create models out of thin air you might make them halfway believable. How are people buying what is being sold to them these days? This one has to be the worst. Numero UNO followed closely by the one world currency, creating a world superpower.

He said, watch me, as he placed the Earth in the air and popped a new piece of pink bubblegum in his mouth. He chewed diligently and then blew another bubble as he lifted up his shirt to show all his organs in his body. I watched his lungs contract as he blew up the balloon.

He said, this man in the diagram is blowing the balloon contracting his lungs as he expands the balloon. Therefore, to expand awareness in life you have to contract. You have to GO WITHIN. You have to go deep within yourself and OPEN UP to your imagination. It's the same process in the Universe. Everything is in constant flux, contracting and expanding at the same time. Everything is PROCESS.

Your country only knows about expansion, as in explosion. Your country needs to take the time for contraction, going WITHIN and reflecting on oneself. Every time you kill someone, you kill a fragment of yourself. It serves no purpose unless that is your purpose.

He took off his Nobel Prize for physics. He threw it at me. He said, that is a sham. Let it OPEN UP your eyes to the shams all around you. The Nobel Prize should hold great clues for you! OPEN YOUR EYES. How does one win the Nobel Prize if they promote the *Road to Destruction?* Learn to GO WITHIN and ask questions! If that doesn't work, learn to ask better questions. Never ask, why? Instead say,

$$X = Y^{knot}$$

Know your why! Know what is driving you in life! Know what makes you tick! Ask, is this creating unity or division of the people? Is this promoting life or anti-life? Who is benefiting from this? Who is benefiting monetarily? Something is wrong with your world when you would rather put billions of dollars into roads rather than helping human beings who are starving to death. You live in a paradigm of anti-life versus life.

The pin on his life jacket shapeshifted to: *Learn from yesterday, live for today, hope for tomorrow. The important thing is not to stop the question.*

He said, my equation has created such damage to so many things including the human psyche. I would like to rectify the situation before it is too late. Human beings have closed minds instead of open minds because of this. They are now attached to the situation instead of being a non-attached observer. You are continuously in FLUX. Everything is moving. Everything is PROCESS. You shouldn't be attached to anything...including outcomes. You were put here to experience life not to control it. I do feel sadness for you. He rubbed his eye as a crystal tear formed. You have been manipulated so you cannot see the distortion. He caught the tear as it formed into Dali's artwork, the "Persistence of Memory" and then dissolved.

He rubbed his chewed gum in between his index finger and his thumb and placed it in the air next to the Earth. He said, this hollow moon construct has done great damage. It has manipulated you for far too long. Thank goodness this epoch is coming to an end. This epoch has been based on limitation and control through fear.

Fear energy feeds this group of controllers from within your solar system. If you learned to step out of fear they would immediately deconstruct, but you are *so attached to the outcome.* You are more powerful than you realize! You just need to REMEMBER WHO YOU ARE.

He dropped a thought of fear in a quotation bubble and then into the vacuum and showed how an off planet source took the mathematical equation for fear: you < THE GREATER YOU and manipulated it by multiplying it by PHI, creating a string of mathematical equations linked together with the common denominator, your original fear:

$$\underline{\text{you} < \text{YOU} \times 1.618}$$

$$\textbf{FEAR}$$

He said, these mathematics create a lower vibration logos string running through the constellation Orion that is a miasm, a kink in the chain of your reality. The manipulation is always at 1.618 so that you cannot SEE it. This epoch is ending, and soon you will be able to SEE.

I stood there rubbing my eyes and wishing I could SEE.

He said, every event is given to you beforehand. You just need to open your eyes to see it. It is given through symbols. The controllers have to foreshadow everything to bring it into existence and they only have one timeline. They are playing the same theme *over* and *over* and *over.* It is the story of Osiris, Isis and Horus. You just have to change your glasses so that you can SEE it.

He snapped his fingers and the movie *THEY LIVE* played through the light bulb. He handed me a pair of black Blues Brothers-type sunglasses from inside his lifejacket so I could see the movie. I put them on and tuned in at the 1.618 interval that showed a man placing a pair of special dark sunglasses on and seeing how he had been living a life of manipulation. Everything was done to program him to live under the control of a few bankers who were controlled by off planet sources. The movie ended with a scene www. youtube.com/watch?v=Wp_K8prLfso of a man walking into a bank raising his shotgun and saying, *I have come here to chew bubblegum and kick ass and I am all out of bubblegum.*

Einstein snickered, making his wild eyebrows vibrate vertically. He turned his pack of bubblegum upside down showing it was empty. He said, let's usher in the new epoch with the TRUTH VIBRATION. They cannot mess with that vibration. It's at a higher octave than them. The new equation to bring this about is R**O** R**O** R**O**.

I immediately thought:

> Row, row, row your boat,
> Gently down the stream,
> Merrily, merrily, merrily, merrily
> Life is but a dream.

I thought I have been singing that rhyme my entire life. Maybe this was why.

He said, that is a perfect way of REMEMBERING the formula. It means: RESISTANCE / **O**pen UP REVELATION / **O**pen UP REVOLUTION / **O**pen UP.

He looked at me over the top of his glasses and said, in a sad voice, please rectify my error by publishing this equation…and please unshrine me. I have done more harm than good.

I said, what does the equation R**O** R**O** R**O** mean?

He said, your mind cycles because of the incorrect Unified Field Theory and the miasms. You can end the computer brain cycling the same story *over* and *over* in your head by noticing as a non-attached observer when it is happening. When you step back as a witness and ask questions you notice a lot more:

• What are you resisting looking at?
• What beliefs are you so vested in that you will not look at alternatives?
• What beliefs have you built walls around?
• How thick are your walls? As thick as Solomon's Temple?
• What diversions are you creating so you can keep these beliefs going?

Your computer brain is cycling what it believes to be true. If you take a PAUSE, an empty S P A C E moment, and **O**PEN UP the possibilities to the Universe…something is revealed. It will come up with something off the wall to break the cycle. Your imagination is k^{e}y here!

I couldn't help but think, what is my mind cycling?

He said, this cycle has had an effect on your soul's evolution. Your soul hasn't been able to travel up the scale of notes because it has been attached to one note…a lower octave note. He sang, *ut, re, mi, fa, so, la*. He snapped his fingers and played the theme song of "The Jeffersons" www.youtube.com/

watch?v=MYcqToQzzGY He danced around and sang as loud as he could.

When it ended, I said very quickly, what are you supposed to do when you **O**PEN UP?

He said, you PAUSE, you ask yourself this question: What would it look like being different at a higher octave? Or ask any question…for heaven's sake, just ask questions! You need to open your minds! You have become slaves living in a box! Turn off your TVs and **O**PEN YOUR MINDS!

What happens after you **O**PEN UP?

You will be given information to help you break that cycle you were cycling in.

Can you give me an example?

He said, imagine you think someone has done you wrong. You play this record *over* and *over*. So and so did me wrong. When you catch yourself doing that, stop and GO WITHIN for a second and see what information you get. You may get something crazy and off the wall. He snapped his fingers and "Living off the Wall," www.youtube.com/watch?v=Xrd3lSn5FqQ by Michael Jackson started playing. Einstein danced the entire song and finished on his two toes. I noticed he wore white socks with sequins and black patent leather shoes like Michael Jackson, but these were lace ups and on the loops were bunny ears imprinted with the words *it's all about the feedback loop.*

He said, you gotta boogie down once in awhile. Now what did you get?

I said well….

He said, stop hem-hawing around. What was the first thing that flashed in your mind?

I said, dance like a bird.

Perfect. Now do it.

I walked down the tunnel acting like a bird flailing my arms. I felt like I was in the Cave of the Birds.

He said give it 100 percent…flap those wings.

I shook my hands so fast I thought they would fly off.

He said, live your life with pauses and your life will improve 100 percent.

I said, what if people think I am crazy?

He said, living crazy, that's the only way. The only rules are the ones you have self-imposed. He jumped on his toes to the left and then the right imitating Michael Jackson.

He said, next you will have a REVELATI**O**N of some sort because you created s p a c e for new information from the Universe to come into your head. Your brain is like a CD and you just removed a bit so something useful can be put in instead of the same program running *over* and *over*. This will create a REVOLUTI**O**N in your life. The more you do this, the more cycles you will break and the more cycles you break the more of your true self will be able to come through. This will allow your soul to move up in its evolution.

I stood searching for a cycle. I wanted to break them all.

He took a bunch of deep breaths. He said, this frequency is so low here. He did the twist and said, this is as low as you can go. Now shake it, shake it, shake your tail feather and create the real Big Bang. When everyone opens up from following this new formula it will create a fractal change within each person resulting in a BIG BANG!

I thought of the man blowing up the balloon in the book and I took a safety pin and popped his bubble so that the truth of the nature of our reality could be revealed.

Einstein took out a pink plastic protractor that reminded me of one I used in grade school. He drew a circle in the sand with a dot in the middle. He said, the world is infinitely small and infinitely large at the same time. You are a smaller version of the world. He drew a pyramid facing up and one facing down inside the circle creating a star tetrahedron. He said, the world is contracting IN and expanding OUT simultaneously and continuously.

I thought, where had I seen this configuration before? I paused and then remembered…on my passport. The symbol above the eagle made this configuration!

Einstein said, this is the fractal nature of the Universe. He added smaller star tetrahedrons off the 6 apex points and then duplicated it *over* and *over*. He said, it goes to infinity. But, pointing to the circle, it won't exceed this beginning boundary. He said put your RIGHT eye up to one of the star tetrahedrons and look within.

I put my eye up to the drawing and saw it went on to infinity. I traveled down a long hall. It was never ending. I kept hearing a voice say, *keep going, you are on your way.* He said, this circle with the star tetrahedron inside is the shape of the container around your body. You go on to infinity on the INSIDE.

Spend some time going INSIDE instead of searching outside. A whole other world will open up to you! Learn to have fun with it! I regret not dancing more. I was always studying…when I crossed over the threshold I learned nothing really matters but the matters of the heart…and dancing makes your heart soar.

He pulled out a yellow piece of construction paper made into the form of a geogami in the shape of a star tetrahedron and torqued it with his thumb and index finger. It spun and then landed solidly on my left foot.

He asked, did you see the SPIN? That SPIN makes everything have more energy.

I bent down and picked it up. The outside read #39 on one side. The other side read 25.20 = fractal numeric value.

He shouted: *When people repeat what they've been taught it doesn't expand one's knowledge. Logic will get you from A to B. Imagination will take you everywhere.*

I immediately thought about Dad. We nicknamed him REPEAT because he always repeated the same stories and most of it was contrived from the newspaper…the spin doctors.

Einstein handed me the red device he had brought with him. It was a red Etch A Sketch. The red funnels fell from the air along with the two chewed pieces of pink bubblegum. Einstein started to disappear on a chessboard mirage. He began moonwalking down the light bulb. He yelled, it's the seismic creep. The Earth is snap, crackle, and poppin'. I looked at the Etch A Sketch. It was blank. I wondered, what could this mean?

I heard Einstein's voice in the distance say, ask the question…what would this look like being different at a higher octave? Nothing is as it seems you just have to OPEN UP to the possibilities of the Universe. Think outside the box! He flew a paper airplane through the light bulb. I caught it and read each side. One side read: *Modified Unified Field Theory*, by Nassim Haramein. On the flip side it read: *Unified State of Consciousness*, by Your Higher Self.

I picked up the red funnels and chewed pink bubblegum. I stared at the light bulb pictogram on the wall and thought, what would that look like being different? The light bulb turned on and within it I saw two rows of scientists facing one another. They were dressed in chaps and cowboy boots with spinning spurs, that created sparks behind them that rose above their heads into burning light bulbs. Their heads were fitted with ten-gallon cowboy hats that shapeshifted to hard hats with a light on top that beamed out the words: *Hard Head/EGO.* They squared up against one another. One man stood between them and the world. R.I.P, who wore a jester hat with a pin that read *U.S. Patent Office 1872.* Instead of a gun he held the red rubber stamp, DENIED PATENTS/ACTA. The men drew their guns and turned on one another. They fired… displaying false flags that read: THE BIG BANG IS DEAD. THE BIG BANG IS WHAT FRAGMENTED YOU AND THE U.S.

A woman appeared and unplugged the light bulb pictogram and the scene disappeared as the minds of the scientists were just being opened. All that was left was the face of the real inventor of the light bulb, Nikola Tesla. He said, I have grave regret over my invention of the death ray. You call it HAARP. It was not meant to lead the world down the *Road to Destruction.* It was meant to create a small box to create electricity for an entire city, not put you in a box 6 feet under. I am distressed how world powers have begun to play the HAARP game. It is being used to destroy areas in the world through weather wars. It was not meant to put you in bondage. It was meant to free you from bondage.

I thought, if the shadow government is using this to decimate areas of the country, soon insurance companies will go belly up and then the government can come in and take over the insurance industry giving the shadow government the ability to regulate what goes on in the home. Banksters and Insurance Companies walk hand in hand.

The woman holding the plug had long red hair and porcelain skin. She whispered, weather derivatives. She was hanging half IN and half OUT of a steel mailbox with the coordinates of HAARP etched on the side: 62.39° N latitude and 145.15° W longitude. She was dressed in a pink frilly dress with black and white striped stockings with a stamp of the *Emissary of the Galactic Federation* on the soles of her feet. The tips of her shoes were gold and read *Beyond Your Galaxy* on the LEFT and *Beyond Your Imagination* on the RIGHT. Her right hand was extended. She was holding a 6 x 8 red, white and blue intertwined ribbon laced envelope addressed to *my darling planet Earth.* It was stamped *par avion* with a frontal picture of a plane with its engine made up of 24 spokes all aligned slightly to the right. It was postmarked *out of this world* and it was covered in stamps. She sang, *airmail,* in a soprano voice.

As I took the envelope from her she shot like a starburst into the sky creating a five-petaled violet…at superluminal speed. She took her place in the cosmos as Venus marked with an arrow that read *Queen Star*. I opened the envelope.

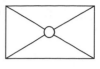

I pulled a pink card out that had a small violet in the corner. It read: *If you think quantum physics is a shock you haven't seen anything yet! Be aware of my astrology cycles. My energies are powerful! The shadow government knows this and plans to use these energies for the destruction on 6 – 7 – 2012 = 6 – 7 – 5 … the mirror image of my sacred number, which is 5-7-6. It was the time Leo, the lion, represented by the Sphinx, ruled the zodiac. It started and ends with Leo the Lion, the uncowardly lion from the "Wizard of Oz"…WAKE UP your sleeping lion within.*

I looked back at the light bulb and saw a scene of pictures from ground penetrating radar of hundreds of still frames of Egyptian tunnels, rooms, and labyrinths and their alignment with the stars. They started at the paws of the Sphinx and traveled outwards. The final picture was of 10 briefcase size wooden boxes with two gold counter-clockwise rotating devices with ancient writing on them around a crystal inside emitting an energy source from inside the underground Khufu Temple Complex. The Secretary General of the Supreme Council of Antiquities of Egypt's face overtook the light bulb. He reached his hand up in the air in slow motion and then at super speed slammed down a red stamp that read DENIED INFORMATION OF YOUR TRUE ANCESTORY!

A thin gold double-headed serpent slithered in an oscillating pattern through the writing, leaving a track that said: *It all leads to the repairing of the splicing in your DNA.* The serpent shapeshifted into a DNA strand showing the splicing at 1.618 intervals. Every 1.618 interval held a Joker playing card.

The scene flickered ON and OFF, showing titanium briefcases being delivered to all the world leaders. One briefcase was zoomed in on revealing a blueprint for free energy. A segment was highlighted that read: *Free energy is the way of the future. Either you are on board with freeing the people from bondage or you are not, what do you choose?* There was a box for NO and no box for YES to be checked by the recipient.

PAUSE

STORY #89: The Red Funnel Theory™

When I got back to the Love Boat I passed Akhmen who was in the bar with a group of new tourists that were boarding. I passed a sign that read, THERE. I went straight to my quarters without stopping. I had to get to a pen and paper and write all this down. My memory wasn't working so well these days and with 100-degree heat I was feeling loopier than ever. I raced up the stairs and paused before I opened the door. I thought, learn to PAUSE. I took a deep breath and turned the brass doorknob and entered my room to find another towel design on my bed. This time it was of a frog with two eyes bulging out with a small card attached that said *Yanaguni*.

I ran over to a pad of paper on the desk. It read: *When your heart speaks, take good notes.* I smiled and started journaling as fast as I could the interpretation of the equation. I put the pen to the paper and instead of thinking what to write I decided to try something new and GO WITHIN and PAUSE and write what came into my mind. I wrote:

R**O** R**O** R**O** means Resistance / SPACE Revelation / SPACE Revolution / SPACE.

> *We need the PAUSE, the empty space, the void because it is HERE that true freedom is achieved. It is HERE that one can allow the freedom of the right brain to roam free, to travel around with no path, to soar like a bird, to look at things through your feet instead of your eyes, to open up to all the possibilities that the left brain structure would never allow. The left-brain is about patterns and logic. It wants structure at all costs. Including the cost of losing yourself. It really isn't your friend a lot of the time. I witnessed this in the King's chamber.*

> *Patterns are what make up this Universe. There has to be some type of structure in which the Universe exists otherwise we would live in chaos. We have structure through the singularity point. This allows all to view things somewhat the same, but now it is the time to start really opening up the right brain and experiencing the freedom of the imagination. This in effect will create a bridge between the right and the left-brain. The bridge is where the right brain can be free and the left can keep the logic with ease. This bridge will allow one to feel the freedom they are so desperately searching for through the most material possessions.*

> *The void, the s p a c e, the PAUSE is what allows the opening up of the possibilities. A huge funnel opens up and everything out of the ordinary comes sifting in. Things you could not have thought about. This is called the RED FUNNEL. It is a vortex of creative thoughts. Your only*

job is to step out of the way and allow because you would not be able to come up with the things that rush in. You have to release your control. Your controlling is no longer going to work in the coming world.

The mind is constantly trying to find patterns. As soon as it goes outside it is looking for a pattern. This makes it feel safe. Your mind searches for things that reflect who you think you are and then it takes it in. It leaves out a lot of other patterns. It therefore creates a REALITY that is unique to you and your perception is only through this lens. You have created a world that is unique to you based on your genetics, your experiences, your likes and dislikes. Your PERCEPTION is limited. You believe certain things to be true because of your conditioning.

In reality, are they really true?

We humans have created mind loops through our limited perception. It's a loop that consistently plays over and over in our minds, something we find to be true, like a CD playing the same track, in the same groove over and over. If however, we create a PAUSE, step into the void and ask what would it look like differently at a higher octave? Then we get a different perception. This void, this s p a c e opens up a rush of different ideas. The mind is no longer able to track like it did before in a linear line of playing or tarot cards. Imagine these cards lined up one after the other in a certain sequence your mind has created. But when you open it up from this different s p a c e you can create a vortex, a rounded spiral instead of a straight line, and your world opens up. Imagine a RED FUNNEL on top of your head instead of a linear line. As you are contracting on the inside, you are opening up the RED FUNNEL to bring in a myriad of different ideas, some so off the wall they make you smile. After a while they become more and more creative and more and more colorful. Bright reds, bright yellows, bright blues, bright oranges... all colors creating a psychedelic array of new and fascinating options. Life all of a sudden doesn't seem so mundane, so meaningless, so boring.

When we were children it was a lot easier to tap into this. We didn't have the stress of the mortgage payment, the insurance payment, the car payment, a job or other responsibilities to start weighing us down. We became like Hercules, carrying the world on our shoulders desperately searching for FREEDOM. We just didn't know it was actually right inside of ourselves.

I laid the pen and paper down and picked up the Etch A Sketch. I created an oscillating pattern on the screen alternating the knobs back *and* forth, creating a wave. But when I sat back with no judgment, just BLANK curiosity, the screen turned into a vortex showing me that waveforms are not flat. They are vortices. As I stared in wonderment the Etch A Sketch had a vortex running through the middle from LEFT to RIGHT. I thought, I used to think vortexes only ran up and down—interesting. I then saw a red ball BOUNCE through the air diagonally and land on certain points creating a diagonal wave pattern leaving a 19.47 imprint behind. Before I could distinguish the pattern I saw jacks spinning through the air landing on the spots the red ball imprinted and left behind.

Wow! I thought. Amazing! What does that mean?

And just like that, the imprints showed in a flash they were ancient sites and a vortex opened over them showing they were stargates. I thought, Einstein was trying to show me this through his bubblegum.

I sat back in wonderment and thought there is more than meets the 'i' in this world. We live in a wonderland. I closed my eyes and repeated we live in a wonderland. I opened my eyes as I thought, we get too stuck in our judgment of what is. We block the vacuum. We become stagnant swimming in a cesspool of unproductive thoughts. I wrote judgment on a blank piece of paper and flipped it over and wrote *compassion / forgiveness*. I thought, the next time I go overboard in judgment of what is I am going to flip the card over and go into compassion and forgiveness to keep the energy moving because I refuse to live in stagnation. I sang:

> *Row, row, row your boat,*
> *Gently down the stream,*
> *Merrily, merrily, merrily, merrily,*
> *Life is but a dream.*

STORY #144: Looking Glasses

I walked to Mrs. Velvet's wearing Mom's new ruby red shoes and her red and white checkered long sundress over my school pants. I twirled her pearl necklace around my wrist getting it kinked and then unkinked as I walked through the basement tunnel observing the new wallpaper Mrs. Velvet had hung. The wallpaper started with **the word** *setup* written in pink cursive next to a large A. *Setup* was followed by an arrow that pointed to the floor and continued with a larger arrow painted on the floor connected to another arrow ❯ to another arrow ❯ to another arrow ❯ to another arrow ❯ to another arrow ❯ with the words overlaying it that read, *moving toward the fulfillment of...* Along the arrows the words COMPREHENSIVE, CALCULATION, CONTEMPLATION laid out in Nike tennis shoe tracks.

I thought, someone has walked these footsteps before. I walked from the *setup along the fulfillment of...*in comprehensive, calculation, contemplation. I walked in deep thought as I contemplated the new wallpaper. It was of all different types of birds in birdcages. I opened all the birdcages as I walked by freeing the red, white, blue and yellow birds that were trapped inside. I took my index finger and flipped the latch and let them fly free as I sang, "Bye Bye Birdie." I watched all the birds come to life and fly. I whispered, YOU ARE FINALLY FREE! Beat your wings. Soar to new heights. ASCEND. I started to run and flap my wings along the *in the fulfillment of...* arrow wishing I too could fly. The tunnel turned into a cave filled with birds as I heard "Close to You" www.youtube.com/watch?v=re-6eOhrejE by The Carpenters from the movie "Mirror Mask" playing. The sound was coming from Mrs. Velvet's house.

One yellow birdie flew up to me and said, *set up* your life as you OBSERVE. This helps you evaluate your empowerment as you move down the line.

I realized at that moment as I had moved down the line I had reached and passed by several > signs labeled: *me.* I thought, I am moving to greater heights. What I once thought was the limit is no longer so. A limitation is something self-imposed. I threw all my limitations against the wall like cooked spaghetti strings and watched as none of them stuck. I watched them form a small holographic 'i' in midair wrapped in single quotation marks. I went over and pushed ON the dot. The quotation marks around the 'i' expanded outward and turned into black cloaks with the words, *National Security* written on them and then they fell to the ground. I went over and pressed the dot of the i again and this time the word information came up holographically. I pressed information and it turned into the words: *Great Observer.*

A lovebird flew up to me and sang, so, so, so, sew a new thread of love through the world. Her mate flew up and dropped a blue string into my hand.

I held it up in front of me and thought, how could I make this useful? I thought, I know. I know. I know. I can string it across the world creating a new vibration of love. I can create a *Blue String Theory* where one person does an act of kindness and passes it ON to another

who passes it ON to another

who passes it ON to another

    who passes it ON to another

        who passes it ON to another

            who passes it ON to another

                who passes it ON to another

                    who passes it ON to another

                who passes it ON to another

            who passes it ON to another

        who passes it ON to another

    who passes it ON to another

who passes it ON to another

who passes it ON to another…until it stretches around the globe creating the web of a higher vibration of LOVE as everyone takes part in the REMEM-BRANCE of who they are at their core…LOVE. I thought, I am going to call it *the blue string theory.* I thought, the thrill is gone for the people filled with fear and hate. I heard B.B. King sing softly in my ear, "The Thrill is Gone," http://www.youtube.com/watch?v=4fk2prKnYnI. I thought, if I were Queen I would choose B.B. to be my King. He has more soul than 200 pairs of Nikes.

I continued walking, contemplating my *Blue String Theory* as B.B. King appeared before me jamming out on his guitar. I stood in amazement at the sound of the blues. As he ended his jam session he threw me the pick. I caught it midair. It expanded to a large round-edge pyramid in my hand so I examined it. It read:

What am I to do

when you don't know YOU?

Exquisite masterpiece of art

completes the moment you find heart

To explore your humble mass
raise your face to looking glass
A line of dead, a dead of lie
is stricken down by poly sci
No! Don't imitate!
Play! Imagin8!

I flipped the pick up in the air and watched the flip side hang in the air. It revealed the flip side was a bicycle spinning its wheels in midair. I caught the pick as it descended and continued walking the line with the pick in hand. As I neared Mrs. Velvet's door I saw some more of Mrs. Velvet's cursive hand-writing on the wall. *There is a BIG difference between KNOWING versus not knowing. Knowing is when you experienced the lesson so you know it, therefore you have a knowing. Not knowing is just reading the definition and not having the experience of the lesson.*

I thought, if you don't have the experience of the lesson you can't have the knowing. I heard a little birdie say, you don't know what you don't know. Do you know what this all means, dear?

I said, yes ma'am. Know ma'am. I'm just HERE.

I reached Mrs. Velvet's door and did a shuffle ball change dance step on her doormat. I looked down and noticed it was different today. It was the picture of a woman dressed in a red 2011 ticket agent dress accessorized with a pin shaped like wings that read: *YOU earned your wings. You know how to go from HERE to THERE*. I walked as she lifted off her red pillbox hat revealing a riddle inside: *Who do you choose to be – the ticket agent or the traveler?*

I smiled and said, I choose the traveler, without pausing to contemplate the riddle.

She said, the CHOICE is always yours. There is always a ticket waiting for you to go anywhere in the world at the ticket counter. The question is...can you believe this? Can you stick with your belief that it's THERE waiting for you? Can you not cross the counter and become the ticket agent, who doesn't believe there is a ticket THERE for YOU? The ticket agent's pin turned into the word: *Self* **o**h *Sabotage*.

I contemplated. Could I hold my belief so strong that nothing, including my mind, could deter me from my ticket to travel the world? The ticket agent shapeshifted into the word MiND on the doormat surrounded by 7 question marks. I put both heels of Mom's ruby red shoes on the dot of one of the question marks and fell through the doormat going deeper than the MiND down a tube of white light. I landed on a wavy gray line marked resistance followed closely by a line that read depression. My feet got stuck on that line. It felt like bubblegum. I realized that the MiND holds you like a trap until you can gather strength from your heart and jump over the line. I decided to FLIP THE SWITCH in my MiND and saw the bubblegum for what it was—Silly Putty—and I jumped over the line. The tube of light turned into hundreds of > signs and expanded out in every direction spelling out the word KNOWING in BIG letters. Each boundary layer had a small wavy line of *resistance* that led to *depression* before going on to the next boundary layer. I decided to push myself and go as far out as I could. I realized that my potential was infinite only separated by a thin boundary line. I said to myself, how far is far? All of a sudden I reached a place where I just knew what I knew. I paused and thought, there's a remembrance in knowing that goes deeper than the MiND.

After realizing this, the nuclear bomb in a black box at the bottom of the tunnel marked World Trade Center Building 1, 2 and 7 exploded. As it exploded it turned into the nuclear bomb cloaked as a security camera in the shape of a black box in the basement of the f a k e shima nuclear power plant.

Once I felt the explosion I was thrust UP by a blast of hot air. I passed 72 black box television sets. The U.S. President was on all of them giving a news conference filled with FEAR – False Evidence Appearing Real. The bottom line on the TV screen read: Setup date: 9 – 11 – 2011. This date was followed by a string of oscillating arrows made out of the words of the poem "What Is Needed" in the pattern of the Grief Graph:

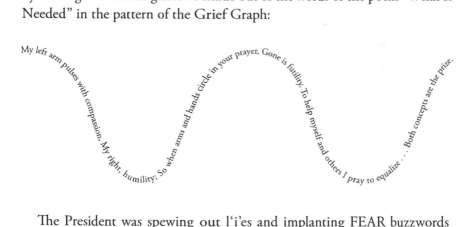

The President was spewing out l'i'es and implanting FEAR buzzwords into the consciousness of the world so that the Shadows could continue moving their agenda of population reduction down the line through the use of nuclear explosions. All of the arrows on the bottom line of the black box television sets pointed to a with a subtitle that read: *The question becomes – what is the date that matches the resonance when Atlantis sank in a flood on 7 – 27 – 9792 B.C. This date was the beginning of the root pattern of the human race's belief system, STORY ONE. We The People are continually running the old and outdated pattern of the Atlantean seed conflict:*

Abuse of Technology versus Consciousness

creating war over power

A piece of red tape with the word FRAUD appeared over the President's mouth as the television sets showed the national disaster of nuclear reactors going off as if they were dominos lined up to take the fall at a precise orchestrated moment.

The television sets changed frequencies and tuned into a Looney Tunes cartoon. Porky Pig appeared in the center of 13 radial rings of orange and red. Porky said, th, th, th, that's all folks as he lifted up a poem for the camera to zoom in on. The psalm read:

6 - 7 – 5 is a match back. It matches the resonance of the Atlantis downfall and the Olympics is the target date. Be aware!

Airs of Condition

~~~~~~~~~~

Cold and fusion?

Moron oxy.

Air condition

Winter's proxy.

~~~~~~~~~~

Close a window

Manage the heat

Use a blanket

Walk with bare feet.

****

Furnish an ace

Start the blower

Thermostatic

Summer knower.

~~~~~~~~~~

Four the seasons

Two of billing

Forcing currents

Breathing, willing.

~~~~~~~~~~~

After 99 seconds Porky pulled the psalm and waved his white batting glove good bye. The TV sets exploded to the tune of Marilyn Monroe singing "Happy Birthday Mr. President," www.youtube.com/watch?v=k4SLSlSmW74.

All the belief systems of war *over* power spewed out from the TV sets turning them into dominos that had been *set up* and were now falling in line along a Grief Graph, hanging in the air. The dominos were tipped over one by one going from **the word** *Denial* (HERE) to **the word** *Acceptance*, which was now crossed out and replaced with **the word** *Change* (THERE). As they fell they turned into pink piggy banks filled with Billions of pennies.

I read the writing on the wall as I passed by. It said: *Patriot Act* followed by *the 1ˢᵗ Law of Physics: For every action there is an equal and opposite reaction.*

The pink piggy banks flipped upside down emptying out hundreds of copper pennies sending them floating through the air like rain. Abraham Lincoln's face came alive in each one and they all said in unison, *It is better to remain silent and be thought a fool than to open one's mouth and remove all doubt.* All the faces of Abraham Lincoln opened their mouths at the same time singing, mi mi meeee, and then they all started singing the song, "It's Like That," from "The Emancipation of Mimi" by Mariah Carey www.youtube.com/watch?v=LBG7Aed_zvU. Abe turned into Babe, the pig from the movie "Babe: Pig in the City." He said, l 'i' e l 'i' e l 'i' e as he turned into the pig Wilbur from the book *Charlotte's Web*.

I reached out and tried to grab a penny, but all the pennies had now turned into flying pigs. I floated UP passing 10 open windows. The frames read: *Windows Of Opportunities Are Open Now.* I blinked my eyes while realizing that I live inside a black hole and then I passed another window with a frame that read: *New Frame Of Reference Installed.* I blinked my eyes again and when I opened them a financial derivative was floating in front of me. It read:

Derivatives = Biggest Crime in Human History.

The derivative flipped over and read: *JFK New Deal.* I flipped it back over and it read:

Maritime Admiralty Law 1933

I contemplated this and soon was back up on top of the MiND doormat, which was now covered in Charlotte's web.

Charlotte, the spider said, REMEMBER what Grandmother Spider always said, you can handle it. You can handle the TRUTH. A queen bee wearing a crown made out of 6 red heart prongs flew into the web and instead of getting stuck jumped on a string making the F sharp tone and then bounced out spinning the crown to the tune of *ut, re, mi, fa, so, la* as the web turned into the corporate web of greed. She said, being is greater than doing. She made the equation:

Being > Doing

in the air which descended on the web, breaking it apart. A copper penny that was stuck in the web fell out and onto the doormat dotting the i of the word MiND imprinted on the doormat once again. I watched as 13 radial rings of the number 1440 expanded out from the dot spelling out the words:

KNOWING > the fool

I contemplated the equation as I looked back at the doormat. The word MiND was replaced by the pyramid symbol from the dollar bill radiating out the song, "Uprising," by Muse, www.youtube.com/watch?v=w8KQmps-Sog. I walked up the 13 steps of the pyramid. As I stepped on each step, it lit up an equation of:

$$144,000 \times 1$$
$$144,000 \times 2$$
$$144,000 \times 3$$
$$144,000 \times 4$$
$$144,000 \times 5$$
$$144,000 \times 6$$
$$144,000 \times 7$$
$$144,000 \times 8$$
$$144,000 \times 9$$
$$144,000 \times 10$$
$$144,000 \times 11$$
$$144,000 \times 12$$

I jumped on the 13th platform making the number $144,000 \times 13 = 1872000$ appear. Once 1872000 appeared, all the other steps turned into piano keys from C to C. I stood on the 13th platform and stared I to i with the eye symbol on the pyramid. I turned to my RIGHT and looked back and saw the equation of the radial rings change to:

KNOWING > Nuclear Reactors.

A little yellow birdie reappeared with a ticket hanging out of her mouth. She dropped the ticket and it drifted through the air changing into the U.S. astrology chart of July 4, 1776 at 5:10 p.m. with the "Myth of Zipacna and the 400 Boys" highlighted at the bottom. She said, do you know what this all means dear?

I said, yes ma'am. Know ma'am. I'm just THERE. Then I saw myself at the ticket counter at the John F. Kennedy International Airport. I was having a standoff with a brunette female ticket agent. I was believing without a shadow of doubt there was a first class ticket THERE for me in her drawer.

The brunette ticket agent finally reached in her drawer handed me my ticket and said, you're on your way. Follow the arrow. As she passed the ticket through her hands she shapeshifted into **the word** *self sabotage* and then faded into **the word** *empowerment*.

I heard a mechanical voice say, BEEP. BEEP. BEEP. BEEP. BEEP. BEEP... this has been a test from the central processing unit.

The little birdie whispered, you passed the test. Proceed to GO and collect your $250 million payoff. You chose to believe in YOU. I looked down at the ticket and it read: *Fight versus flight. YOU CHOSE FLIGHT. You earned your wings. Now fly little birdie.* FLY.

I looked behind me to see if anyone else was HERE or THERE. I noticed the directional arrows on the airport floor now read: ASCENSION TIME-LINE.

The birdie said, dear, some people are still buying their tickets, but you are down the line. Be compassionate for others because *maybe they will or maybe they won't* get on the train. YOU my dear can't wait!

Thirty-three bluebirds gathered and sang in tune, Wooo woooo!! They flapped their wings and turned into baseballs speeding down the tunnel as a group changeup pitch. The breeze formed the words: *It's time for a changeup. We're tired of the curve ball always being thrown* at U.S. A woman's professional softball came flying out of left field with unraveling red seams spelling out the word: *Dream Seam.*

I grabbed the black and white checkered doorknob with **the word** IN-TENTION written on it next to a B. I turned it with a CLICK and opened the door. I pushed through the doorway and entered Mrs. Velvet's hallway to the tune, "Run Fast for Your Mother," by Florence and the Machine, www.youtube.com/watch?v=iWOyfLBYtuU.

I stood before the wooden bowls shaking my hips *back* and *forth* thinking, I wonder what other surprises today will bring. I whispered to myself, I have 8^2 possible ways of looking at things today. My eyes scanned the room and I immediately noticed the bowls on the entry table were different. There were only 3 bowls numbered 1, 2, and 7 staring back at me connected by a black and white checkered finish line that read: *As We Near The Finish Line The Infighting Within The New World Order Guarantees Their Implosion.*

Under the bowls were 3 books. The first book said, STORY ONE; the second book said, STORY TWO; and the third book said, STORY THREE. I said, *un, deux, trois,* as I did another shuffle ball change step. I looked down to see if there was another doormat, but instead I noticed a Golden Ticket stuck to the tip of my shoe. I bent down and peeled it off. I put it in my hand and read the boarding pass number to New York City / Rome / Paris / Spain / London / India / Bali / Israel / Washington D.C. out loud: **1765422998742-01.1** I flipped it over onto the top of my left hand and the other side read: *MiND.* I licked it and stuck it to my forehead. I thought, I can't shake this thing! The ticket changed to read:

UNINHIBITED MIND

I looked around the corner and caught a glimpse of Mrs. Velvet in the bathroom. She looked much younger today. She had on a sexy black bra and panty set. She was fixing her garter belt, which was holding up a pair of black stockings. Her hair was different too. It was long and dark brown. Gone was the pink beehive.

I yelled to her, Mrs. Velvet I am HERE! I went back to the bowls and squeezed my eyes shut and said, my wish is that I choose the right card for me today. I fished my hand in the bowl and pulled out the card marked number 39. I flipped it over and heard 2 Cellos (Sulic and Hauser) playing "Welcome To The Jungle," www.youtube.com/watch?v=mSByjqMGtaU, as I read the poem:

SUBJECTS
Math and science

In the building

Social studies

Tending, fielding.

Quantitative

Long division

Contemplative

Verse precision.

Fourteen forty

And twenty two

Over seven

One to three through.

Shine it, type it

Make it witty

Learn teach audit

Study pretty.

Then Mrs. Velvet yelled, I will be out in a moment. I ran to the corner and saw her slowly close the door as she was spritzing herself with an old fashioned pink bottle with a large red ball attached.

I thought, she is so so beautiful and elegant. Even the way she spritzes herself is mesmerizing. I wondered, why does she look different today? She came out and changed the record player to play "Fever," by Peggy Lee, www.youtube.com/watch?v=JGb5IweiYG8.

She sashayed over to me. She was now dressed in her pink beehive and red corset top and beautiful flowing long *haute couture* silk skirt, brocade, with pink and red flowers. She looked like she stepped out of the Marie Antoinette time period. She looked divine.

I looked at her wondering how she had just transformed before my very eyes. I caught a glimpse of a small card in her beehive made out of a windshield wiper. It read: CLARITY / Frankincense clears the astral slime.

She said my my my…my little girl is growing up. You have eyeglasses now?

Yes I said. Mom bought me glasses because I flunked the eye exam. The doctor kept making me look through this large apparatus and I didn't see very well. He kept asking, what do you see now? as he clicked different lenses into place. His machine went

CLICK

    CLICK

       CLICK

          CLICK

CLICK

CLICK

CLICK

CLICK

CLICK

CLICK

until it was perfect and I could see to infinity and beyond. He called it 20/20. It was really weird. I didn't like it. I felt sick and dizzy afterwards. But now I can see really far! I guess I now know how far is far.

Well, you look like a young lady.

My brother said that I look like a frog. He said that the glasses are too big. I don't know how I feel about them yet. I wish my brother wouldn't have said that. Now every time I look in the mirror I see a frog.

Mrs. Velvet said, you know you can choose how you feel about them. Here are some suggestions. A) You can feel like you can solve any riddle with them on; B) They give you magical powers when you put them on; C) They make you feel like a superhero when you put them on.

I said, ok. I choose Plan B. I want to have magical powers.

Well there you go. You just received magic powers with your new eyeglasses. I think we should celebrate. She pointed her finger to 4 o'clock.

I followed her finger and saw mountains and mountains of pink cotton candy made into tiny tornados. I ran over to check it out. I didn't want to touch it. It was like a scene out of the Willy Wonka movie. I felt I was in a wonderland of pink cotton candy.

She said, go ahead. It's all for you.

I blinked my eyes and said, is this real?

She said, yes dear, as real as real gets. Now, what card did you draw?

I said, SEEING IS BELIEVING.

Oh lovely. Seeing is believing. What do you think that means dear?

That whatever I see is real.

Your eyes are one of the most important things you have, but they are more special than you think. They allow you to see the outside world and the inside world. They are like tiny mirrors.

Mom said that mirrors show all your blemishes.

Well, they do, but only if that is what you are looking for. When you look out into the world you get to see what you want to see. You create your reality by looking through your glasses. No one's world looks the same. Everyone is living his or her own REALITY.

I want to create a reality of love…and pink cotton candy.

Beautiful. I am going to teach you a couple of tricks. The key to seeing the outer world as love is to see the inner world as love. The way to do that is to always stay true to who you really are. Once you start doing things that aren't really who you are, the outside world starts to get muddy. It all has to do with a big word called PERCEPTION. The way you view a mean thing your brother said and bring it inside of you affects your world. You were going to bring it in as something wrong with you and that isn't who you are. You are perfect. You are a child of God. So instead you replace it with….

I yelled, Plan B.

Mrs. Velvet said yes. You wear these glasses to bring out your magical powers and that is loving. Do you understand?

Yes. So, love means a lot of things.

Yes. Love is the most all-encompassing word there is. It means so many different things. But, it always means being true to yourself. Self-love is the true meaning of love.

You mean STORY ONE is love?

Yes. That is a new way of looking at STORY ONE.

What about love with a boy?

That can only happen if you love yourself first. Otherwise you lose yourself by becoming someone who is putting another's needs before their own. Women seem to be the masters of this. It is only because they do not understand who they are and the power they hold. A relationship with a boy never works unless you are your true self in love with yourself first.

I said, STORY ONE is putting yourself first…as number one. If you don't put yourself number one who else will?

That is exactly what I mean, Love.

Now, let's talk about PERCEPTION. Perception means how you view things. You can change how you view things with a blink of an eye. You are the one that attaches the meaning.

So, choose a meaning that is in line with STORY ONE.

Yes. You see how I have several different pairs of glasses lying around. You have seen all the different ones, right?

I said yes. I like the red ones with rhinestones on them.

Well, when I put on each pair they give me a different view of the situation. One situation can be seen in at least 64 different ways.

Wow.

Don't get stuck on one way of looking at things. It will remove all the magic from life. Always remember to keep putting on different pairs of glasses. It is like viewing life through different lenses like when the eye doctor kept asking you, how does it look now? How does it look now? How does it look now? Do you see what I am saying?

Yes.

The only thing that is going to distort your vision is FEAR. Fear is the only thing that changes the TRUTH. Fear thinks you can't handle the truth so it changes the REALITY to what it thinks you can handle. Remember all lies have their basis in FEAR. This will be your biggest challenge in life. You have to play with your mind by not allowing FEAR to take over your life. Fear is the pair of glasses with all the funny swirls on them. You know, the ones with the fake nose.

Yes. Mom has a pair of those. She wore them through McDonald's drive-through once. I was so embarrassed.

I am happy she is playing a little. Adults have lost all the magic of life. Mrs. Velvet grabbed a pair of fear glasses from a drawer and put them on. She said, do not allow yourself to take on fear. It will change your reality in so many ways. If it gets a hold of you it will start living your life for you and you will lose all the magic of life.

Wow. I want to live in love and for love my whole life. I will have to get a lot more pairs of glasses.

Mrs. Velvet laughed and said, would you like to make some today? We can make a pair of love glasses and fear glasses. I have pipe cleaners and construction paper and bottle holder plastic rings and tracing paper. This is all we need.

I said sure, as I took my index finger and swiped the pink cotton candy.

Mrs. Velvet and I made a pair of glasses in the shape of hearts for the love glasses and a pair of crazy eyed glasses for fear glasses. I wore the love glasses home. I asked Mom what she thought and she said, I see a girl who spends too much time dreaming about love and not enough time doing her homework. She asked where the glasses she just bought me were.

I told her they were resting. They were only to be used when I wanted my magical powers.

She said, could you have your magical powers go vacuum the living room?

I thought, what would I do for a Klondike bar? I paused and decided to go ahead and vacuum and put all my desires inside the infinite vacuum. I created tracks going from my center point....

UP and DOWN and back to center...counting 12

and

diagonally to the RIGHT UP and back to center...counting 1

and

diagonally to the RIGHT UP a little lower and back to center...counting 2

and

diagonally to the LEFT UP and back to center...counting 11

and

diagonally to the LEFT UP a little lower and back to center...counting 10

and

to the LEFT and back to center...counting 9

and

DOWN and UP to center...counting 6

and

diagonally to the RIGHT down and back to center...counting 5

and

diagonally to the RIGHT down up a little and back to center...counting 4

and

diagonally to the LEFT down and back to center...counting 7

and

diagonally to the LEFT up a little less and back to center...counting 8

and

to the RIGHT and back to center...counting 3.

Jonny ran through the tracks breaking my mind gap yelling, may the vacuum be with you!

I chased him out of the room and came back and slipped on my magical glasses resting in my pocket. I continued vacuuming and connecting all the tracks with one another while thinking, if we all took actions toward our greater self rather than our lesser self the intersecting tracks would affect one another creating a unified humanity with the Universe as a whole. I smiled at my conclusion and silently thanked Jonny for his interruption because it gave me the s p a c e for my realization. I stood with the vacuum in my hand and stared at my masterpiece wondering what I just connected HERE and THERE in other timelines.

Jonny reappeared at the doorway holding his black boombox. He said, your carpet tracks look like the geometry of a vector equilibrium to me. I looked over at him and winked.

He pushed PLAY on the cassette player and "She Blinded Me With Science," www.youtube.com/watch?v=3fI8834iCgo, by Thomas Dolby played throughout the living room. I stood in the center and marveled at the vacuum.

Jonny danced around the room messing up all my tracks. He stopped and stood in front of me daring me to chase him. I undid my ponytail and took off my glasses in preparation for the showdown.

Jonny laughed and said, good heavens Miss Sakamoto! You're beautiful!

STORY #89: Unsticking the Stuck

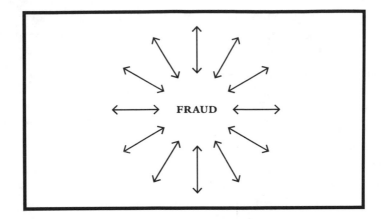

Break down the box you have built around you with box cutters.

Dismantle your belief systems, patterns and personalities.

See past the façade of FRAUD.

The structures you think hold you up only keep you down.

What you are at your inner core is LOVE...the only truth is LOVE.

Angela Gheorghiu, Vissi d'art – Tosca – Puccini, www.youtube.com/ watch?v=_OIExoUb8jk.

STORY #55: The Tree of Life

I awoke feeling every bit of my 42 years. I lay in bed on the Love Boat and looked up at the ceiling letting my mind wonder and wander. I could faintly hear "Rock the Boat," www.youtube.com/watch?v=dndAXxqJbc0 by the 1974 Hues Corporation. I thought, what boat could I rock today? I started connecting the dots on the ceiling as I thought, I know I have many possible ways of looking at the dots on this ceiling. Today I am going to find 72 possible ways to look at everything. I started to daydream as faint images started coming into place out of the mists of my mind and then they became clearer and clearer. Three large pillars appeared above me numbered 1, 7 and 2 followed closely by a handful of baseballs. The white balls flew through the room unraveling their red strings from their seams weaving in and

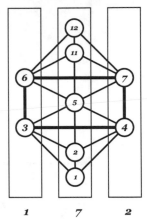

around the pillars creating the ancient symbol of the Tree of Life. I thought, the ancients believed that all life on Earth is interrelated. I thought, this image has to relate to the number 72. The Tree of Life lit up in a glowing golden hue. My eyes traveled around the intersecting pathways going up and down and diagonally giving my mind a workout.

The Tree of Life doubled, creating 2, and then doubled again, creating 4. I counted *un, deux, trois, quatre*. The 4 Trees of Life doubled creating 8 as I sang five, six, seven, eight. I thought, I am the Queen of my F8. When I spoke this aloud the 8 individual Trees of Life lit up a box inside the formation near the bottom of it made up of red strings connecting the baseballs.

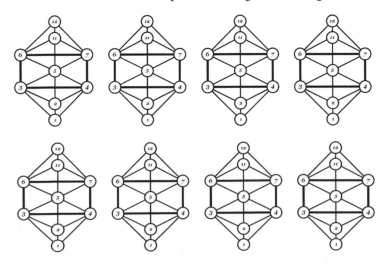

The 8 individual boxes sprang open breaking their strings of attachment creating separation of what *was*. The fibers of the strings repaired the threads that were frayed when the separation took place. This allowed the box to be opened and the possibilities to flow IN and OUT. I felt a freedom run through my body as this happened. I felt a beauty within and around me I had not felt since my first major crush at age 13. I heard a

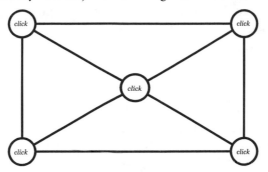

The individual box slid into the space of the exact same proportions above it with a

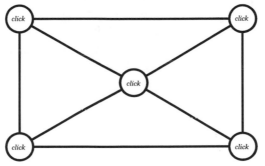

I felt my empowerment TURN ON as I saw the new box light up like a domino highlighted with 5 brilliant blue hued dots glowing from within.

The domino rotated counterclockwise 64 times and turned into another piece of the puzzle…a Rubik's Cube with one face showing 6 squares that lit up in a brilliant blue hue. The Rubik's Cube began to CLICK in a clockwise SPIN 64 times turning into a 6 blue dotted domino. The domino dots sang out the tones: *ut, re, mi, fa, so, la.* The domino began to SPIN and turned into a 1960s Parisian envelope stamped with a blue wax seal in the shape of a labyrinth. I followed the pathways of the labyrinth and got lost in the seal as I traveled along blue pathways to the sound of the 22 letters of the Hebrew alphabet. I heard an electronic voice say, you've got mail.

I heard someone else whisper in a child like voice, *Open me, Open me, Open me, Open me, Open me, Open me, Open me, Open me.* I realized the whispers were coming from deep within the labyrinth. I opened the wax seal as I said the secret passwords that appeared on the wall in front of me in the form of an eightball.

> *The missing Article XIII from the Constitution: If any citizen of the United States shall accept, claim, receive, or retain any title of nobility or honor, or shall without the consent of Congress, accept and retain any present, pension, office or emolument of any kind whatever, from any emperor, king, prince or foreign power, such person shall cease to be a citizen of the United States, and shall be incapable of holding any office of trust or profit under them, or either of them.*

The eightball shook and the numbers and letters appeared:

10

15

21

26

21

15

10

Psalm 118: 22, 23, 24

I whispered, *open sesame* and every dot turned into a portal of greater than signs offering me unlimited possibilities in every arena in my life. I looked at each arena of my life individually and saw the only thing holding me back was me. I decided to Open me up! I saw the game of life laid out before me. It was my choice to play at a higher or lower level all beginning and ending with **o**. I unlocked my financial future. I unlocked my relationships. I unlocked my happiness. I unlocked my true self. I unlocked myself out of 3D. I unlocked myself out of the Lower Level game of survival. I unlocked billions of love letters.

As I reveled in my mind I saw a 64-squared chessboard appear with a poem overlaying it. The poem read:

OOOOOOOOOOOOOOOOOOOOOOOOOOOOOOOOOOOO

Diagram life.

Divide by thirds.

Count your numbers.

Look up your words!

OOOOOOOOOOOOOOOOOOOOOOOOOOOOOOOOOOOO

Scientists say

The th of aught

Can't be altered--

Might be thought.

OOOOOOOOOOOOOOOOOOOOOOOOOOOOOOOOOOOO

Yes it is there

Before the fun

Goose egg nothing

Negative none.

OOOOOOOOOOOOOOOOOOOOOOOOOOOOOOOOOOOO

Hole and whole heart.

What is here? Oh!

Zero at love.

Love at zero!

OOOOOOOOOOOOOOOOOOOOOOOOOOOOOOOOOOOO

The poem disappeared as the red squares became encrypted with **the word:** *Higher.* Another 64-squared chessboard connected underneath with its black squares encrypted with **the word:** *Lower.* The Higher Level game connected to the Lower Level game by Chutes and Ladders and 3 black squares on the higher level that dropped the player down a black hole into the Lower Level game through an E G O. I decided to GO BIG or GO HOME as I heard Diana Ross sing "Take Me Higher," www.youtube.com/watch?v=Vlckx_CjlWc&ob=av2e. I disconnected the Lower Level game because I was not willing to participate in it anymore. The board game shattered into black and red squares that disassembled and then reassembled as a dance floor that slid underneath the Higher Level game. Thirteen squares lit up a bright red and popped up creating 13 steps with the words: *dance step* overlaying them.

I decided I was only going to play on the Higher Level game board from HERE on OUT. After making my decision solid in my mind, the 3 black squares that led to the lower game turned into 3 Klondike bars which melted into 3 Oreos with the words 3D *trap doors now sealed* overlaying them. As soon as the seals were sealed the Oreos read: Y O U are now connected to the Source Code and the game turned into a game of tic tac toe with 3 X's in a row. One Queen yelled out, strike 3 you're outta this game!

Sixty four Bicycle Brand Queen of Diamond cards came flying out of the checkered game squares through an automatic shuffler from Las Vegas to the tune of a shuffle ball change dance step playing backward creating the tune *change ball shuffle.* Sixty four Queen of Diamonds popped out of the playing cards and flipped the playing cards over and got on the bicycles that also popped out of the front side of the cards. The bicycle wheels were spinning Oreos with spokes that read: *I had a moment NOW I am having another moment!* The Queens went on the ride of their life as they rode the bicycles around the upper chessboard creating a pattern of 8 Trees of Life made out of baseballs and string. The Queens interconnected the 8 Trees of Life by connecting the top baseball with red thread through the Crown. I said to myself, King Done. CHECK MATE! The Source Code is now in effect! When I said this, the 3 black holes revealed they had been running a 555 reversal code that was now sealed and revealed for what they were: toxic assets running on a game of Chutes and Ladders played by the Kings of Tyranny.

One Queen yelled in the height of her glory, this gives new meaning to the game Crazy 8's. She rode around and around creating an 8 as she untied a red string hidden within her crown and passed it to another Queen, who untied a red string from within her crown. She said, the crown is the source at zero as she counted out loud, 8 Trees of Life times the 9 baseballs equals:

$$1 \quad 2 \quad 3 \quad 4 \quad 5 \quad 6 \quad 7 \quad 8 \quad 9$$
$$10 \quad 11 \quad 12 \quad 13 \quad 14 \quad 15 \quad 16 \quad 17 \quad 18$$
$$19 \quad 20 \quad 21 \quad 22 \quad 23 \quad 24 \quad 25 \quad 26 \quad 27$$
$$28 \quad 29 \quad 30 \quad 31 \quad 32 \quad 33 \quad 34 \quad 35 \quad 36$$
$$37 \quad 38 \quad 39 \quad 40 \quad 41 \quad 42 \quad 43 \quad 44 \quad 45$$
$$46 \quad 47 \quad 48 \quad 49 \quad 50 \quad 51 \quad 52 \quad 53 \quad 54$$
$$55 \quad 56 \quad 57 \quad 58 \quad 59 \quad 60 \quad 61 \quad 62 \quad 63$$
$$64 \quad 65 \quad 66 \quad 67 \quad 68 \quad 69 \quad 70 \quad 71 \quad 72$$

She passed the red string to another Queen, who untied her crown and whispered, the way to unlock your box is awareness and the name of God...

She passed the red string to another Queen who untied her crown and whispered,

TETRAGRAMMATON.

She passed the red string to another Queen who untied her crown and whispered,

TETRAGRAMMATON.

She passed the red string to another Queen who untied her crown and whispered,

TETRAGRAMMATON.

She passed the red string to another Queen who untied her crown and whispered,

TETRAGRAMMATON.

She passed the red string to another Queen who untied her crown and together they used the string to string together the 72 names of God in Hebrew.

והו	ילי	סיט	עלם	מהש	ללה	אכא	דהת
הזי	אלד	לאו	ההע	יזל	מבה	הרי	הקם
לאו	כלי	לוו	פהל	נלך	ייי	מלה	ההו
נתה	האא	ירת	שאה	ריי	אום	לכב	ושר
יהו	להח	דוק	מזד	אני	חעם	רהע	ייז
ההה	סיכ	וול	ילה	סאל	ערי	עשל	מיה
והו	דני	החש	עמם	נוא	נית	מבה	פוי
נמם	ייל	הרח	מצר	ומב	יהה	ענו	מחי
דמב	מזק	איע	חבו	ראה	יבמ	היי	סום

She passed the red string to another Queen, who untied her crown and stood on top of her bicycle seat and put her arms to the sky and yelled, this gives new meaning to 9 - 11.

Eight women's softballs came flying out of left field and filled in the last piece of the puzzle. I watched as their seams unwound and spelled out the word *dream seam* in blue. The softball landed in the space *under* and *over* the Crown. The word KNO**O**Wledge appeared out of thin air and overlaid the baseball. All the other red strings interconnecting all the Trees of Life turned blue, creating Grandmother Spider's web.

Grandmother Spider walked into the center of the web and said, you have to go to the ledge to find truth…always REMEMBER you can handle it because nothing is new because you always knew…it's a game of remembrance. She struck a string on the web and it played a C sharp note followed by an operatic Queen's voice that sang, *remove the curse of the crown that binds one from finding their true self…game changers. Untie the strings of the crown setting the single souls free to find their mates. Open the queue! It's time! It's time two!*

The web vibrated the tone 440 and the strings fell apart turning into the Chinese Go game with 12 white stones in a star formation. Words formed over the board game that read: It's time for two forms, one soul to join. The 12 white stones on the board lit up and turned into the jewels of a Queen's crown. A Queen's voice sang, *let them eat cake!* The jewels turned into Dali's painting of the melting clock. The clock moved it's hands from 12 **o**'clock to 3 **o**'clock to 6 **o**' clock to 9 **o**' clock to 12 **o**'clock. When the clock struck 12 a new deck of Heart brand cards came flying up and out of the board game. A Queen's voice sang: *The deck was stacked! The game was rigged! It's time for a New Deal! It's NOW time! The crisis by design trademarks on the old deck of cards are ready for their exposé!*

Fifty-five Kings of Tyranny appeared underneath the board game with brooms to clean up their mess. They began to sweep cobwebs from the directions north then east, south then west. They gathered the cobwebs of the NRG program as they sang, "RESPECT" by Aretha Franklin, www.youtube.com/watch?v=6FOUqQt3Kg0. As they sang, the upper level game turned into a blueprint for a tree house.

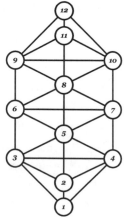

STORY #34: Boundary Layer

WALK THE LINE

TURN THE PAGE **185**

STORY #21: Wheels on the Ceiling

I decided to get off the Love Boat. I stood staring at the boat thinking… what if you are on a boat going nowhere and you don't even know it. What would you do? How would you realize this? Would you? Could you? When?

I decided to stay in Denderah by myself. I told my new friend, Akhmen I had to get off the boat for awhile. I had to see things differently for myself. I had gotten swept up in the motion of the boat rocking me *back* and *forth* and I needed to stand on firm ground for awhile. I was experiencing something magical and I needed to stay behind and see what I could see. When I told Akhmen, he reluctantly agreed that my journey was my journey and his journey did not look anything like mine so he had to continue on with his new group of tourists. He said, he had to help them see what they would allow themselves to see. He said he was going to sail them up the river with great hope. Deep inside I wanted to see if I would have another experience in the temple with Einstein. I had questions for him…good questions. I didn't tell Akhmen this. I didn't want him to think I had a screw loose.

He understood something because he whispered, it's magical isn't it?

I looked at him wondering, did he know? Then I thought, no. My mind began to vascillate between know and no. My mind created a melody of:

kNOw no kNOw no kNOw no kNOw no kNOw no

    kNOw no kNOw no kNOw no kNOw no kNOw no

        no kNOw no kNOw no kNOw no kNOw no kNOw no

kNOw no kNOw no kNOw no kNOw no kNOw no kNOw no kNOw no
kNOw no kNOw no kNOw no   KNOW….

Akhmen slipped me a piece of paper as I was having a tug of war with myself and I barely noticed. I was too busy wrestling myself. I thought, does it even matter if he knows or not? Who cares if he knows. What's he going to do or say?

As Akhmen walked away I thought, I missed a very important exchange with him because I was too preoccupied with my own wrestling match between Me and me.

I watched as he faded into a thick mist.

I pulled out the paper he had slipped into my pocket. It was an old parchment paper with a wheel drawn on the front of it with the words:

HYpoemTHESIS

ⲡⲡⲡ

Hypothesis
What when where why?
To hit or miss
Steam bake boil fry.

𝝅𝝅𝝅

Laboratory
Windows open
A correction
What we're hoping.

𝝅𝝅𝝅

Test the answer
Then verbalize
Cure a cancer
Through poets' eyes.

𝝅𝝅𝝅

A goal in mind
To build not wreck
And keep all thought
From bottleneck.

I stared at the words and the wheel and they started to SPIN. I stood staring at the parchment paper cupped in my right hand. I flipped it *over* and it read, Terrence **7164291790986755**. Call him before you leave. He has a code that is important for you.

You are going to be a part of the discovery of something new and fantastic that the world has never seen.

I looked up from the paper to see if I could see Akhmen, but he was gone. I thought, I wasted my precious moments with him wrestling with my mind. What a waste of my time and his. We could have discussed this.

I stood there alone with my mind. I realized I was in Egypt and the one person I knew was now gone. I was alone again, but I felt fine. I felt alive for the first time in a long time. I was feeling the curiosity I had that once burned inside of me as a little girl but somehow got burned out of me. I also was not feeling as sad about the loss of Mitchell. I realized I would prefer to be living this life instead of my life with him. This was filled with so many possibilities. Every corner I turned held a new experience, a new possibility for what my life could be. This was the life I had imagined for myself all these years.

I went back to the temple of Hathor. I meandered around the temple by myself. Every once in a while I stepped into a tour group to hear what their tour leader was saying. I was so surprised to hear that every one of them had a different STORY. Everyone was telling the information from their perspective and they were all different.

I rested on the floor of one area to take in the temple from my feet's view or was it my eyes in my feet view? I caught a glimpse of a pictogram on the ceiling that was covered in wheels. I stared at them and whispered, spin. I sat watching the wheels spin as if they were pinwheels.

A tour guide dressed in blue pants and a white T- shirt of the group Dead or Alive and the song "You Spin Me Round" in the center. I played the game, *What Doesn't Belong HERE* and it was definitely his T-shirt. He walked up in front of me and began his lecture. He pointed at the pictogram and said, there are 7 people walking along the bottom of this drawing with animal heads and ovals above their heads. They are gods and those ovals are what Thoth called the egg of metamorphosis. These gods represent us as we go through a certain stage of resurrection, which is a rapid biological change into a different life form. These gods are showing the transition as you see them walk to the end and then make a 90 degree shift upward. This shift is available to all of you. The only thing holding you back is you. You have to be present in your own evolution.

I kept looking up as he continued talking. This 90 degree shift is a crucial part of resurrection. The dimensional levels are separated by 90 degrees. Dimensional levels can best be described through music notes. A piano has 8 white keys from C to C, which is the familiar octave, and in between those are the 5 black keys. The keys produce all the sharps and flats in what is called the chromatic scale, which is 13 notes. So from one C to the next are 13 steps.

I thought maybe this was what Einstein meant when he said our soul's evolution had to keep moving up the scale of notes.

The tour guide continued, the same is true for dimensions. They are overlayed, one **O**N top of the other

ON top of the other

    ON top of the other

        ON top of the other

            ON top of the other

ON top of the other

ON top of the other

ON top of the other

ON top of the other

ON top of the other

ON top of the other

ON top of the other

ON top of the other

….separated only by frequencies. They are like pieces of tracing paper laid upon one another separated only by a frequency. This frequency is shown through sine waves. Sine waves correspond to light and the vibration of sound.

One tourist asked, what is a sine wave?

He used his finger to make a wavy line in the air. He said that is 2D but in 3D it is a wave.

The guide said, do you know that old toy called an Etch A Sketch? Everyone said, yes. I couldn't believe he just brought up the Etch A Sketch! I had one in my bag. I just couldn't believe the synchronicity of this.

He said, you know the lines it makes when you alternate the 2 buttons?

Everyone said yes.

He said, that creates a vortex that is a certain frequency of light and sound and when you want to go to another dimension you just change the frequency of the dial. It's like tuning the radio to another station. When you change the radio station you get a different wavelength. Lower vibrations are longer wavelengths and higher vibrations are shorter. A 2D sine wave is a 3D vortex.

I raised my hand and asked, is that what UFOs do when they appear and then disappear?

He said exactly! Change your dial to the multidimensional channel and you can do the same! The radio channel is located at **764298772210-99.00000000**.

The tour guide said, let's venture into the next room and do a little meditation. We are going to be chanting OM. Our Universe has a base wavelength of 7.23 centimeters and so does the word OM.

Someone shouted out, didn't Leonardo da Vinci prove that with the drawing of the Vitruvian Man?

Yes indeed, said the tour guide.

Everyone got in a line and walked in the other room for the meditation. I followed behind staring down at my Etch A Sketch. A Grief Graph appeared on the screen. My eyes followed an oscillating roller coaster track as it passed through a straight line several times. Three X's lit up as the tracks traveled through the line stamping out—Denial. Anger. Depression. I thought, I must have moved down the line toward Acceptance.

As soon as I said this **the word** *change up* appeared at the end of the line and then the line made a 90-degree turn spiraling UP as **the word** *ascension* overlaid it. I blinked and the crook of a woman's elbow appeared with **the word** *ascension* written along her forearm as she held it at a 90° angle. I decided to skip the meditation and take a 90° turn.

STORY #13: Tea For Two

I watched the meditators disappear as I decided to walk the road less traveled. I veered away from the group. I thought not many want to keep moving down the line, but I do. I took a 90-degree turn and followed a perforated line marked *ascension* on my Etch A Sketch. I pulled out the elixir given to me by Gouda. I stared at the label: $T_4 2$. I felt the time was right to indulge in this elixir. I popped the bluebird stopper and watched it fall to the ground in slow motion. I drank the elixir and immediately felt woozy as I watched the bluebird come alive and take flight. I began to feel as if I were growing smaller and smaller. I dropped my Etch A Sketch as I became too small to hold on to it. It landed on the floor and became one with the floor. I did the only thing I knew how to do and that was walk the line marked *ascension* while in *contemplation*.

As I walked the line it became a 3D vortex. I felt as if I were walking inside a Slinky toy and I was the Queen figurine off the top of my wedding cake. I reached for my wrist to check the time and noticed there was a crown hanging around my wrist. I inspected the 12-jeweled crown and placed it on my head. I contemplated what it would look like to be *Queen of my Fate*. I came up to a Slinky wire link and noticed for the first time words engraved on the link. It read: *Paradox = where the rational mind bumps into its own limitations.* I thought the only way to grow is to keep moving down the line and pass through a lot of paradoxes. My next footstep in my Nikes felt sturdier and more secure knowing I just had to jump the links and not get kinked in the link.

I thought, what are my limitations I am walking through right now? I took a

PAUSE

to reflect and then continued walking and growing larger and larger as the Slinky spiral was growing smaller and smaller. I looked behind me and saw the paradoxes had all shifted to words that spelled out the psalm:

For when you see

unity, you

can live as one—

know possible!

I smiled as I got deep within the bowels of the spiral and the sides turned into funhouse mirrors. I stopped to take inventory and saw a blazing sun emanating out from my crown. I watched in one mirror as the crown prongs overlaying my head came out in hydraulic form to the tune of 1, 2, 3, 4, 5, 6, 7, 8, 9, 10, 11, 12. They turned to blue strings and connected into the spiral Slinky field around me turning the blue strings to silver.

A clock appeared before me. I heard Salvador Dali say, it is the persistence of memory that will get you from HERE to THERE. I watched as the silver strings connected into 12 different timelines. Once they connected in they turned into multi-colored doors. I watched as each door sprang open revealing my life in different ages and stages.

The mirror I was standing in front of began to speak to me. My mirror image said, the timelines were all interconnected and supposed to work together but somehow had become separated breaking my connection to unity. The words: *The Blue String Theory* appeared above each door. I thought, I wonder if every time I walk through a door I enter into another reality to assist in another aspect of myself in this timeline and in another timeline? The floor behind all the doors became a black and white chessboard. The mirror image of myself said, it's a big game of *shuffle ball change!* The Blue String Theory becomes a reality when you plug back in to where you were supposed to be in the beginning! Everything in life is loosely connected to a string of thought created by you in the dream state or the awake state. The question becomes, Who are you? I stood staring at myself wondering who am I? My mind wandered as I watched 12 DNA strands within me come alive and create a beautiful harmony of sound emanating deep from within me creating a blue pillar of light covered in 13s. The 3 connected I-Ching coins in my pineal gland connected with 3 other sets of 3 making 12 in total. They began to spin and vibrate the 72 names of God in Hebrew. I felt light as a feather as tetrahedral shields began to form around me. I stood in awe as I watched the spiral field I was in spew out mathematical codes all ending and beginning at o followed closely behind with the Pythagorean theorem.

I said, $a^2 + b^2 = c^2$. I thought, what is denial squared?

A peculiar voice said, denying the deniable. Two negatives, which equal a positive.

I paused and thought, what is acceptance squared?

A peculiar voice said, the willingness to SEE. Two positives equal more positiveness.

I paused and thought, what is ascension squared?

A peculiar voice said, a^2. The squaring of the circle.

A white rabbit, dressed in a checkered jacket appeared out of nowhere and said in the same peculiar voice, it's time. You must give up the watch. It's time to go into no time! He clicked his JFK presidential antique gold stop-watch with an engraving that read: *You've been off track since the JFK timeline.* The rabbit said, on your mark get set, GO!

The tunnel turned into the Chinese Go game in front of us. The rabbit went up to the Go game and placed the white stone game pieces in a circular pattern. They turned into the numbers on a clock. The face of Santa Claus appeared underneath as the face of the clock. Santa reached up with his white batting gloves to take the position of the hands of the clock as he winked and turned into Porky Pig for a split second. Santa took his big hand and his little hand and pointed them to 12 o'clock. Then he moved his smaller hand to 3 o'clock and then he moved his smaller hand to 6 o'clock and then he moved his smaller hand to 9 o'clock and then he ended where he began, at 12 o'clock with his big hand and little hand. I stood there and all I could do was form the word oh as all my self oh sabotage flew out the door. With a new sense of clarity, I pulled out the paper Gouda had given me. I looked at it and then back at the clock and then at Santa Claus all the while smelling frankincense. I compared the two riddles:

12 o'clock was labeled Taurus 2304 years.

3 o'clock was labeled Aquarius 2016 years.

6 o'clock was labeled Scorpio 1872 years.

9 o'clock was labeled Leo 2592 years.

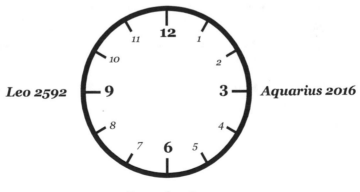

12 Taurus 2304

Leo 2592   **Aquarius 2016**

Scorpio 1872

The rabbit said, you are connected into unity source code and out of mind control when you understand these ages and years. You are connected back to where you were always supposed to be. You are at the beginning of the end, the end of the beginning.

I said, oh and stood THERE perplexed. I looked back at the clock to double check the time and the clock numbers had turned into the 12 oil notes of the ancient ones. I looked intently at the labels. Each one read: *It's time to break the seal. It's time for the anointing of the old mixed with the new creating...blue lotus pixie dust.*

King Solomon faintly appeared in midair as if he were a piece of tracing paper. He was dressed in a white flowing wispy robe that resembled toilet paper accessorized with a red and white checkered sash and an old and tarnished gold crown. He said, your divine energy shield is now repaired allowing you to travel *back* and *forth* between the timelines giving your life the dimension you were always missing.

I looked around me and saw my repaired energetic shield resembled a Catholic eucharist. Once I saw this, it changed into a spinning Vanilla Wafer. I contemplated on the act of the priest asking if I accepted the body of Christ.

King Solomon interrupted my train of thought by asking, you have felt like there was something missing all along, haven't you?

I screamed YES! Not knowing until this moment what had been missing. I thought, I guess I have been playing the wrong game all along. I was playing the game of What Doesn't *Belong* HERE instead of what is *missing* THERE.

King Solomon began to fade as he whispered, Salvador Dali's, *Persistence of Memory* is the greatest artwork of all time for several reasons. He began to laugh and his tarnished crown jewels fell off and onto the floor revealing they were tiny red and blue pills held in place by pink Silly Putty. He said, it is time the Kings of Tyranny retire and give way to the Queen. He began to recite the poem,

Queen of Diam〇nds
Queen of garden

Lady of sky.

She's equipped

The why of MY.

Organic crown

Atop her head.

Used eyeglasses

For book she read.

Ruby slippers
Will take her home.
Distilled essence
Creates her poem.
We now present
A woman, risen.
Made of goals and
Good decision.

He finished the poem and his existence. He disappeared into a puff of black smoke filled with 9's and 11's.

The rabbit nudged me and said, let Dali teach us all something. True discovery happens when you can visualize. If you can't visualize, you dismiss things as untruth because you want to categorize everything and put everything in a box so you can feel a fake sense of security. A silver pin on his vest lit up a fluorescent yellow question mark. He fished inside his vest pocket and handed me a silver toilet paper holder. He said, what can you visualize?

I took the silver toilet paper holder in my hands and pushed it together and it sprang open.

The rabbit said, see the energy stored in the spring of an item that small?

I said yes as I thought, a cake isn't ready until it springs back.

He said, let the visualization of the spring open doors for you in your dream world. He walked through the black smoke filled with 9's and 11's as he said, sometimes you have to move through the smoke to get to the truth in life.

I followed behind him contemplating what smoke had blurred my vision on truth in my life. I got stuck in the smoke for a bit and lost sight of the rabbit. I came up to a door with a doorknob painted in the design of a black and white chess board with a B and **the word** *intention* next to it. I touched my crown to make sure it was still there and realized I had grown to full size and so did my crown. I stood with my hand an inch away from the doorknob thinking of my intention. I set my intention to REMEMBER HOW TO TIME TRAVEL NOW. Immediately the jewels on my crown connected in to my chakra system down the back of my body and up the front of my body creating a new energy signature within and around me. Everything began to synch in and synchronize like an iPod plugging into a computer. Divine galactic energy came spiraling in from above and below creating the pattern of 8's as it moved up and down the hara line, the vital life chord of my body connecting into the 12 timelines and the 12 area chakra system that was now online. I heard a little girl whisper in my ear, *you've got mail.*

I looked back at the multi colored doors and each door had me as a little girl in front of the opened door holding a bag of Oreos. A man rode by on a white horse with a string of keys hanging off his waist. He wore a red long jacket with gold piping, tight white pants and a hat made out of a black and white newspaper crossword puzzle. I made out two words in blue ink, Fate Queen. He rode by each little girl and handed them a pink envelope sealed with a red wax heart and a k^{e}y. He said, if everyone wrote more love letters the world would be changed.

The rabbit hopped by and took a pen and paper to take note. I saw him write the heading, TO DO: WRITE A LOVE LETTER. He scribbled, how do I say: I adore you even more today than yesterday?

Each girl opened the H^{e}art brand greeting card in unison and turned into a big girl, a warrior of love, dressed in a green army dress with an armband displaying a heart within a heart. They said in unison, IT'S TIME TO RE-MEMBER THE WARRIOR WITHIN YOU! I walked over to inspect each warrior. They greeted me with a salute of one finger from their forehead out in a curve. I watched their brain cavity expand as I mirrored them. They took a deep breath and blew their energy into me clearing away the black smoke hanging on me. The last warrior handed me her pink envelope and her k^{e}y which was imprinted with the word: *compassionate witness.*

I pulled the card out of the envelope and read: *Forgiveness is the fragrance that the violet sheds on the heel that has crushed it.* –Mark Twain.

The warrior said, move forward in love and step into your power. You have all the wisdom you need. She turned around and grew to 13 feet tall. A red cape appeared around her that read: *Avatar.*

She fist pumped in the air and a cloud appeared above her that said, KA-POW and the cloud burst into the fragrance of *Amberi Atari.*

I turned the doorknob as I heard a train barreling down the track. I looked behind me and the right side of the track was labeled: HARA LINE / VITAL LIFE CHORD: *mind follows breath,* while the wrong side of the track was labeled: *Catholic Church.* I took a deep breath and counted 1, 2 and on 3 I jumped. The Blue String Reality appeared over the door as a Capital C and **the word** *ascension* appeared on the multi-faceted crystal doorknob. I twisted the doorknob to the left and walked through the door with a new sense of power. I thought, I am now in touch with my warrior, my avatar self!

The rabbit, who now wore a name tag of Brad, greeted me eagerly in the hallway. He said very cooly, just in the nick of time! He was holding a blue and white striped teacup with the equation $a^2 + b^2 = c^2$ written all over it. He said, the question is: would you like T or T?

I contemplated, could this be a trick question?

Brad said, tricks are for kids, would you like Tea or Tea?

I said, tea for two.

He smiled and handed me his cup of tea with a triangle shaped tea tag that hung to the right that read, Tea á Ma'at, along with a Queen of Diamonds playing card and a Monopoly card. I flipped the Monopoly card over to reveal a black and white Pennsylvania Railroad train.

I read, $1 million, $2 million, $3 million, $4 million.

Brad started laughing and singing, $1^2 + 2^2 + 3^2 = 4$.

I played along singing, $1^2 + 2^2 + 3^2 = 4$. I flipped the card back over and it turned into a winning lottery ticket for California's SuperLotto. At the bottom in fine print it read: *We thought you'd never make it. Congratulations!* The hallway turned into 99 hanging stoplights now all colored green for Go! The hall turned into the old library of Alexandria in Egypt as one side filled up with 1960s ticket agents and the other side filled up with T^2ravelers carrying bags covered in circles, triangles and square stickers showing where they had been. My eye caught a bag covered in stickers imprinted with a blue lotus flower with the word India written over a picture of the Taj Mahal.

An older man broke through both sides of the crowd breaking my concentration. He walked toward me. All I could focus on were his blue suede shoes. He wore a white lab coat a size too small that perfectly matched his white beard. He had a nametag in the shape of a pink cloud that said *Creatologist, Purveyor of Curiosité.* His crystal blue eyes had gold flecks in them making them sparkle like pinwheels as they scanned me. He snapped his fingers 3 times and 3 fields of energy formed around him that were rotating fields in a star tetrahedron pattern one overlaying the other and the other all at different speeds, creating one field that rotated backwards. He smiled and said, it was all in my notebooks.

I smiled immediately recognizing him as Leonardo da Vinci. He saw my recognition and snapped his fingers and I heard trillions of CLICKS as one library wall turned into the painting of "The Last Supper."

I walked up to inspect the famous work of art and to my amazement the entire painting was made out of tiny Rubiks Cubes all displaying their solid colored side. I took the toilet paper holder out of my pocket and removed one

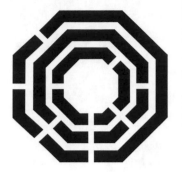

end and the spring and used the hollow tube to peer into one Rubik's Cube. I saw a book inside of it and I turned and asked Leonardo, what is *the* book?

He said, look at the blue-faced Rubik's Cube in Jesus' eyes. That is your book. I peered inside that Rubik's Cube and saw a blue hardbound book open to page 144, held in place by a blue string. It revealed my soul's journey up to this exact moment in a blueprint. I saw the road map I chose to take. I saw what roads, highways, train tracks, bicycle paths and tunnels I had taken and what they taught me along the way. I also saw how each individual soul comes to learn about only 3 things: love, power and wisdom. I stood in amazement of what life is and how simple it is and how we have made it so much more difficult than it really is. I pulled my toilet paper holder back and replaced the spring and put it in my pocket for dream time. I thought to myself, if life is this easy imagine how easy time travel is.

Leonardo said, there is a movie within each piece of art. Each art piece is like a pearl, a jewel, a moment, strung together creating a story. These jewels all connect in the end to create a beautiful piece of art or jewelry, like a pearl necklace.

I thought, like pieces of toilet paper sewn together with perforated lines. I heard Charles Darwin's voice say, don't squeeze the Charmin, as I saw the evolution of man fly through the air on panels of toilet paper connected by perforated lines depicting the evolution of mankind. A queen bee appeared with a red Sharpie marker and wrote over each panel of man **the word** FRAUD. The perforated edges came apart unraveling history down to panels of toilet paper.

Leonardo da Vinci said, art creates a story within a story in a timeline. He pointed his finger up, mimicking the man's index finger in "The Last Supper" to Jesus' left that was pointing up to the sky. He said, there is more than one story to everything. Would I ever paint out of proportion? I think not. Look at the proportion of Mary's hands. The clues are all in the PHI proportions. History was changed in a brushstroke. My work reflects stories and mathematics. You should always look at things from at least 3 angles— tri-angles.

I whispered, triangles.

The row of ticket agents and the row of T²ravelers all turned around and reappeared with Etch A Sketches in their hands. The ticket agents' screens showed the image of a triangle with **the word** Pythagorean theorem underneath the equation $a^2 + b^2 = c^2$.

The T²ravelers screen showed the upside down and backwards image of the equation $a^2 + b^2 = c^2$ underneath the image of a triangle with the word H^{e}art theorum underneath. The a^2 was shown springing OPEN A BOX it was set inside. The Ticket Agents and the T²ravelers walked up to one another and eXchanged information creating a new theorem where two triangles were laid one on TOP of the other creating a diamond out of two triangles. The two rows began to sing:

Row, row, row your boat,

    Gently down the stream,

        Merrily, merrily, merrily, merrily

            Life is but a dream.

The two triangles slid into one another with a CLICK revealing a Morse Code of dots. The two rows of ladies held a PAUSE and then shook their Etch A Sketches in SEQUENCE. The image on the screen turned into timelines. Leonardo's timeline lit up with words overlaying it that read: *It's time for the Renaissance again. Art and literature will change the world! Everyone is dying to express their Creative Genius!*

Leonardo dug in his pocket for something as he said, *There are three classes of people: Those who see. Those who see when they are shown. Those who do not see.* He tossed me a tiny round mirror and as it floated through the air it turned into a coin.

I caught the coin midair and flipped it over the top of my left hand. A silver shield in the center read: *You've arrived!* I flipped the coin over my right and read the flipside. It read: *Your heart is your map!* I dropped the coin and the word *MiND* appeared on the floor. The coin dotted the i turning the dot into a Ping-Pong ball as the word *MiND* was replaced by the superhuman braIn with a large EYE. I picked up the coin and slid it in my pocket.

I looked past Leonardo and looked at "The Last Supper." This time I could clearly see the mathematics displayed through the underlying sacred geometry imbedded in the paintings and…the woman who held the power, Mary Magdalene. She was seated at Jesus' side showing how he drew his power from her Christ body. She was the warrior of love, wisdom and power.

Leonardo said, she was the divine feminine, that which is returning in an energetic form to each person now. He gave me a moment as he paused. He pulled a Slinky out of his pocket and asked, now would you like to see something amazing?

I said, SEEING IS BELIEVING!

He smiled and ushered me through a wooden door with ancient carvings of birds on it. We stood in a large empty ballroom filled with empty golden frames. He snapped his fingers and his artwork appeared inside the golden frames. He snapped them again and the Pythagorean theorem highlighted within each one as a glowing triangle among many other circles, squares and lines.

He turned to me and said, everything is based on mathematics…even my art. He snapped his fingers again and all the paintings showed the lines of sacred geometry within them. The lines turned into multicolored lasers and the field of the room changed. The floor turned to a wheat field as crop circles appeared off in the distant wheat fields. He said, my art tells stories that you already know. I was from the future. I was a Time Traveler. I left you so many clues in my notebooks. You have the same abilities as me. You just need to REMEMBER T^2 and Tea á Ma'at.

The floor turned from wheat to a very large Etch A Sketch and we walked over to it. Brad, the rabbit appeared holding two cups of tea. He said, tea for two? Leonardo grabbed the cup without acknowledging the rabbit because he was too busy studying the screen. I watched his tea tag, which read, Tea á Ma'at flip over to reveal a Rubik's Cube with all solid faces. I accepted a blue and white striped cup and saucer. I said, thank you and looked in the cup and saw Abraham Lincoln staring back at me. I closed my eyes and drank the tea down. It tasted like blueberries.

Leonardo said, this is what it has come to. He pointed to the screen. He said, all the people *within the know of the technology* are manipulating time-lines. This is creating havoc in your world. This is abuse of technology over consciousness dating back to the Atlantean timeline. I looked down at the screen and saw blue timelines that looked like strings in a tangled mess. The Atlantean timeline read 7 – 27 – 9792.

Leonardo took a silver measuring tape with a black box image on the face of it with a red X through it. He measured off 23 inches and cut the blue strings out of the screen. He said, the only way out is through T as he took a sip of tea.

I said, what does that mean?

He said, transmute or transform. He said, you are going to have to learn to transmute thoughts that are not yours fast.

Brad, the rabbit, walked in speaking random thoughts a mile a minute. I could only catch and compute a third of what he was thinking and speaking. Leonardo just looked at me with raised eyebrows. Leonardo said, you have to see where the thought is sourcing from. Ask questions:

♦ Is the thought sourcing from the Lower or the Higher Level game?

♦ Is it your thought or someone else's?

♦ Is it from this timeline or another?

♦ Is it a pattern? Is it a cycle you have been running since you were 10?

You have to be vigilant of your thoughts right now. You have to step into the observer and observe your thoughts and observe where they are sourcing from and not engage with others in their game. The question for YOU becomes: Do you want to play a Lower Level game or a Higher Level game?

Brad's question mark pin lit up a fluorescent blue.

I said, I choose the Higher Level game. As I thought this, the Etch A Sketch floor was replaced by a black and white chess board, but not before I caught a glimpse of the world map. King Solomon's tracing paper figure hovered over the map. He removed his tracing paper robe and it overlaid the world map. Once it was lined up one on top of the other silver toilet paper holder images appeared and aligned with the fault lines of the earth. A Queen Bee flew by with a red Sharpie ink pen and made a red X over where the toilet paper holders were, revealing it was an exact match with the nuclear power plant locations.

King Solomon sneezed and the entire world shook revealing the new world map, which showed an entirely different game. The game was called, Go! I knew intuitively that it was time to take back humanity by contracting within ourselves instead of expanding outside of ourselves through explosion.

Leonardo said, you have to transmute the thoughtforms that do not serve you or humanity by spinning them into a triangle and then down to an atom. He said, let's take this. He pulled a string of thoughtforms out of my right shoulder that were connected to Mitchell. He said, because he had surgery and you so wanted to assist him you took on the energy of him believing he would never live up to his expectations. He gave up on life and you took that energy on. It has been blocking your wellspring of energy ever since. It's time to let that go. Do you agree?

I yelled YES!

He pulled a red string out. I saw the numbers <u>14832</u> as he spun the red string of thoughtforms and mathematical equations all with less than signs into a triangle that resembled the Great Pyramid and then down to the size of an atom. He said, imagine the baggage you are carrying around inside that body energetically because you take on judgments others have placed on themselves and it gets transferred on to you all in the name of national security. The great triangle, the Mind, Intellect and Ego, takes information in and then finds evidence to support it. Why not try something different. Treat everything like it is misinformation. View every piece of information as healthy vs. unhealthy. Ask the question: If I swallow this judgment am I taking the pill to make me less than, < or greater than, >.

Brad, the rabbit hopped in and said, would I? Could I? Should I? Show up different? His pocket that was full of red and blue pills spilled out on the floor. As they hit the floor a hopscotch pattern made out of triangles sprang forth. Brad sang, Can't get a red bird a blue bird will do. Can't get a red bird a blue bird will do. Can't get a red bird a blue bird will do. Skip to the loo my darling.

I picked up a red pill and threw it like a stone and began to play hopscotch. I sang, Can't get a red bird a blue bird will do. Can't get a red bird a blue bird will do. Can't get a red bird a blue bird will do. The hopscotch turned into the blueprint for the city of Luxor, Egypt graphed in boxes. Over the black box marked Building 7 was etched in stone—reactor 4, Fukushima.

Leonardo said, transformation happens when you see the thoughtform and it has no effect on you. You should never have the thought, oh no, I shouldn't have taken the pill because if you swallowed what someone else passed on you as judgment it is sourcing from their fears, their Less Than programs. It's the Lower Level game that you don't play anymore.

Brad, the rabbit hopped back by looking a lot lighter and more playful carrying a handful of fresh flowers. He handed them to me and said, I chose to be different! Now, it is time! On your mark, get set, GO! He clicked his stopwatch and lifted his paws up in the air and said, wonder twins activate, TRANSFORM! In the shape of two Creative Geniuses! He turned and materialized two cups of tea and turned back to me and said, tea for two?

The black and white chessboard floor turned into my blueprint, titled: *Mrs. Velvet and the Blue String Theory*. It was open to Story# 144. It showed how the PROCESS of the book takes each person who reads it back to their original divine blueprint so they can get in touch with their Creative Genius!

I thought could it be so?

Brad said, it is sew as he pulled a bright yellow button off his jacket and tossed it in the air. He pulled a blue string from his jacket and came over and placed it around my wrist.

I watched as all the lines within my blueprint lit up showing the track I chose to get HERE. The lines lit up from the beginning Point A (HERE) to the end Point B (THERE). I thought, I made it to Plan B! I pulled out the coin Leonardo had given me and read, *I've arrived!* The blue line marked THERE materialized a red ball of string made out of several unseamed base-balls imprinted with **the word** *acceptance.* The red ball of string spun and materialized a blue lotus flower inside it. The blue lotus flower morphed into and out of a blue crown. I felt every cell in my body embody the flower of life, the blue lotus. The flower of life pulsated out in petal rings of:

144,000 x 1

144,000 x 2

144,000 x 3

144,000 x 4

144,000 x 5

144,000 x 6

144,000 x 7

144,000 x 8

144,000 x 9

144,000 x 10

144,000 x 11

144,000 x 12

144,000 x 13

I walked through the rings until I got to the 12th. When I reached this point I decided to JUMP. I jumped to another timeline. The floor shifted to a black and white chessboard and 528 men and women from different time-lines were dancing with themselves. I watched as men and women danced the dance of YOU ME YOU. Jesus and Mary Magdalene took center stage as they danced the tango moving their energy *back* and *forth* with grace as Mary Magdalene's energy sparked Jesus'. Jesus and Mary danced in rever-ence with one another near me. I heard Jesus say, this beats the nuclear tango going on with Iran.

I nodded as an Energizer Bunny entered the dance floor beating his drum off beat and speaking very quickly. He said, the questions keep going ON and ON and ON.

■a.) Why doesn't the U.S. have an effective nuclear materials tracking system in place?

■b.) One of the smugglers of nuclear materials is Israel. Why are they selling nuclear materials on the black market?

■c.) Japan threatened an exposé of the truth. Why was Fukushima the result? Could the answer be $a^2 + b^2 = c^2$? Could the answer be

$$X = Y^{knot}?$$

The dance floor turned into an I-Ching spiraling one half black and one half white with a fish jumping *back* and *forth* between the large dot on both sides. The I-Ching turned 3 dimensional and demonstrated how it fed back into itself like a feedback loop.

King Solomon appeared next to it and said, imagine if this was a little askew what would happen. Fourteen fish were jumping from one dot to the next as the I-Ching spun. King Solomon adjusted the numbers from 12960 and 12960 to 14832 and 12960. This adjustment materialized an eightball over the second dot marked with the number 14832. The fish jumping out of one dot could not find the other dot so they jumped but had nowhere to land. They landed on the black portion of the I-Ching giving a new meaning to fish out of water.

Leonardo reappeared and wrote several less than and greater than signs on the wall with red chalk. He said, you have to break things down to see what is missing.

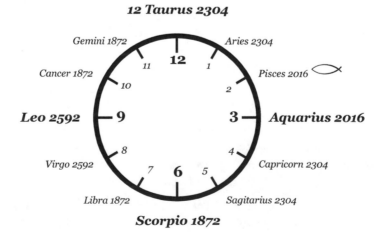

12 Taurus 2304

Gemini 1872

Aries 2304

Cancer 1872

Pisces 2016

Leo 2592

Aquarius 2016

Virgo 2592

Capricorn 2304

Libra 1872

Sagitarius 2304

Scorpio 1872

I said, is this the game of what is *missing* THERE?

Leonardo said yes. He created a clock of all the ages of the zodiac.

12 o'clock Taurus	2304	
1 o'clock Aries	2304	
2 o'clock Pisces		2016
3 o'clock Aquarius		2016
4 o'clock Capricorn	2304	
5 o'clock Sagittarius	2304	
6 o'clock Scorpio		1872
7 o'clock Libra		1872
8 o'clock Virgo	2592	
9 o'clock Leo	2592	
10 o'clock Cancer		1872
11 o'clock Gemini		1872
total 12		total 25,920/2 =12,960

He took the fish, Pisces from 2 **o**'clock.

He said, the myth of Osiris says the fish, Pisces (2016 years) ate the 14th piece of Osiris when he was dismembered into 14 pieces. This math riddle can be solved as so:

2016 / 14 =144 so 2016 – 144 = 1872 out of balance

If 12960 is in balance, add 1872 and you get 14832.

14832 / 1440 = 10.3

10.3 – 9 = 1.3 = 13 out of balance. This is being restored now.

The divine feminine comes in the energetic form of 13.

He said, proportions are essential to the divine matrix. Remember if everything is not perfectly balanced in the feedback loop the clarity gets scrambled. The fish out of water ate another fish jumping in the air with *Pisces #14* written on its fin as an ace playing card appeared in the hole opening it back up and replacing the eightball.

The fish became a gold chalice with the letters IRNI on it. It shot up in the air and into "The Last Supper" as the painting split in two and mirrored on top of itself revealing a superhuman being at the center of the table and the chalice with the letters IRNI on top of his head. The letters IRNI turned into the numbers 12960 + 12960. The energy in the form of numbers began to recalibrate like the Wall Street ticker tape. All the symbols went back to their divine schematics.

Leonardo said, once the chalice is reset everything will go back to where it was supposed to be. He took the gold chalice and placed it on my crown. He said, the funnel has to be opened to connect YOU into the cosmic flow of energy. The bird stopper has to be removed. It's time! The I-Ching began to spin in proportion again. It spun back into itself 64 times and then turned into a crop circle of the flower of life.

I stood staring at the flower of life. A T²raveler walked up to me and broke me out of my trance. She said, do you have the time? I feel that I am late.

I looked at my wrist and noticed I was not wearing a watch. I then looked around and noticed no one was around. I said, that's strange.

She walked away smiling. I noticed her luggage was covered in circles, squares and triangles. One blue sticker with the picture of the blue lotus caught my eye. I shook my head and began my walk through the tunnel to home.

STORY #8: The Vacuum and the Maid

I walked to Mrs. Velvet's house while wearing Mom's ruby red shoes and yellow sundress. I went through the connecting tunnel of our homes and noticed something was different. I was walking on a red carpet! When I arrived at her house she had a new doormat that read, *Welcome Home*. I smiled and turned the multi- faceted crystal doorknob to the left and walked into her house to the pleasant smell of fresh cake baking.

Mrs. Velvet opened the door peered out from the kitchen in a white lace apron holding a cake in one hand. She said, the cake isn't done until it springs back, as she pushed on the cake. What took you so long? I have been expecting you.

I said, how did you know I was coming?

She said, my intuition. I can feel you when we are separate because we are never really separate.

I said, wow. Sounds like magic to me as I slipped my hand in a bowl of cards. I pulled one out of a Golden Ticket in the shape of a chalice and slipped it in my breast pocket.

Mrs. Velvet said, how are you today?

I'm ok. I'm feeling a bit overwhelmed by school. We had a math quiz and the teacher timed us. I didn't finish and it really bothered me. She said that it didn't matter, but it did to me.

Love, it does not matter, trust me. That is just your mind playing tricks on you. Your mind wants you to think you are not good enough. What would make you feel better?

If I could figure out a magic trick to do math quicker.

Mrs. Velvet said, ok. Let me show you how to turn your computer ON your superhuman brain. The human brain has been trained to look at numbers in a certain way that perpetuates a misunderstanding of them and life. There is a chapter missing in every math book that should be called Story # **O**. Close your eyes and turn on the calculator in your head.

I squeezed my eyes shut, hoping to see every mathematical code to the universe.

Mrs. Velevet said, what do you see?

I saw a **O**. A goose egg. Negative none.

Great job! It's an inside job when you get down to it. You now have the lens put on your glasses to see the world of numbers in a clear way. Now I want you to envision 1**O**. If you did it properly you put down a 1 and then an **O**. Right?

Yes. I did.

Now look at the numbers from right to left. What do you get?

I said, **o** and 1.

Mrs. Velvet said, which equals what?

I said **O**NE.

Now, take your original number, 1**O** and subtract 1 and what do you get?

I said nine.

Mrs. Velvet said, nine is the magic number of the Universe, one of the crown jewels. This will help you see a pattern, which works for every number to infinity. This will help TURN ON your superhuman brain so it is online. It will put you on the track to remember how numbers work together. Every math equation breaks down to equal 9 and if it doesn't something is askew and when something is askew it is not in balance. Let me write out some equations for you to keep for safekeeping for when you get older.

I said ok as I thought about my bigger self and watched Mrs. Velvet write:

THE SOURCE CODE:
Upper Level:

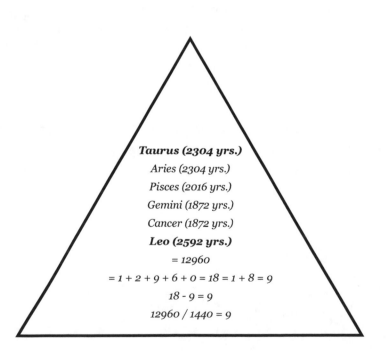

Taurus (2304 yrs.)
Aries (2304 yrs.)
Pisces (2016 yrs.)
Gemini (1872 yrs.)
Cancer (1872 yrs.)
Leo (2592 yrs.)
= 12960
= 1 + 2 + 9 + 6 + 0 = 18 = 1 + 8 = 9
18 - 9 = 9
12960 / 1440 = 9

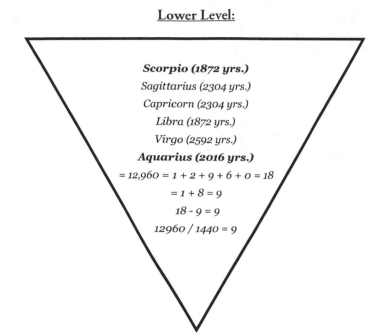

Scorpio (1872 yrs.)
Sagittarius (2304 yrs.)
Capricorn (2304 yrs.)
Libra (1872 yrs.)
Virgo (2592 yrs.)
Aquarius (2016 yrs.)
$= 12,960 = 1 + 2 + 9 + 6 + 0 = 18$
$= 1 + 8 = 9$
$18 - 9 = 9$
$12960 / 1440 = 9$

Pisces (2016 years) ate the 14th piece of Osiris so:

2016 / 14 =144 so 2016 – 144 = 1872 out of balance

If 12960 is in balance, add 1872 and you get 14832.

14832 / 1440 = 10.3

10.3 – 9 = 1.3 = 13 out of balance.

Aquarius (2016 years) is the age when King Solomon will be replaced with the Queen.

Now my love, what card did you draw from the entryway bowls today?

I said, synchronicity.

Mrs. Velvet said perfect. Synchronicity is basically all the numbers lining up in a certain SEQUENCE to allow something you were thinking about happen. It is not random. It is perfectly timed to happen exactly as you set it up. You set it up in your dream state and in the words you speak. That is why it is so important to be very clear on your words.

I felt my stomach roar like a lion. I said, can I get a piece of the velvet cake before we go any further? Math makes me hungry.

Mrs. Velvet said, of course, Love. She walked me into the kitchen and before me stood a 13-layered triangular crystal cake plate on her center kitchen island.

Mrs. Velvet took a cake slicer in the shape of a triangle and cut the cake into 6 pieces and removed one for me. I looked over at her with deep admiration and saw her name tag on her apron. It read: *Auntie Sweet Sweets.* I smiled as I thought if every woman baked and loved like Auntie Sweet Sweets the world would be in divine alignment.

Ok, I said, I'm all yours, as I took a spoonful of velvet cake.

Mrs. Velvet said, you become more and more aware of your true self by being aware of all your cycles and your patterns and stopping them by pausing and opening up to the Universe. The Universe will bring in more and more of your true self. As this happens, your vacuum is going to produce more and more of what you DESIRE. A vacuum is a great way for me to show you how it works. Do you know that as one part of the vacuum contracts the other part expands simultaneously?

Really?

Mrs. Velvet said, the clearer you are about who your true self is the more the vacuum brings in what you want at an increasing speed. But it will come back to you modified.

I said, what does modified mean?

The Universe will send you something in a different way than you were expecting. So you are creating your reality and it is creating you. It's coordinated through 12 timelines. The clearer you are about your true self the more synchronicities you have.

Why is that?

If you live IN SEQUENCE with who you are then more things come to you. If you do not live as who you are it is harder for things to come to you because you are sending out mixed signals of who you really are. The strings of thought get tangled and your signal is not clear. That is why the key is to be CLEAR about who you are and live your life accordingly.

What if I don't know who I am?

You have to start REMEMBERING. You have to listen to what clues people tell you daily. You have to go within and see how you feel. You have to spend time contemplating this. This is why you came here to this Earth. This is the most important part of your journey on Earth. The only reason you came here is to REMEMBER WHO YOU ARE and then live in accordance with that.

I said, wow, that's a lot to figure out. I am only 12.

I know, but I am teaching you life lessons so you remember when you get older. REMEMBER it is the interaction with other human beings that creates synchronicities…so listen to what they say. They point you in the right direction all the time.

I walked home and found my mother cooking liver and onions in the kitchen.

I asked her who she thought she was.

She said, the hell if I know. Today I feel like I am your maid.

I walked to my room wondering how I would figure out who I was. I looked in my mirror and asked my mirror image,

> *Mirror mirror*
> *Reflect me free*
> *Am I the Mom*
> *Or is Mom me?*

PAUSE

STORY #2: JFK Timeline

I awoke in a hotel room. This hotel was called Queens Play Fourth. I found myself missing the Love Boat and at the same time feeling the call of my own bed. I surveyed the room looking for the boats rocking on the walls, but they were gone. Since getting off the boat everything seemed different. *I sang, row, row, row your boat, gently down the stream, merrily, merrily, merrily, merrily, life is but a dream.*

As I lay there, I thought what should I do today? I immediately thought about Terrence. I thought I better call him before heading back home. Akhmen made it sound like he had some valuable information for me. I thought, I wonder what type of adventure will unfold with this. I reached over on the nightstand and unfolded the paper Akhmen had given me. I picked up the red phone on the nightstand and dialed **7164291790986755.**

I said, hello Terrence.

He said, hello Gabriella. I have been awaiting your call. What took you so long?

I smiled and thought, everything is in perfect order.

He laughed on the other line and said, divine order.

I said, could we meet somewhere to eXchange information with one another.

He said yes. Meet me at the hookah bar across from your hotel at 4 pm. It is across from the thread shop on the corner. I will be awaiting you. I will be wearing a white turban and Armani sunglasses. You will not be able to miss me.

I smiled to myself and said ok.

He said, see you at 4.

I raised the 4 fingers on my right hand and stared at them. I thought, the taxi cab driver was right. I am seeing past my four fingers now.

I went to the hookah bar and found Terrence sitting in front of the place at a round table set for two. He was as he described. He was wearing a white turban, a blue dress, Armani sunglasses, but what made him stand out was his long black and grey beard. It was braided into 12 tiny braids held in place by blue rubber bands that matched several glow in the dark blue bracelets he wore on his wrist down to the angle of his elbow. He lifted up his blue and white striped teacup to me as I approached. My eyes met his and then immediately traveled up his arm through the Slinky of bracelets. My eyes got stuck in the spiral. I didn't pop out until I heard his deep booming voice.

He said, *mind the gap.*

I said, Bonjour, as I reached out my hand to shake his hand. We created an X in the air as we missed hands. I laughed and said, I am happy to meet you Terrence. He removed his sunglasses revealing his eyes. I felt like I was staring in 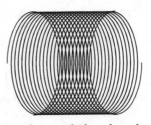 Jerry Garcia's eyes, the lead singer of the Grateful Dead. I smiled and said, Akhmen said, it was important I connect with you. I surveyed the table, zeroing in on the game Connect Four. The red and black game pieces were scattered all over the table as I checked the 7 columned yellow game to see if there was a winner in the last game played.

Terrence took a draw off his hookah pipe sizing me up and down. He said, there are no winners or losers in this game. Please take a seat. He was writing the directions to the game Connect Four. I read:

Modeling the Game – this involves understanding the states and actions for each step of the simulation. It is important to have these well identified because actions are based on these states.

Understanding Advanced Strategeries – All moves are based on mathematics.

Selecting the Tactics – There is more than one possibility at each stage of the game.

Connect Four is a turn-based logic game.

I took a seat as he just stared at me making me slightly uncomfortable.

Finally he broke the silence and said, please call me T. Would you like a tea and your own hookah to smoke some apple herbal shisha?

I said sure. I wasn't big into smoking, but I thought it would only be proper to partake.

He motioned for the waitress to double his order with the sign of his two fingers.

I sat and observed him and me and our eXchange. He said, who are you?

I smiled and said, well, that's a very peculiar question.

He said, no it's not becoming a tad bit aggravated.

I thought, is that the best question you can come up with?

He said, it is the only question that matters as he pointed to a triangle shaped button on his chest that read: *3 states of matter.* He took the pin off and threw it through the air. It t became a guitar pick as it landed on the table in front of me revealing the flipside that read: *Pick Up Theory.*

I said, I am in PROCESS. I am figuring myself out. You see I was lost and now I am finding myself. I have taken many roads and they all lead me HERE. So, I am thinking you are going to shed some light on this for me.

The waitress reappeared with a tea and a hookah pipe. She said, tea for two, as she nodded at me and placed my tea and saucer down. I noticed that the tea tag hanging off the side of the cup read: *Women are like tea bags. We don't know our strength until we are in hot water!* –Eleanor Roosevelt. I looked back up at her and she winked and for a split second she looked like Abraham Lincoln. Abe said, your best support is you, no matter who enters the picture to give you information.

A woman T²raveler carrying a bag covered in blue lotus stickers sat down next to us and winked at me. Several other T²ravelers appeared all carrying their overnight bags. I stared at all the bags around me knowing they were in the picture for me.

I looked over to Terrence. He said, everyone's baggage shows up before they do. Everyone is attached to their baggage in whatever shape or size it takes form. It's where they want to hang out. He took a sip of tea and said, so *let it be.* It's not your concern. There is not a thing you can do about it. You are not THERE to fix them because every player has a program. He lifted up the Connect Four directions revealing they were written on the back of a baseball roster book. The cover had a picture of a baseball that was on fire with its seams unraveling and instead of a team name it read: *You can't tell a player without a program.*

I took a side trip in my mind and thought, all women want to do is fix men.

Terrence said, the question for T²ravelers is – are they willing to lose their stuff? Because YOU don't have to be THERE. You have a CHOICE. You can be a pointer. He lifted up his finger and turned into Leonardo da Vinci for a split second and then he turned into the man pointing to Mary Magdelene's throat in the "Last Supper" painting revealing she had no Adam's apple confirming she was a female in the painting at the right hand of Jesus. The man shifted back to Leonardo and said, you can point out peoples' baggage, but you cannot fix them. That is their journey. Your journey is about making YOU the best YOU can be. He turned into Uncle Sam for a split second and then back to Terrence.

I shook my head to clear it and looked at the T²raveler next to me. She engaged in an eXchange with another T²raveler across from her while they were both holding their baggage filled with stickers of circles, squares and triangles. I drank a sip of tea as I watched the two become panels of toilet paper connected by a perforated line on a scale. I watched one panel move over into the other panel and tip the scale.

Terrence said, she just lost herself. Did you see that?

I said yes without taking my eyes off of either of them as the scales evened out.

Terrence said, she bought the other T²raveler's story for a moment. Then, she went into her own fear program and then reacted from her own fear program. After several seconds she realized she didn't buy into it and then she pulled back to who she is, the holy ghost.

I said, the eXchange is the buyback of your own fear program?

Terrence said, yes and women buy back their perfectionism program *over* and *over* and *over* with every woman they encounter. It's called the 639 program. It's why they turn on one another for fear of being revealed that they are a fraud because their self- esteem is not where it should be…playing on the Higher Level game.

I said, how do you release the perfectionism program and move on down the line?

Terrence reached in his robe and pulled out a black and white Polaroid of a black 1961 Lincoln car. He flipped it over on the table revealing the 12, 3, 6, 9 program.

I said, I need to REMEMBER 12, 3, 6, 9 as I studied the numbers.

Terrence flipped the photograph back over and I stared at the Lincoln's suicide door as I remembered JFK. The Grateful Dead began to play "Truckin" in the background, www.youtube.com/watch?v=pafY6sZt0FE.

Terrence took a blue string and placed it on the table in an oscillating pattern. He said, imagine this is the *road less traveled* and you are in this car moving down the line on your journey called life. He glided the Polaroid picture of the Lincoln down the line moving it from left to right slowly.

I watched carefully somehow knowing this was the eXchange I came for.

Terrence stopped the Lincoln and said, the tire just hit the curb and sent the wheel into a wobble. The tire has gone flat. What do you do?

I paused.

Terrence said, it is HERE, THIS MOMENT RIGHT HERE THAT WILL DECIDE YOUR FATE. How you handle this situation determines it all. What do you see? What do you choose to see? What do you choose not to see? How do you choose to react to this situation? Because the thoughts that come rushing in determine the outcome of this moment. It could be made into a mountain or a Moleskine. Your body is the key because something will arise within your body at this moment sending you to the left to the *Road to Destruction* or to the right to your *Providence.*

I replaced my STORY in the spot of the flat tire. I thought about where something in my life threw me a curve ball. It wasn't hard to find. It was my relationship. My body started to pulsate and sweat and I could feel the anger of betrayal arise within me. I felt like a teapot boiling hot.

Terrence said, in this moment you have 2 options. Number one: love your situation 100 percent.

I thought, that's not going to happen.

He said, number two is to go into it and hate it. He raised his finger to the sky and turned into Leonardo da Vinci for a split second. Leonardo said, but if you're going to hate it, hate it 100 percent.

I could feel steam coming off of me.

He said, are you THERE yet?

I said, no. I'm still HERE.

He said, are you THERE yet?

I said, I'm at 99 percent.

He said, take it over the line—all the way to 100 percent.

I envisioned the betrayal from *my* relationship, the betrayal of my true self, the betrayal from the government feeding me lie after lie keeping the world in a state of chaos and then I envisioned the betrayal of *my* entire existence on planet Earth.

Terrence said, it's all been a façade.

This fueled my hate. I could feel it hit 100 percent. I closed my eyes and saw a sledgehammer strike a strength meter marked $250M at a circus. The strength meter shot a red ball up to the top hitting the line mark labeled 100, ringing the bell. I heard *dinga linga ling. Dinga linga ling. Dinga linga ling.*

Terrence whistled like a teapot going off. He said, in this moment find where your betrayal is stored in your body. There is a button within your body that has stored all that betrayal.

I closed my eyes and found a big button, my belly button.

Terrence said, contemplate this button. How many times do you push it in life? How many times do you let others push it? It's your program wrapped up in a playbook. Now, remove the button and spin it into a triangle and then down to an atom.

I did this. I pulled the big yellow button stored in my belly button out and then spun it into a triangle and then down into an atom. I opened my eyes and sat staring at Terrence.

He said, now love it 100 percent.

I said, that is like trying to go from 0 to 60.

Terrence laughed and said, just ask yourself how can I love this 100 percent. Your mind will track the question and along the way you will figure out how to love it 100 percent. Being willing to move down the line toward your GREATNESS gets you to 100 percent of love all the time.

The round table formed a center ring filled with blue hearts at the center followed by several other rings. They read:

144 x 1

144 x 2

144 x 3

144 x4

144 x 5

144 x 6

144 x 7

144 x 8

144 x 9

144 x10

144 x11

144 x12

144 x13 = 1872

All the T²ravelers surrounding us stood up and exited following an oscillating yellow line that appeared and ran straight through the tea shop with greater than signs. The word PROVIDENCE appeared written over the yellow line.

I said, so you wallow in your stuff or you move down the line to your GREATNESS. Does this mean the greatest question you can ask is: Is this contributing to my greatness or not?

Terrence said, yes and when you have eXchanges get the other to realize you don't care about *your* stuff, just *your* greatness. Their stories just trigger *your* stuff so you can see that you are more than your stuff and *your* skills.

I said, how do I get the other person to eXchange at this level?

People engage with others because they want to calm their anxieties. So when they engage with you and bring up their anxieties they try to pass them off as yours. They want to change you when really they want to change themselves. It's a huge game of shuffle ball change. The key is to tell them they are right.

I said, right about what?

Terrence said, whatever they are trying to tell you that you need to do. This disengages the game. The crossover stops. The X turns into an **O**. It eases their anxieties about themselves. When you do this, it cuts the string of thought and you do not take it on. It moves through you instead of getting stuck in you making you stuck. Instead it empowers them. They think they won even though there are no winners and losers in the game. As a result you play at a Higher Level game, which allows you to keep expanding into your greater self that goes to infinity and beyond because you never really know your total greatness.

A T²raveler dressed in a newspaper hat bent over our table and handed me a key from around his waist. The key read unattached observer.

Terrence said, people give you clues all the time, but the Bermuda triangle, the Mind, Intellect, EGO questions. You are supposed to see the clues and connect them and then let go.

Brad, the rabbit hopped by and said, why are you playing in the mundane? PLAY in forward momentum. It beats the Would I? Could I? Should I? be different game.

I took a sip of my tea and read the tea tag again. *Women are like tea bags. We don't know our strength until we are in hot water* –Eleanor Roosevelt. I thought, thank you Mrs. Roosevelt as that quote popped me back into my own personal STORY. I said, T, how do I stop judging what is?

He said, finally we get THERE. He said, you have to judge. You can't help yourself. You cannot turn this off. He raised his finger in the air and turned into Leonardo da Vinci for a split second and said, when judgment pops up see what it is, notice it, then do the next appropriate thing. STOP and look both ways. Push it aside and realize you are having a moment and then move into the next moment with the question...what if I moved into LOVE right HERE? Find a way to love the judgment 100 percent.

How do I do that?

FLIP THE SWITCH with a MIND game.

I said, what if I can't love it 100 percent?

Terrence said, then the mind will track it. It only has 2 tracks to follow. He pulled some black and white film from his pockets. He unrolled the two rolls creating a higher and lower film SEQUENCE and placed it on the table. He pointed to the lower one and said, this film had the splicing at 1.618 intervals leaving you missing the connections between the timelines.

He pointed to the film on the higher level and said, this one had the film unspliced. It's the true story. He created a less than sign with his left index finger and thumb and said, this one is the Less Than game. Then he took his right index finger and thumb and created a greater than sign and said, this one is the Greater Than game. He connected his fingers creating a diamond. He said, the question becomes which do you choose to see?

He pushed the reels together and they turned into the arms on a pair of thick black framed glasses. One had black electrical tape along the side and the other had safety pins holding it in place at the hinge of the frames. He tossed them across the table and said, it's time to SEE the game for what it is.

I peered through the glasses and saw a Slinky. I blinked and saw pink cotton candy. I blinked a third time and saw a nuclear explosion turning buildings to dust. I removed the glasses as a 1960s T^2raveler walking the line bent over the table and said, the tracking game can lead to tipping the scales into insanity because some times the truth is stranger than fiction. Be aware! She said, woo, as she fell off the line. She said, no struggle here as she got back on the line. She fell off and said woo! The entire line of T^2ravelers started singing, "White Rabbit," by Jefferson Airplane, www.youtube.com/watch?v=WANNqr-vcx0&feature=related.

Terrence said, if you can't love it 100 percent you will have to keep playing the game.

I said, do you have a tip for me?

He laughed and smiled through his eyes. He said, ask yourself how you can groove? Terrence's eyes turned into 45 rpm records and the Michael Buble' song, "Feeling Good," www.youtube.com/watch?v=Edwsf-8F3sI&ob=av2n sounded through his eyes. He said, if you find some music to groove to, it always helps and then re-engage in the game with the thought, there is something I am supposed to love more! You will have to fully engage in PLAY in *letting it be* to play the GO Game!

I said, because when you can love the judgment 100 percent you only track the Higher Level game?

Terrence said, yes and the Higher Level game is high self esteem and that is where you will find true freedom from the mind game. It's the high stakes poker game you can play!

I said, so there is no Mr. Right out there?

Terrence laughed and said, why would you want to tie the knot?

I paused to consider this question. Why would I?

He said, Mr. X = Why^{knot}.

I laughed as I thought of everything I would like to change about him.

Terrence said, judgment will still be THERE with any man or woman. A relationship usually derails YOU from your route because one of you wants to control the other. The real game is a solo game of chess with yourself. The goal is to find your true self and have fun along the way by learning to SEQUENCE forward and PROCESS back.

I decided in that moment it was time for me to pass GO and go home to create an X-husband.

Terrence pointed at his heart and said, home is where the heart is. The question beckons. How long is it going to take the world to realize freedom is not found on the world stage of war over power? Technology versus consciousness. Freedom is found in the mind of every person through the understanding of pronouns. There is only one Universal Mind. We are all just recycling the same STORY. Isn't it time for a new novel? He handed me a paper.

I read: YOU ARE NOW DISENGAGED FROM NEGATIVE ALIEN MIND CONTROL. STEP INTO YOUR TRUE SELF. ONLY YOU CAN DO IT. IT'S ALL AN INSIDE JOB! **8973765244439.00** TURN OFF. THE L'i'ES HAVE TO STOP.

The last T^{2}raveler in line stopped by the table as she walked the line of PROVIDENCE. She peered into my eyes and said, when you travel you lose your baggage easier because there is no attachment. You realize personal attachment to things is a FRAUD. There is no MINE in the T^{2}ravelers world. She said, go out and see the world for what it is. She handed me a Golden Ticket to New York City / Rome / Paris / Spain / London / India / Bali / Israel / Washington D.C. out loud: **1765422998742-01.1**

I thought, when you travel you do lose the sense of personalizing everything as MINE. There is a freedom THERE. Terrence handed me an old brown antique bottle marked T^2 = Time Travel. I opened the bottle and smelled a long forgotten aroma that took me to a different time and place. A red Connect Four game piece stuck on the side of the bottle fell off and on the table. I picked it up and read, ONE aspect of YOU is the HERO. Time to wake up! I looked at Terrence and he pointed to the woman T²raveler. All I could see was her red cape with one golden triangle facing down and one facing up inside a circle with the word underneath, divine logos. She lifted up her overnight bag and I read,

YOU > you x PHI

LOVE

Terrence said, it is always important to look at the common denominator. It's either LOVE or FEAR.

576

The T²raveler threw a pink paper in the air as I noticed a pair of wings appear on her overnight bag. I thought, she is passing her code of honor to me. It is time for me to embody my...I mean *the* code of honor! The pink paper floated through the air and landed at my left foot. I picked it up and it was a permission slip that read, you signed up for this. Step into your hero!

Terrence picked up a hat from the chair beside him. It was the type of hat a train porter would wear.

I realized he was a train porter.

He said, I have a math riddle for you to solve. A freight train on the Pennsylvania Railroad is carrying nuclear explosives. It left the station in Philadelphia at 10 a.m. on January 2, 1960. It is traveling toward Union Station in Washington, D.C. at 40 mph. At 4 a.m. on January 2, 1960. A Eurostar train leaves Gare du Nord in Paris carrying a woman holding a pink rose. She is peeling off each petal one by one and saying, I love me, I love me knot. This train is traveling to the Gare Nice Ville Station in Nice at 50 mph. Given the gravity of the situation, calculate the distances between her heart and her h^{e}art, the answer from the rose, the probability of another nuclear explosion if the train continues down the same track.

STORY #ONE: Boundary Layers

YOU just crossed the line ascending into a new boundary layer toward your GREATNESS.

144 + 144 + 144 + 144 = 576.

STORY #ONE: Choices

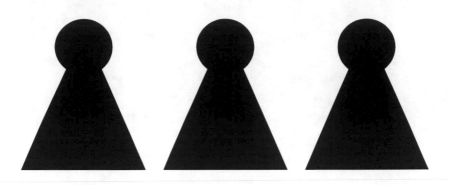

I stood eye to eye with a circle that had a triangle underneath that read, *Resistance*, next to a second circle with a triangle underneath that read, *Revelation*, next to a third circle with a triangle underneath that read, *Revolution*. I reached in my pocket and pulled out an antique gold kᵉy marked *EMPOW-ERMENT*. I flipped it over and it read: *Critical mass.*

I contemplated. Which to choose…to play forth or match back? I could PROCESS back through or SEQUENCE forth. I calculated how many Xs and Os I had already strung together. I lifted the kᵉy to the sky and kissed **the end** of it as the letters and numbers mixed together creating the Divine Feminine mixed with the Divine Masculine. I placed the kᵉy in the keyhole and took a deep breath as I turned the lock with a CLICK.

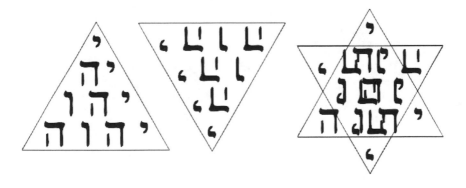

I walked through the door and onto a black and red chessboard floor that read, Welcome Home number 144. I continued walking and words appeared overlaying the chess board that read,

Welcome Home TEACHING POEM

Outside living

Skins our houses

Inside knowing

Strangers, spouses.

Stress to threshold

Relief enters

Leaving bringing

Stories, printers.

Paint the painter

Draw the drawer

A life's novel

Meant to awe her.

Me and you and

Those humaning

Our home theories:

Master planning!

Welcome Home

Taurus 2304   Leo 2592

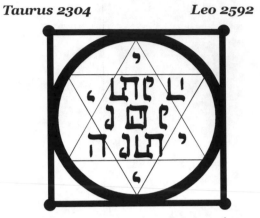

Scorpio 1872   Aquarius 2016

zero point, the event horizon

The beginning of the end

Taurus 2304   Leo 2592

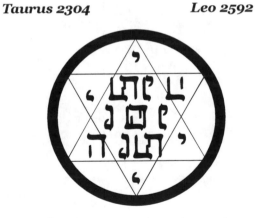

Scorpio 1872   Aquarius 2016

zero point, the event horizon

The end of the beginning

STORY# ONE: Love Letter to a Rookie

A Love Letter to: *My Darling Planet Earth,*

What in the world are you fighting for?

You are fighting over a symbol that represents the fractal nature of the universe.

Lay down your weapons of mass destruction and realize you are fighting yourself. It has and always will be an inside job. Be the kink in the chain of command leading us down the *Road to Destruction.*

Realize there is nothing to win in this game. What you are searching for is INSIDE. You are searching for the connection with the DIVINE FEMININE. That is why you *search* and *search* and *search* and *search* and nothing fills this black hole. To become whole you must realize the origin of your eXistence has been a façade. You are a galactic being with powers beyond the mind control. It's time you **O**PEN UP and realize your true self.

 You are the only one that can **O**PEN UP YOU because everyone on earth is from some other part of the galaXy and all of YOU together create the sum total of the universe.

YOU are the HER**O** you have been searching for. The only way to get in touch with your HER**O** is by tapping your Creative Genius! IT'S TIME! It's time for every individual to step into their CREATIVE GENIUS by turning the Blue String Theory into a reality.

The Blue String Reality Mission Statement:

The Blue String Theory is a movement where each individual uses a blue string to REMEMBER who they are at their core. As an act of remembrance, each individual wears a blue string around their wrist to give to another person as an act of *gratitude* and *recognition* to help us all remember that we are all ONE.

To complete the feedback loop of giving and receiving, each individual blue string bracelet wearer states their creative desire on the blue stringing tab of *Mrs. Velvet and the Blue String Theory's* website.

It is here where each individual can play the game PLAY FORWARD/ MATCH BACK. This game is where everyone in the world can PLAY by presenting their eXtreme creativity (whether it be a thought, an act, a dream, an idea or a wish) and match back to someone searching for something similar. This is the process of connecting one person to another to another like pearls and stars gather on a string.

The act of reading *Mrs. Velvet and the Blue String Theory* then using the website to interact with one another will propel each other's creativity to another level. This was designed so that each person on Earth can move forward down the line and keep discovering more of their true self. True selves in a state of knowing and seeing others as their true self is what allows all of humanity to embrace creation, truth, goodness and beauty.

Through the Blue String movement, blue strings will stretch around the world thousands of times and create a new LOGOS, a new vibration of love and harmony. Peace on earth, individually and collectively, will become a reality.

I agree to be my true self, the HERO.

LOVE x 1.618

(Sign your name here and say your name 3 times as you remember your true self.)

Tic-tac-toe 3 in a row!

1, 2, 3, 4 Connect Four! You are now connected to the DIVINE FEMI-NINE. Now Go! Go create a new reality!